Breakthrough
Nonprofit Branding

The AFP Fund Development Series

The AFP Fund Development Series is intended to provide fund development professionals and volunteers, including board members (and others interested in the nonprofit sector), with top-quality publications that help advance philanthropy as voluntary action for the public good. Our goal is to provide practical, timely guidance and information on fundraising, charitable giving, and related subjects. The Association of Fundraising Professionals (AFP) and Wiley each bring to this innovative collaboration unique and important resources that result in a whole greater than the sum of its parts. For information on other books in the series, please visit:

http://www.afpnet.org

The Association of Fundraising Professionals

The Association of Fundraising Professionals (AFP) represents over 30,000 members in more than 197 chapters throughout the United States, Canada, Mexico, and China, working to advance philanthropy through advocacy, research, education, and certification programs.

The association fosters development and growth of fundraising professionals and promotes high ethical standards in the fundraising profession. For more information or to join the world's largest association of fundraising professionals, visit www.afpnet.org.

AFP Publishing Advisory Committee

Chair: Nina P. Berkheiser, CFRE
Principal Consultant, Your Nonprofit Advisor
Linda L. Chew, CFRE
Development Consultant
D. C. Dreger, ACFRE
Senior Campaign Director, Custom Development Solutions, Inc. (CDS)
Patricia L. Eldred, CFRE
Director of Development, Independent Living Inc.
Samuel N. Gough, CFRE
Principal, The AFRAM Group
Audrey P. Kintzi, ACFRE
Director of Development, Courage Center
Steven Miller, CFRE
Director of Development and Membership, Bread for the World
Robert J. Mueller, CFRE
Vice President, Hospice Foundation of Louisville
Maria Elena Noriega
Director, Noriega Malo & Associates
Michele Pearce
Director of Development, Consumer Credit Counseling Service of Greater Atlanta
Leslie E. Weir, MA, ACFRE
Director of Family Philanthropy, The Winnipeg Foundation
Sharon R. Will, CFRE
Director of Development, South Wind Hospice

John Wiley & Sons, Inc.
Susan McDermott
Senior Editor
AFP Staff
Jan Alfieri
Manager, New Product Development
Rhonda Starr
Vice President, Education and Training

Breakthrough Nonprofit Branding

Seven Principles
to Power
Extraordinary Results

JOCELYNE S. DAW

CAROL CONE

WITH ANNE ERHARD

AND KRISTIAN DARIGAN MERENDA

WILEY

John Wiley & Sons, Inc.

Published by John Wiley & Sons, Inc., Hoboken, New Jersey.
Published simultaneously in Canada.

For general information on our other products and services or for technical support, please contact our Customer Care Department within the United States at (800) 762-2974, outside the United States at (317) 572-3993 or fax (317) 572-4002.

Wiley also publishes its books in a variety of electronic formats. Some content that appears in print may not be available in electronic books. For more information about Wiley products, visit our web site at www.wiley.com.

Library of Congress Cataloging-in-Publication Data:

Breakthrough nonprofit branding: seven principles for powering extraordinary results/Jocelyne Daw . . . [et al.]
     p. cm. – (The AFP/Wiley fund development series; 188)
Includes bibliographical references and index.
ISBN 978-0-470-28691-3 (cloth); ISBN 978-0-470-91866-1 (ebk); ISBN 978-0-470-91867-8 (ebk); ISBN 978-0-470-91868-5 (ebk)
   1. Nonprofit organizations.   2. Branding (Marketing)   3. Advertising   I.   Daw, Jocelyne.
HD62.6.B735 2010
658.8'27–dc22

                                                                                  2010023299

Printed in the United States of America

10 9 8 7 6 5 4 3 2 1

This book is dedicated to the millions of ordinary individual men and women who through their tireless work and voluntary actions are making extraordinary contributions to the quality of life and communities around the world. People are the final embodiment of a brand.

Contents

Acknowledgments

It is a little-known truth that few books are written alone and this book is no exception. *Breakthrough Nonprofit Branding* resulted from the combined contribution and talents of many individuals and organizations.

NON PROFIT CONTRIBUTORS

This book would not exist without the significant involvement and generous contribution of the 11 nonprofit case studies showcased in this book. The 11 are recognized leaders in their field, respected by peers and experts, and celebrated through awards and extensive media coverage.

They willingly and generously shared their branding stories, outlined their special way of doing things, and revealed the secrets of their success. This book presents their remarkable efforts to enhance our collective lives. They graciously provided their time and expertise because of a deep belief in the value of enhancing the work of the nonprofit sector. A sincere thank you for your commitment to the greater good.

American Heart Association

Gordon McCullough, Chief Operating Officer

Robyn Landry, Executive Vice President of Field Health Strategies

Kathy Rogers, Executive Vice President of Consumer Markets

College Forward

Lisa Fielder, Executive Director and Co-Founder

Emily Steinberg, Associate Director

Christine Torres, Development Manager

Remy Cofurd, Public Relations Coordinator

Melody Kaney, Operations Manager

Ashley Aaron, Fund Development Coordinator

Joe Vladeck, Organizational Advancement Manager

Food Bank For New York City

Lucy Cabrera, President & CEO

Gregory Boroff, former Senior Vice President, External Communications

Lisa Jakobsberg, Vice President of Marketing and Business Partnerships

Goodwill Industries International

Ryan Kuhn, Director of Marketing, Goodwill Industries International

Wendy Copeland, Vice President, Mission Service, Goodwill Industries International

David Hadani, Nebraska Heavy Industries, former Board Chair, Goodwill Industries International

Gidget Hopf, President and CEO, ABVI-Goodwill, Rochester, NY

Kim Zimmer, Vice President Communications, Goodwill Industries International

Memorial Healthworks! Kids' Museum

Phil Newbold, President & CEO, Memorial Health Systems

Reg Wagle, Senior Vice President, CEO, Memorial Health Foundation

Diane Stover, Memorial Health Systems, Vice President, Marketing and Innovation, and Chief Experience Officer

Rebecca (Becky) Zakowski, Chief Infection Agent, Healthworks! Kids' Museum

Sarah Seales, High Flying Kid Motivator, Healthworks! Kids' Museum

Laura Garvey, Conductor of Creative Chaos (General Manager), Healthworks! Kids' Museum

Inspiration Corporation

Diane Pascal, Director of Development & External Relations

John Pfeiffer, Executive Director and CEO

Lisa Nigro, Founder

Shannon Stewart, Chief Operating Officer

Kids Help Phone

Ellen Réthoré, Vice President, Marketing and Communications

Meghan Reddick, Director, Marketing

Alyson Waite, Manager, Student Ambassador Program

NatureBridge

Jason Morris, Vice President of External Affairs and Programs

Susan Turner, Communications Director

Dr. Stephen Lockhart, Regional Vice President and Chief Medical Officer, East Bay Region, Sutter Health, San Francisco, CA; Chair, Board of Directors, NatureBridge

David Placek, President and CEO, Lexicon Branding and Board of Directors, NatureBridge

Stratford Shakespeare Festival

Antoni Cimolino, General Director

Anita Gaffney, Administrative Director

Susan G. Komen for the Cure

Emily Callahan, Senior Vice President Global Marketing and Networks

Katrina McGhee, Senior Vice President, Global Business Development and Partnerships

Susan Carter Johns, Strategic Relationships Vice President

U.S. *Fund for UNICEF*

Caryl Stern, President & CEO

Jay Aldous, Former Chief Marketing and Communications Officer

Kim Pucci, Former Marketing Director

Ed Lloyd, Executive Vice President and Chief Financial Officer

Stevan Miller, Director, Partnership Development

Alisa Aydin, Director, Interactive Marketing

Anthony Pantaleoni, Partner, Fulbright & Jaworski L.L.P.'s New York office; Chair, U.S. Fund for UNICEF Board of Directors

Lisa Szarkowski, Vice President, Public Relations

Jennifer Dorian, Senior Vice President, TNT/TBS (Turner Broadcast Systems), Volunteer Committee Member, U.S. Fund for UNICEF

EXPERT INTERVIEWS FOR THE BOOK

Ten experts recognized for their work in branding—in both the nonprofit and for-profit worlds—were interviewed. We tested our hypotheses with them, learned from their knowledge and know-how and sought their recommendations. Their focus on Breakthrough Nonprofit Brands gave us real value in our analysis. Thank you to each for your time and expertise.

Sue Adkins, Director Cause Related Marketing, Business in the Community, UK

Suzanne Apple, Vice President of Business and Industry, World Wildlife Fund

Kurt Aschermann, President and Chief Operating Officer of Charity Partners

Thayne Forbes and William Grobel, Intangible Business, UK

Cheryl Heller, CEO, Heller Design

Kash Rangan, Professor of Marketing, Harvard Business School

Mark Sarner, President, Manifest Communications, Canada

Alan Siegel, Founder & Chairman of Siegel + Gale

Ron Strauss, Brandzone

Research and General Support

The Association of Fundraising Professionals, American Marketing Association, Nonprofit Special Interest Group, and Imagine Canada generously facilitated our omnibus survey of their members. The survey enabled us to glean nonprofits' understanding, attitudes, and practices towards brand and branding. It also significantly contributed to finalizing our 11 Breakthrough Nonprofit Brand case studies.

We are indebted to Mike Wallace, Abby Schmidt, Carolyn Pisarri, and Stephanie Gurtman, Cone interns who provided important research support at critical points throughout the development of the book. Claire Malloy, long-time and highly supportive assistant to Carol Cone, provided critical support for the best part of the book project. Stephanie Sutton, assistant to Jocelyne Daw, was invaluable at the project's end. Grateful thanks goes to the Alberta Museums Association for a grant to Jocelyne Daw that facilitated research travel.

A special note of appreciation is due to Cone LLC and Imagine Canada, our employers during much of the research and writing of this book, for their support. Cone LLC (www.coneinc.com) based in Boston, is a strategy and communications agency engaged in building brand trust. Cone creates stakeholder loyalty and long-term relationships through the development and execution of Cause Branding and Nonprofit Marketing. We are grateful to Edelman, the leading independent global PR firm for their support in marketing the book.

Imagine Canada (www.imaginecanada.ca), based in Calgary, Toronto, and Ottawa, is a national registered charity whose mission is to support and strengthen charities and nonprofits so they can, in turn, support the Canadians and communities they serve.

When the writing phase was completed, our talented freelance editors aided enormously. Talya Bosch helped streamline our thinking. She sweetened our prose, helped make sense of our core messages, and enhanced the flow of chapters. Pamela Brandt stepped in at the last minute and added great editorial insights and support to the final three chapters. Thanks to the team at Wiley, Judy Howarth, Susan McDermott, Kevin Holm and others who strongly supported the book's development and contributed considerably to the final result.

A Special Co-Authors' Acknowledgment

A heartfelt thanks goes to the contributions of my co-authors, Carol Cone, Anne Erhard, and Kristian Darigan Merenda. In writing this book our over-arching goal was to provide new ideas and new thinking about the impact of strategic branding. We wanted to create a practical guide with actionable knowledge that could power extraordinary results for nonprofits—of any size and type.

Research and writing the book was a two and a half year journey that was a unique Canadian and American collaboration. Operating in large measure from Calgary, Alberta and Boston, Massachusetts, we met in person four times and then worked together through e-mail and countless phone meetings.

Together we built the book's framework and themes, implemented the research study, and undertook expert interviews that led to the final selection of the case studies—nine American, two Canadian. Each co-author joined me in multiple interviews with our nonprofit case studies and provided critical intellectual input as the chapters developed. Each contributed to the writing of several individual chapters by adding vital insights and enhancing messaging. A final review of the book by each sharpened and strengthened the overall manuscript. Without a doubt their deep knowledge, extensive experience, and strategic thinking enhanced the quality of the book enormously. It would not be the book it is without their involvement. It was a privilege to work with them.

Jocelyne Daw, lead author
Calgary, Alberta

Personal Thanks

In a two-and-a-half-year period much personal support is needed to undertake a project of this size and continue day-to-day work and life responsibilities. We are all genuinely appreciative and thankful for the support of family, friends, and colleagues.

A few additional special thanks . . .

To my husband and son, Brian and Will, for making me laugh as I attempted to work, write, and become a new mom at the same time.

—*Anne Erhard*

I am deeply grateful to my husband, Justin, for making the world a brighter place and to my family, friends, mentors, and colleagues who have been a constant constant source of inspiration.

—*Kristian Darigan Merenda*

Many thanks to my sweet cat Minty, who purred in my lap during writing days. Love to my dear husband Harry, who knew when to stay away, hold my hand, or offer a hug when support was needed.

—*Carol Cone*

Much love to my husband, Bob Page, who supported me for almost a year when I left my position as vice president, Marketing and Community Engagement at Imagine Canada, to dedicate myself full-time to complete the research, writing, and coordination of this book.

—*Jocelyne Daw*

Introduction: The New Nonprofit Imperative

KOMEN FOR THE CURE: REALIZING THE NEW NONPROFIT IMPERATIVE

Can one person really make a difference? That was the question Nancy Brinker asked herself after her sister Susan G. Komen passed away from breast cancer at 36, following a three-year self-described war with the disease. Throughout her diagnosis, treatment, and seemingly endless hospital stays, instead of worrying about herself, Susan spent her time thinking of ways to make life better for other women battling breast cancer.

The year was 1980, and little was known about the disease. Even less was said publicly about what were considered two delicate subjects: breasts and cancer. Yet, breast cancer killed more women during the Vietnam War years than that war killed soldiers. Before Susan died, she begged her can-do sister to help the half million women worldwide diagnosed with breast cancer every year. Moved by Susan's compassion for others, Nancy

G. Brinker promised she would do everything in her power to end breast cancer forever.

With great determination, she launched the Susan G. Komen Breast Cancer Foundation in 1982 and its signature event, the Susan G. Komen Race for the Cure®, in 1983. By 2010, what was a cherished promise between sisters had grown into a movement that has raised and invested nearly $1.5 billion for breast cancer awareness, research, and programs. Komen is an extraordinary leader in the breast cancer arena, not just in its research and education investments but also in transforming the way people have thought, acted, and spoken about the disease.

From its early days with a handful of employees, by 2010 Komen had expanded to a force almost 200 strong, with 120-plus affiliates. Its Race for the Cure event series has mushroomed from one race of 800 participants to more than 130 race events with more than 1.5 million participants annually, including 16 events in 2010 outside the United States.

Yet, during its first two decades, Komen spent little to no money on advertising or lavish communications outlays. Instead, Brinker and the group she founded defined a clear cause—finding a cure—and focused all of the organization's activities around it. Its impressive results stem from a powerful brand meaning backed by a compelling story; a focused, integrated approach to its programs, marketing, and development activities; and its ability to inspire internal and external communities to join in the breast cancer cause crusade. Instinctively following this successful formula, in just 28 years, Komen has built a breakthrough brand and galvanized a powerful social movement.

The Changing Landscape

As time passed, things had changed significantly since its founding. Komen's activities had grown beyond its signature event, and its core audience had expanded exponentially, but its internal structures and communications remained largely unchanged.

The competitive arena also had evolved. A growing number of new and successful nonprofit organizations like the American Breast Cancer Foundation and for-profit companies like Avon[1] were doing great work in and outside the breast cancer community, leading to clutter and confusion in the breast cancer space.[2] Research undertaken by Komen in the early

2000s demonstrated an acceptable level of awareness of the nonprofit but a troubling lack of connection between the organization's key programs and the Susan G. Komen brand. It also indicated that the organization wasn't resonating with certain audiences, particularly younger women and certain ethnic groups, among whom breast cancer was increasing at an alarming rate.

Komen was determined to connect with broader audiences in new ways to rise above the crowd. The programmatic mandate had an accompanying aim of investing an additional $1 billion toward finding a cure in the next decade. Its goal was to stand for something that Komen could uniquely own. Its approach was as daring as ever. In 2002, it began a five-year journey to revitalize and transform its brand.

The new brand message would need to differentiate itself in the marketplace and increase its impact, including reaching out to new audiences in a fresh and progressive manner. "We thought a more sophisticated and timely approach to branding could take us into the public policy area; reach new audiences where they lived, worked and played; and evolve the way we talked about our role—repositioning ourselves from leaders in the breast cancer fight to leaders in the global breast cancer movement," elucidated Katrina McGhee, senior vice president, Global Business Development and Partnerships.[3]

"It took time, effort and commitment. The journey was not an easy one, but it has been so worthwhile," explained Susan Carter Johns, Strategic Relationships vice president. "It has defined what our organization stands for, launched us in new directions, and helped us double our fundraising in just four years. Our brand has become more inclusive, and people internally and externally have embraced it and rallied around our common beliefs, shared hopes, and faith that cures can be found."[4] That is the power of building a breakthrough brand.

WHAT THIS BOOK IS ABOUT

Breakthrough Nonprofit Branding is about the impact a strategically built, focused, and compelling brand can have for an organization of any size. In an age of nonprofit proliferation and increasingly finite resources, this book is designed to help charitable groups enhance their ability to build and strengthen their most important asset—their brand.

As practiced in the real world, many nonprofits define branding as logos, names, and trademarks produced to aid in awareness and fundraising. However, this limited perspective leaves a significant unrealized value on the table. This book will show you how to capture that value by building a breakthrough nonprofit brand from the inside out.

More than simply a cosmetic makeover, at the base level, branding is about identifying what your organization stands for—the unique, differentiated idea that sets it apart. To build your brand requires forging an emotional and personal connection with your core stakeholders. Your brand must stand for a cause—something bigger than organizational activities, something that your constituents care about and believe in. Yet, to truly break through calls for you to rally a community around your brand's meaning and inspire action.

Komen, for example, goes beyond a focus on organizational survival. It stands for empowering women, giving them a voice around the issue of breast cancer, and finding the cure. That approach transcends the disease and even the nonprofit itself. By emphasizing a greater cause, Komen galvanizes constituents and motivates them to take action around a common goal, shared values, and commitments. As a nonprofit, standing for a broader cause will infuse your group with the higher purpose essential for your organization to thrive. It acts as a rallying flag for current and new supporters.

A "Brand" New World

In a 2007 Association of Fundraising Professionals study, branding and increased competition for the charitable dollar were the two biggest concerns of respondents. Those findings were echoed by the authors' extensive 2008 survey, in which 94 percent of nonprofit professionals said building and managing their brand had grown in importance during the past three years. Similarly, almost 94 percent rated branding as extremely important or very important to their organization's success. Yet, a majority felt they still weren't getting it right. They told us few of their internal colleagues knew about branding, what it could do, or how to go about it.[5]

Branding for the nonprofit sector is an important yet overlooked issue. Many don't have the experience or understanding to deliver effective branding strategies.

—ASSOCIATION OF FUNDRAISING PROFESSIONALS
SURVEY PARTICIPANT

Branding is critically important for the nonprofit sector. However, spending human and financial resources on this important task is a low priority, often regarded as a frivolous investment.

—AMERICAN MARKETING ASSOCIATION
NONPROFIT SPECIAL INTEREST GROUP
SURVEY PARTICIPANT

Branding is important for social change, not just fundraising! Branding is important to all organizations—large or small!

—IMAGINE CANADA
SURVEY PARTICIPANT[6]

Key Concepts in This Book

Breakthrough Nonprofit Branding shows how a constituency-focused, compelling brand can revolutionize an organization and the way people view and support it. It is about transferable ideas and practices, ones that nonprofits of any size, scope, or experience can use and implement. Through case studies of 11 visionary nonprofits, this book reveals seven principles for transforming a brand from ordinary trademark to strategic competitive advantage. The groups profiled in the coming chapters reflect a variety of sizes, breadths, regions, ages, and issues. The common thread is that their brand work has resulted in greater social impact and vibrant results.

The chapters that follow contain stories that showcase:

- How a nonprofit with inconsistent community support—but a strong record of mission achievement and efficient management—used its renewed brand to propel the organization forward.
- How renewed brand meaning heightened stakeholder commitment and stabilized an organization's financial position, allowing it to weather a roiling economy.

- How a small organization's focus on branding resulted in exceptional growth, expanding its core programming, geography, and impact.
- How a rebrand transformed a nonprofit, enabling it to expand from a regional to a national footprint.
- How even one of the largest nonprofits lost momentum and regained direction through a revitalized brand process.

The Power of a Breakthrough Brand

As the Komen example and other case studies will demonstrate, a breakthrough nonprofit brand can:

- *Drive direction and higher performance:* A breakthrough nonprofit brand articulates its mission in a way that is focused and relevant for the times. Its brand meaning provides a uniform direction for all programming, communications, and development activities. When everyone is working toward a shared vision, it creates greater returns.
- *Change perceptions, preferences, and priorities:* A breakthrough nonprofit brand fulfills deep-seated personal needs for connection with an issue or cause. It unites groups of strangers in kinship through shared hopes, values, aspirations, and commitments.
- *Strengthen a nonprofit's capacity to attract, motivate, and retain the best staff and volunteers:* A breakthrough nonprofit brand makes an organization more attractive to passionate people who believe in and want to be part of its cause. This is critical for long-term success, since nonprofits derive strength from the energy of their people.
- *Build deeper relationships with current supporters:* A breakthrough nonprofit brand stands for something that constituents believe in. By building an enduring brand that showcases its mission and values in action, an organization will attract like-minded volunteers and donors. By consistently delivering on its brand promise, it inspires action and establishes a foundation for long-term success.
- *Foster visionary ideas and innovation:* A breakthrough nonprofit brand provides the freedom within a framework necessary to spark and test new ideas. Branding is an investment in the future.

- *Connect with new people and generate new resources:* A breakthrough nonprofit brand masters the art of retaining longtime supporters while cultivating new relationships by carefully balancing historic priorities with new initiatives.

- *Hold the organization steady, even in turbulent times:* A breakthrough nonprofit brand anticipates and adjusts to inevitable financial and political ups and downs. By grounding the organization in enduring values and focusing it on long-term cause goals, brand meaning makes the path forward clear and direct.

A Sustainable Competitive Advantage

In *Good to Great and the Social Sector,* Jim Collins argues that brand and reputation are more critical in the nonprofit sector than in the for-profit world. In the business sector, customers give financial resources in return for a tangible product or service. In the nonprofit sector, supporters provide financial resources based on the knowledge that their money will be used to achieve important but often intangible social goals, and they do not necessarily receive something concrete in return. Therefore, reputation and a sense of purpose and connection become critical differentiators.

Built on tangible results and an emotional sharing of heart, brand reputation encourages potential supporters to believe in a charitable mission yet also in a group's ability to deliver on that mission. It helps people decide which appeal to answer, given a growing list of choices.[7]

A breakthrough brand is an enduring competitive advantage. In the charitable world, the relationship between exceptional results and access to resources is not simple. Yet brands that engage and involve people emotionally, according to *Fast Company,* command prices as much as 20 percent to 200 percent higher than competitors' and sell in far higher volumes. Rational understanding, passionate connection, and personal engagement are the independent sector's secret sauce.[8]

The Growing Force of Nonprofits

The high performers profiled in this book are a testament to the enormous power of nonprofits to solve societal problems and build stronger, healthier communities. Throughout the past 30 years, government has further stepped out of its traditional role of providing public services. Much of the responsibility for ensuring the common good has been driven down to the community level. In response, nonprofits have risen in remarkable numbers to address critical unmet needs.

While social service and humanitarian organizations used to dominate the landscape, the variety of groups and causes is growing. Some are dedicated to improving literacy, feeding the hungry, keeping children in school, or advancing environmental stewardship. The scope and diversity appears almost limitless. So does the potential for impact.

Relatively nimble, nonprofits can act independently and are usually less encumbered by bureaucracy. They are often the first to face emerging societal issues: Consider their role in addressing AIDS, breast cancer, hunger, homelessness, and global warming. Nonprofit organizations were quick to respond in New York following 9/11, in New Orleans after Hurricane Katrina, on the ground overseas in the wake of the Asian tsunami, and in Haiti after the devastating earthquake.

What's more, many nonprofits are moving beyond stopgap solutions and advocating for systems change that addresses the root causes of societal problems. They often move beyond traditional thinking and are skilled at bringing together influentials from the public and private sectors. This approach expedites action and ideas that leapfrog traditional thinking.

Fastest-Growing Sector

Around the world, nonprofits make up the fastest-growing sector. By 2008, there were more than 2 million nonprofit organizations worldwide, with more than 1.5 million in the United States alone and 161,000-plus in Canada. Compare this with 1940, when there were 12,000 American-based charities. As recently as 1998, the number stood at a comparatively modest 733,790.

Today, the so-called independent sector accounts for 5 percent of U.S. gross domestic product (GDP), 8.1 percent of that country's wages, and 9.7 percent of its jobs.[9] In Canada, nonprofits are an even bigger part of the economy, representing just under 7 percent of GDP and employing more than 1.5 million people.[10]

Peter Drucker, the pioneering management guru, summed up this phenomenon: "I am convinced that it is the unconscious, obscure and overpowering drive of millions upon millions of ordinary individual men and women that is the real stuff of history. The biggest story of the late twentieth century could well be the sum of countless small decisions and actions by unnoticed, humble little nobodies out there working in community."[11] In short, nonprofits are the story of our times.

High Levels of Trust

Survey after survey[12] indicates a growing level of trust in nonprofit brands, especially when compared with for-profit or government institutions. Underscoring this trend, the 2002 Edelman Trust Barometer found that nonprofits had approached parity in credibility with business and government. Undertaken again in the dying days of 2008, with no end in sight to the stock market slide, a huge looming deficit, and uncertainty worldwide, Edelman's 2008 Barometer saw a 20 percent decline in trust of business but only a slight accompanying drop in nonprofit trust—with greatest global confidence in NGOs:[13]

- Nongovernmental organizations (NGOs), also known as nonprofits, are the most trusted institutions in every region except Asia Pacific. The global trust total for NGOs is 54 percent compared with business at 50 percent.

- Trust in NGOs is 54 percent compared with government at 45 percent.[14]

Certainly, trust for the nonprofit sector is paramount. As one nonprofit leader stated, "If the communities where we work don't trust us, we have no chance to succeed."

Accelerated Support

Charitable giving in the United States was estimated at $306.39 billion in 2007, when it exceeded $300 billion for the first time in history, according to Giving USA 2008. Two years later the same report estimated that in 2009, giving would rise to $307.65 billion. It was the first decline in giving in current dollars since 1987. Yet, it represented a relatively small dip, and despite the downturn, charitable dollars still represented 2.2 percent of the nation's GDP.[15]

People aren't just donating; they are joining as members and volunteering in record numbers. For example, Amnesty International has 2 million members, and the World Wildlife Fund has more than 5 million. In 2008, about 61.8 million Americans—or 26.4 percent of the population—volunteered through a formal organization.

Businesses and nonprofits are collaborating like never before. While many nonprofits have yet to realize the value of their brand equity, more and more businesses are recognizing the benefits of nonprofit alliances and comarketing efforts. When done right, the relationships with nonprofits help companies stand out and stand for something of importance to their customers and employees.

A growing body of evidence demonstrates the positive impact of nonprofit partnerships to a company's bottom line and reputation. For example, the 2008 Cone Cause Evolution Study revealed that more than 85 percent of Americans say that when price and quality are equal, they will give their business to companies that support a cause they care about. The Datamonitor Group found that a business-community cobranded relationship results in customer acquisition costs 15 percent less than they would be through other means. In other words, connection with a charity provides a halo effect that strengthens companies and can drive additional business.

Nonprofits are also realizing the benefits of company collaborations, which include increased awareness, additional marketing might at no cost to themselves, new revenue streams, and the ability to reach new audiences. Even the *Economist* is touting the benefits and suggests cobranded business and charity relations will become a more common phenomenon, driven by proven mutual gain.

With strong public trust, growing support, and an increasingly prominent societal role, even nonprofits on shoestring budgets can exert outsized influence. Effective branding is often the key.

Changing Donor Decision Making

As nonprofits have grown in number and importance, the charitable marketplace has become more competitive. Donors are becoming more selective and discriminating. Individuals, corporations, foundations, and government all are basing funding decisions on more complex criteria. Examples include values alignment, shared passion and commitment, and the level of trust they have in the NGO's ability to deliver results.

A new breed of supporters is holding nonprofits to higher standards, asking tough questions and looking for outcomes commensurate with the time they commit and the dollars they invest. To stand out, nonprofits must continuously illustrate the ways support is making a difference and increase their relevance through meaningful opportunities for engagement. An authentic brand is a true differentiator and an effective way to connect with supporters. Building a breakthrough brand is the new nonprofit imperative.

How This Book Was Written

In writing this book, we wanted to present the new insights, inventive operations, and leading practices of breakthrough nonprofit brands. We conducted a systematic study, using both quantitative and qualitative methodology, to identify principles that could inform the future of the sector. Our journey was made up of five steps.

On a cold day in February 2008, the Nonprofit Brand Book Team, as we called ourselves, first came together in Boston, bringing more than 70 years of collective knowledge and direct experience with us. We formulated questions that would ultimately help us confirm what it takes to create a breakthrough nonprofit brand. Relying on preliminary background research and our expertise, we outlined seven principles that formed the basis of our hypothesis. We then identified organizational partners and experts to help us test our assumptions and determine which parts of the hypothesis were valid and which, if any, didn't hold up.

Our second step was in-depth research. For this, we administered a major nonprofit survey with partner support from the Association of Fundraising Professionals, the American Marketing Association (Nonprofit Special Interest Group), and Imagine Canada. Specifically, we polled their collective memberships of more than 40,000 nonprofit professionals, gathering responses about sector attitudes toward branding, general practices in the marketing arena, and organizations that are considered to be breakthrough nonprofit brands. (See Appendix A for our assessment tool.)

Paralleling the survey, we interviewed 10 experts recognized for their work in branding—in both the nonprofit and for-profit worlds. We tested our hypotheses, shared survey data, considered their input, and asked them to share their recommendations of breakthrough nonprofit brands for our consideration set.

As we collected original survey and interview data, we simultaneously undertook secondary research using existing information on nonprofit organizational performance, including:

- Top 100 nonprofit organizations list, 2007, *Nonprofit Times*
- Top 300 searches on Guidestar
- "The UK's Most Valuable Charity Brands," Top UK Charities, 2006 Intangible Brands study
- Listing of Top Nonprofit "Philanthropy 400" for 2007, *Chronicle of Philanthropy*
- Charity Navigator efficiency ratings and Guidestar star ratings
- LexisNexis and Charity Village articles
- Publicly available financial data (IRS 990s and annual reports)

From our research, we refined our initial overview of the seven principles used to build, manage, and leverage a breakthrough nonprofit brand; used those principles to help filter candidates from a list of more than 100 leading examples of organizations that embody one or more of those principles; and ultimately narrowed the list to organizations that had clearly articulated their brand meaning and then aligned their mission-based services, communications outreach, and development activities behind the brand. If their efforts had yielded significant demonstrable organizational and social outcomes, they made the short list.

From there, we removed organizations that did not have a formal charitable status—in the United States, a 501(c)(3)—and those that were exclusively grant makers, religious organizations, trade groups, or colleges and universities. Our ultimate selections passed all of these tests and collectively represented a variety of nonprofits of different:

- Ages (pre–World War II, 1945–1980, and 1980 to the present)
- Sizes (under $1 million to $3.3 billion)

- Scopes (local, regional, national, and international)
- Regions (west, east, south, north)
- Types (health, human and social services, education and youth, environment, arts and culture, and international development)

Once we nailed down the final list, we studied web sites, annual reports, articles, and organizational documents. We conducted a series of in-depth interviews with our 11 breakthrough nonprofit brands. In distinctive ways, each had tapped into similar principles to create the tremendous social and organizational impacts they are known for today.

Using rich data, we honed the seven principles they deliberately or, in a number of cases, unknowingly used to create brands that break through in multiple areas. Many of the groups profiled used a combination of principles. Rather than highlight how each organization uses each of the principles, this book will go deep to describe how each organization has used at least one particular principle as part of its brand-building equation.

Our Best Practice Examples

The 11 NGOs are recognized leaders in their field, respected by their peers and experts, and celebrated through awards, extensive media coverage, and/or inclusion in leading indices. They have built and lived their brand in ways that have enabled long-term relationships with corporate, government, and media partners; secured passionate, ongoing commitments from people who have adopted the cause as their own and recruited others to join in; used their brand platform to generate revenue beyond philanthropic gifts; and achieved significant social impact that is constantly propelling their organizations forward.

These extraordinary organizations are quite varied. Some are well established, with storied histories. Others have been formed relatively recently to tackle newer social problems. Some are large, with significant operations worldwide. Others are more modest, with operations focused exclusively on local communities.

Some have mandates to save lives or to advance major social ills. They drive movements and rally large groups of committed people, resulting in widespread social change. Others play a different and quieter role but have an equally important place in the community. They enhance artistic life, help disadvantaged young people make it to college, or support childhood survival around the world. They may not have people marching in the streets, but they compel a critical mass of the right people to help change our communities and the world for the better.

All of the nonprofits we profile understand the importance of connecting with what matters most to their key stakeholders. They have gotten good at unleashing the collective energy residing within a growing group of brand champions. Most importantly, they have found incredible ways of doing things, ways that work better than what existed before.

The authors' overarching philosophy is that a rising tide lifts all boats. With that in mind, this book showcases remarkable efforts to enhance our collective lives. It results from the willingness of 11 outstanding organizations to openly share the secrets of their success with the nonprofit sector as a whole. We sincerely thank them for their generosity and commitment to the greater good.

How to Use This Book

Your brand journey begins with a commitment to leadership: to stand for something that your constituents believe in, care about, and will work to achieve. This book provides the opportunity to learn from gold standard nonprofits by showcasing their practices in action.

In each chapter, we share principles, techniques, and the latest tools to shed new light on challenges your organization may be facing. We also provide a road map to help you move from a base to a build to a breakthrough brand (see Figure I.1).

Base: Fulfills the minimum brand requirements. The emphasis is helping an organization stand out. It presents a focused and differentiated position that is relevant to core constituents. Base-level work provides a foundation for communicating functional benefits, and often includes practical tools and templates. The base level articulates a brand that people can understand and count on. Work at this level helps to solidify support for the organization.

Build: Satisfies a higher-order need and connects to constituents on an emotional level. As an organization moves along the brand continuum, the build level helps an organization stand up for a cause. By

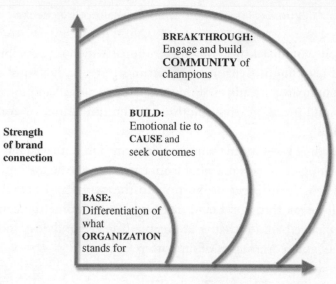

Strength of brand connection

BREAKTHROUGH:
Engage and build
COMMUNITY of
champions

BUILD:
Emotional tie to
CAUSE and
seek outcomes

BASE:
Differentiation of
what
ORGANIZATION
stands for

Brand strength and value

FIGURE I.I   **Breakthrough Nonprofit Brand Continuum**

layering on a passionate commitment that is bigger than organizational survival, build brands connect to the heart of their constituents and what they care about and believe in.

Breakthrough: Reaches the highest level by building a community of owners. The relevant, differentiated brand meaning becomes a rallying point that diverse stakeholders champion as their own. Supporters inside and outside the organization stand together and advance a higher cause. A breakthrough brand engages the hands and yields the greatest return on investment by inspiring action. Long-term sustainability is the end result of brands that consistently follow the continuum from base to build to breakthrough.

Your Brand Journey

Building a breakthrough brand for your organization is a journey, not a destination. It would be a mistake to treat the branding process as a discrete project with a beginning and an end. Branding cannot be checked off your to-do list.

Just as you wouldn't leave your mission unattended or your programs unchanged, branding is dynamic. To remain strong, brands must be purposefully built, managed, and evolved. You need to rally champions to protect your brand meaning from dilution, misinterpretation, or confusion. Focus is a must.

Brand building takes more than a simple campaign with a catchy slogan. It requires a long-term commitment from every part of the institution, and it derives strength in direct proportion to the depth and breadth of its adoption. To break through, brand meaning must become the central organizing principle behind what your organization says and does and how it interacts with your community of supporters.

WHO SHOULD READ THIS BOOK

This book is for all those interested in catalyzing dynamic results for the nonprofit organizations they serve. It provides a practical road map for:

- *Nonprofit leaders* to gain new insights, learn proven best practices, and apply practical approaches to organizational challenges. It is written for and uses examples from organizations of all sizes and scopes— from a health concern with almost $1 billion in revenues to a small education-based nonprofit that tapped its brand to boost annual earnings from $50,000 to over $1 million.

- *Nonprofit communications and development professionals* to deepen their existing knowledge and inspire new ideas. It will help them apply the principles of breakthrough nonprofit branding to their daily to-do lists.

- *Board members and volunteers* to help their charities of choice expand their reach, strengthen their support and influence, and increase their impact.

- *Marketing agencies and consultants* to enhance their guidance. It offers groundbreaking branding practices that are well ahead of generally accepted nonprofit marketing wisdom.

- *Academics and students* to accelerate their learning and bridge the gap between theory and practice.

- *Business leaders* to identify strong potential partners and help propel their work with nonprofits and the causes they support.

If you're reading this book, you're probably open to thinking differently, looking at conventional issues through a new lens, and trying alternative approaches. Whether you need to create, revitalize, or reposition a brand, you will find time-tested wisdom and creative new thinking in the pages that follow.

A Resource to Start Your Journey

What's holding the sector back? In our extensive 2008 survey, nonprofit professionals said the number one barrier to disciplined branding was lack of internal executive leadership support and general understanding from other key colleagues.[16]

Even breakthrough brands experienced this challenge. As Komen's Susan Carter Johns shared, "Not everyone understood our branding efforts. We didn't really gain traction until our senior leadership, including our board, embraced the idea."[17]

Resources, both human and financial, were listed as secondary barriers; a significant number of respondents just didn't know where to start. If that's the case for you, don't worry. You're not alone. This book showcases best practices in building a breakthrough brand and provides tangible examples of each principle in action.

In addition, the authors of *Breakthrough Nonprofit Branding: Seven Principles for Powering Extraordinary Results* have further resources at www .breakthroughnonprofitbranding.com. We encourage you to use both to communicate the benefits of branding among your colleagues. We hope it will help to transform their perspective of brand from a trademark to a true driver of organizational and social good.

The New Nonprofit Imperative

Branding is not a straightforward process; it is an iterative journey. Like all great journeys, it starts with small steps, determination, and a willingness to learn along the way.

As the nonprofit leaders profiled in this book will attest, although branding necessitates an investment of resources, when done right, the benefits far outweigh the costs. Ultimately, it pays huge dividends and is one of the most effective investments in any organization's sustainability and results.

Building a strong brand is no longer something nice to do, but the new must-do nonprofit imperative. It may even determine your ability to survive in today's highly competitive, global nonprofit landscape.

As Peter Drucker predicted, "The 21st Century will be the century of the social sector organization. The more economy, money, and information become global, the more community will matter. And only the social sector nonprofit organization performs in the community, exploits its opportunities, mobilizes its local resources, solves its problems. The leadership, competence, and management of the social sector nonprofit organization will thus largely determine the values, vision, the cohesion, and the performance of the 21st century society."[18]

We agree. Let the journey begin.

CHAPTER 1

From Traditional to Breakthrough Nonprofit Branding

"Brand is not the name, the tag line, or the pretty colors. . . . The brand is the set of expectations and beliefs the marketplace has about what you do."[1]

—David Placek, President and CEO, Lexicon Branding, and Board of Directors, NatureBridge

"Our brand is our key asset. We don't sell widgets; we have a brand and a community tied to it."[2]

—Emily Callahan, Vice President, Marketing and Communications, Komen for the Cure

The world now boasts more than 2 million nonprofits, fueled by a 35 percent increase in the number of organizations in the United States and Canada in the past decade alone. In this complicated philanthropic marketplace, people are overwhelmed by a deluge of overlapping messages from a vast array of organizations—which are often difficult to distinguish.

How can you help your organization stand out among this long list of choices? How can you maintain and grow a vibrant community of supporters through unpredictable political and economic ups and downs? How do you become a charity of choice? The answer lies in building a breakthrough nonprofit brand.

WHAT IS A BRAND?

A brand is a collection of perceptions about an organization, formed by its every communication, action, and interaction. It is what people collectively say, feel, and think about your organization. In short, it's your reputation, identity, and good will with stakeholders and in the community.

A strong brand can be a nonprofit's most valuable asset. It can carry an organization through good times and bad as well as predispose people toward a personal and emotional connection to the group it represents. Because it is linked to reputation, a strong brand drives tremendous economic, social, and political gains for its organization. In fact, in most cases, brand accounts for more than 50 percent of a nonprofit organization's market value.[3]

You have probably noticed the growing global recognition of the value a strong brand can provide to a range of entities, from countries and individuals, to political parties and major multinational corporations, to the local corner store. So it is not surprising that some nonprofits are consciously strengthening their organizations by building compelling brands. This process creates deeper, longer-term, and more loyal relationships with their constituents—and, when it is done with care and consistency, will inspire others to join in. It results in the building of a breakthrough nonprofit brand.

BREAKTHROUGH NONPROFIT BRAND

A breakthrough nonprofit brand (BNB) articulates what an organization stands for: the compelling, focused idea that sets it apart and is meaningful to its supporters. An organization that cultivates a BNB puts its constituents at the heart of its identity. It makes the brand personally and emotionally relevant and creates a sense of community around unifying values, commitments, and concerns.

A breakthrough nonprofit brand has a three-dimensional value proposition (see Figure 1.1):

1. *Convinces the head:* People respond to an organization's need for support only after they understand what it stands for and see how it can be relevant and meaningful to them. Effective nonprofits rationally articulate a unique and differentiated idea that explains what their

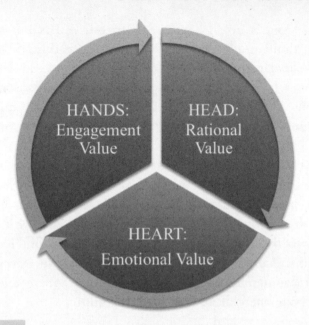

FIGURE 1.1   **Three-Dimensional Value Proposition of**
Breakthrough Nonprofit Brand

organization does better than others. Then, they go further and demonstrate how this core concept is relevant to their supporters.

2. *Touches the heart:* A BNB goes beyond institutional survival to serve a higher purpose. It puts a larger cause and the outcomes they seek ahead of its organizational needs. While this approach may seem risky, it can act as a magnet for those who are passionate about the issue at the core of a nonprofit's mission.

3. *Engages the hands:* People believe what they are told only if their experience is consistent with that message. Stakeholders want the chance to get involved with the entire organization. When asking for support, offer a variety of ways to engage them. Knowing that people like to be around other people who share the same beliefs and care about similar issues, a BNB creates a sense of community, both inside and outside the organization. It unites groups of strangers in an experience of kinship by fostering shared experiences and commitments.

Brand building is not a haphazard process. A BNB is strategically focused and thoughtfully built. As you will see as this book unfolds, a high-performance nonprofit carefully defines its brand and what it means to constituents. It uses the brand to prioritize and make decisions about its operations. And it brings the brand to life by aligning mission-based programs, development activities, and communications outreach around it.

With the backing of the CEO and senior leadership, brand building can become the catalyst for continual self-assessment and innovation. It is a must-do for creating a unique organizational identity that is infused with passion and trust. Forward-looking senior leaders ensure that this brand-centric philosophy is embraced by the whole organization. They leverage the brand to strengthen donor loyalty, recruit top executives, rally staff members, meaningfully engage volunteers, drive diversified funding streams, and, ultimately, make a greater social impact.[4]

TRADITIONAL NONPROFIT BRANDING

Every nonprofit has a brand—regardless of whether it is a priority. As more nonprofits try to set themselves apart, branding is an increasingly hot topic. As suggested in studies by the Association of Fundraising Professionals and the authors, a growing number of nonprofits want a breakthrough brand, but many are not quite sure what such a thing is, how to do it, or how to ensure that the resources invested will benefit their organization.

Traditional thinking is that a brand is more or less just an organization's logo or suite of communications materials. Some nonprofits develop brand usage guidelines that prescribe fonts, color palettes, and design parameters. More sophisticated traditional branding exercises get closer to the heart of the brand by providing a clear statement of values and a unified set of messages that express the organization's identity. Yet, most still lack a compelling, overriding idea that drives strategy and infuses every decision, activity, and communication with a deeper and distinctive purpose.

When nonprofits conduct traditional branding exercises focused on enhancing communications and stimulating fund raising, the result is typically new packaging, which has the potential for moderate short-term gains. However, when these efforts do not yield significant, long-term revenue growth or attract media attention, the organization typically experiences a wave of disappointment and confusion. Ultimately, questions are raised about how other organizations, often with a simpler design and messaging, could have developed the lucrative breakthrough nonprofit brand position the traditional brander aimed to achieve.

Kids Help Phone, a Canadian nonprofit, is one such BNB with a straightforward logo and tagline: being there for kids. And yet, Kids Help Phone is recognized internationally as a leader in the delivery of anonymous, bilingual phone and online counseling for kids. The charity services more than 3,000 communities and handles in excess of 2 million calls annually. It has articulated and lived a brand that has attracted more than 10,000 volunteers in communities throughout Canada, as well as dozens of leading government, education, nonprofit, and corporate partners, including four companies that have been partners for 20 years.

How did they do it? The answer lies in the difference between traditional and breakthrough nonprofit brands.

TRADITIONAL VERSUS BREAKTHROUGH NONPROFIT BRANDING

Breakthrough nonprofit brands know that their brand identity must outlive individual management teams and economic fluctuations to become an enduring embodiment of their organization's essence. This requires a profound shift in philosophy, as well as a sophisticated approach to ensuring that what they stand for is communicated and lived through every stakeholder interaction. You recognize a BNB when you experience one. There is a discernible difference in the way it walks and talks, a palpable shift away from traditional branding practices:

A shift from campaign to commitment: In the traditional view, branding equals a new look, logo, or language and is often expressed in conjunction with an annual campaign. A BNB aligns its brand meaning—and every brand expression—with an aspirational idea and higher cause. It uses that bigger purpose to tell an enduring story that helps unify its actions from year to year. With this shift, nonprofits can avoid the common pitfall of appearing to put style before substance. The breakthrough approach positions the nonprofit as a hero pursuing solutions that advance the cause and as a convener inviting others to join the movement. This is new thinking. Even the American Heart Association (AHA), a large and innovative organization, only in the past decade recognized itself as a brand.

A shift from communicating activities to benefits: There is an old saying that activities tell and benefits sell. Rather than just reporting on activities, a BNB focuses its communications on the benefits and outcomes that deliver value and address values. This involves making a rational case for the value of an organization's work to the individual and the community. It includes making a personal, emotional connection by addressing constituents' values, aspirations, and concerns. The most effective nonprofits take it a step further by inviting supporters to experience the brand in action as a primary benefit of membership. By issuing compelling, personally relevant offers, a BNB makes association with its brand a top choice over all other alternatives.

A shift from transactions to relationships: A traditional fund raiser or marketer emphasizes annual numbers and dollars raised. A BNB invests in and rewards staff for building long-term relationships. It takes the time to engage in a meaningful dialogue with donors. This ongoing conversation helps illuminate what the organization means to its supporters and what their involvement says about them to others. An effective nonprofit builds trust and long-term loyalty by meeting or exceeding supporter expectations, by listening, meaningfully responding, and doing what it says it will do. It goes beyond the easy, one-time ask and works to create mission-aligned donor experiences that delight and engage while building sustainable revenue streams. It creates a true community of believers.

A shift from being well known to well owned: Being better known does not equate to being better understood or valued. Mass awareness is helpful, but it does not necessarily lead to support and even less surely to love. A BNB appreciates the importance of awareness and fund raiser but spends just as much time engaging internal and external communities around the cause. It believes in the power of many and meaningfully engages a critical mass of people in its cause. Inclusive, not exclusive, it creates owner-based relationships with constituents; rather than experiencing themselves as mere names on a list, supporters feel pride of ownership and view the organization as an extension of themselves and a means to achieve goals they value. The most successful nonprofits distribute power to shape the brand through tools, resources, and training that encourage creative engagement. Meaningful two-way engagement accomplishes far more than any controlled message from the top ever could. By empowering an army of supporters who call the organization their own, a BNB causes people to take another look and creates waves of new recruits eager to commit to the cause.

A shift from organizational silos to integration: In traditional settings, the marketing or communications team is singularly responsible for branding. Although marketing is critical in shaping and presenting a brand, brand building and marketing are not the same. A high-performance nonprofit uses brand as the force behind everything that an organization does, making it the central management preoccupation for the CEO, board, executive team, and all staff and volunteers. Brand is at the heart of governance, operations, and mission achievement. Because a BNB views its brand as synonymous with the organization itself, care for the brand belongs to everyone. Breakthrough nonprofit brands make a concerted effort to break down internal silos and bring the organization together for operational effectiveness. All-out efforts are made to ensure that decisions align with the brand's meaning and represent a clear, consistent message to current and prospective supporters. This creates a sense of cohesion and camaraderie both inside the organization and throughout its extended community.

A shift from conventional to innovative thinking: Doing things the way they have always been done does not position an organization for the future. A BNB asks the hard questions, does the research, and takes calculated risks in embracing big, bold ideas and innovation. It makes strategic investments and hard trade-offs, cutting legacy programs that no longer fit to free resources needed for achieving audacious goals. To ensure harmony with the organization's core identity, all potential actions are assessed according to how well those initiatives reflect the brand. Then, the organization dares to live its brand meaning in ways that are innovative and different, creating a new definition of leadership in its field. BNBs know that the excitement and challenge will grab people, inspire commitment, and stimulate forward momentum. Uncomfortable with complacency, BNBs believe that "if we always do what we've always done, we'll always get what we've always got."

A shift from market competition to cooperation: Traditional nonprofit brand strategy generally is to become the biggest, richest, or furthest-reaching organization. Although all nonprofits must carve out a meaningful and differentiated niche, a BNB also partners with other organizations, including government, businesses, and other non-profits working on similar societal challenges. Since it is almost impossible for one organization to fight for a cause single-handedly and win, a BNB doesn't try to own an issue but rather finds the space within a cause movement in which it can best deliver. It reinforces that position and maximizes its effectiveness and credibility through the ways it brings its brand to life. A clear brand identity facilitates cooperation by defining the strengths an organization brings to its relationships, as well as areas outside its core capabilities where new partnerships could be particularly fruitful.

A shift from program maintenance to property management: Although focus is important, it isn't a mandate to do just one thing. BNBs know oversimplification can be a detriment because it can stifle innovation and leave value on the table. With an intensive brand focus, it is possible—and often necessary—to segment audiences and to stand for something relevant to each of them. This is possible through stand-alone campaigns that are logical extensions of the overarching organizational brand. While filtering out disparate programs that do not fit the organization's master brand framework, a BNB invests in subbrands or brand extensions that are distinctly managed yet remain strategically integrated with the overall organization. They can synergistically strengthen the parent (or master) brand, build emotional and lifestyle appeal for different target audiences, and create unique sponsorship opportunities for corporate partners.

A shift from viewing branding as a cost to a strategic investment: While some nonprofits may view brand building as too expensive and best suited to large organizations with ample resources, BNBs of all sizes know that it is one of the most cost-effective, sustainable ways to strengthen and sustain any organization. Branding does not have to be prohibitively expensive for nonprofits precisely because smart branding is about strategy, not costly ad campaigns. In addition, nonprofits have the advantage of being able to engage highly skilled volunteers, obtain professional support pro bono or at reduced fees, and use the insights in this book and other resources as a guide. As the case studies will demonstrate, almost any charitable group can create deeper, more meaningful brands that stand the test of time. However, building the brand is only the first step. The experiences of BNBs show that disciplined and consistent brand execution is required for the biggest return on investment.

Addressing the Skeptics

The growing interest in nonprofit branding has sparked debate. Critics are suspicious about its value and wonder whether charitable organizations should invest in a realm traditionally associated with corporations. Wary of the costs tied to brand development, skeptics question whether branding is anything more than a facade used to manipulate donors. Others see it as the current flavor of the month.

Their hesitation is understandable. Even the high-performance nonprofits featured in this book have wrestled with these concerns at some point. As U.S. Fund for UNICEF's Kim Pucci explained, "When I first joined UNICEF, brand was a dirty word. I had to edit it out of all of my material."[5] Today UNICEF's brand is at the heart of a dramatically revitalized organization.

Yet, brand building is not a panacea. However powerful branding can be, it can't solve basic organizational challenges. Branding enhances the work of a strong organization; it won't fix poor-quality programs or services, change indecisive leadership, or stick without institutional commitment. As Gregory Boroff, the Food Bank For New York City's former vice president, External Relations, emphatically explained, a brand will not take hold without a well-run organization with solid programs and services. It also can't be sustained without a financial investment in its development and implementation.

While a brand can point the way forward, it can't fix an organization overnight—especially one that has frequently changed its strategy and direction. Typically, boards are impatient to discover the underlying reasons for organizational challenges, but that can take time. So decisions are made quickly, and they often aren't the right ones. Often, a new CEO or executive director is brought on and is eager to set a new direction. The new CEO may have strong new ideas about the brand, yet consistency over time is vital to the success of any branding effort.

Trying to redesign an entire brand strategy using only internal resources can be challenging for many nonprofits. As College Forward's executive director, Lisa Fielder, noted, branding has been vital to the organization's growth. They didn't have the expertise or resources to do it on their own. The agency that helped provided not only direction but also important understanding about what a brand is and can do. Few nonprofit organizations have enough perspective to handle all aspects of brand planning without outside counsel. Most organizations that try that approach fail to realize the full potential inherent in the brand-development process.

Branding can be a winning strategy to raise image, strengthen relationships, build loyalty, grow community support, and achieve important social goals. Yet smart branding takes time and shouldn't be viewed as a short-term quick fix.

SEVEN PRINCIPLES OF BREAKTHROUGH NONPROFIT BRANDING

Making the leap from a traditional brand to a breakthrough nonprofit brand requires new thinking and new ways of doing things. Table 1.1 provides a checklist for the shift that takes place in moving from traditional practices to living the principles of breakthrough nonprofit brands.

The goal of this book is to equip you with the insights and tools to accomplish this shift—a road map of the seven fundamental principles used by BNBs. The principles that have set breakthrough brands apart are not simply additions to the traditional views of branding; they represent the emergence of an entirely new way of thinking. A brief preview of the principles that are overturning previous approaches to communications, fund raising, and organizational development follows.

TABLE 1.1	TRADITIONAL VERSUS BREAKTHROUGH TERMINOLOGY

Traditional	Breakthrough
Organization	Cause
Transaction	Relationship
External	Internal and External
Users	Owners
Supporters	Community
Monologue	Dialogue
Messages	Conversations
Information	Stories
Static	Dynamic
Look and Feel	Experience
Simple	Complex
Own	Share
Direct	Quarterback
Command and Control	Empower
Status Quo	Risk Taking
Reach	Engage
Return on Investment	Return on Involvement
Marketing at	Connecting with

Principle One: Discover the Authentic Meaning of Your Brand

Vision, mission, and values should rarely change, but operating principles and practices must constantly evolve. Changing organizational and marketplace imperatives should be reflected in the way any organization's purpose is articulated and lived. A brand is the bridge between an organization's unwavering mission and its evolving strategies. It is the embodiment of the focused, compelling idea at the heart of the organization's identity. By articulating what an organization stands for, its brand enables it to connect with constituents' core values. It brings them together around common interests and shared hope, aspirations, and beliefs. The authentic meaning of your brand provides the focus and framework for building your organization's strategies. It acts as a filter to determine what your organization will and won't do.

Principle Two: Embed Your Brand Meaning across the Organization

A BNB embeds its brand meaning into every organizational function, from people management to information technology systems. It aligns its mission-based services, communications, development activities, and operations with the brand. By integrating the brand across the organization in meaningful ways, it eliminates silos, creates information-sharing channels, and cultivates shared agendas. This principle provides a road map for embedding your brand's essence into your operations and strategies.

Principle Three: Rally Internal Brand Ambassadors

Frequently, nonprofit organizations focus on branding as an external marketing function. Yet, potential supporters are often introduced to nonprofit brands through contact with internal constituents such as staff and volunteers. A breakthrough brand continuously attends to the way its brand is expressed through the actions and attitudes of its internal stakeholders. Breakthrough nonprofit brands carefully craft communications tools and training, and they use storytelling, rituals, and symbols to create a sense of community. They create an authentic and shared internal brand culture that builds loyalty, cultivates champions and ambassadors, and attracts and retains dedicated employees and volunteers.

Principle Four: Develop 360° Brand Communications

Effective nonprofits build brand identities that are clear, relevant, and engaging for all stakeholders. A breakthrough nonprofit brand is an excellent storyteller. It finds authentic, compelling stories that paint mental pictures of who the organization is, the value and values it represents, whom it seeks to attract, and the benefits for those audiences. Utilizing a variety of integrated communications, including both online and off-line tools, the effective brand dynamically expresses its essence and connects with constituents in ways that are meaningful and relevant to them.

Principle Five: Expand Your Brand by Mobilizing an External Community

A BNB acts as a connector. It builds external communities, knowing that a critical mass of the right people mobilized behind its work is the most effective way to propel its cause. A BNB maintains a constant focus on listening and provides a host of opportunities for supporters to interact with the organization in ways that align with its core brand meaning. It learns from every supporter interaction and responds through continuous improvement. This approach builds lasting and trusting relationships and mobilizes communities. Breakthrough nonprofits build their brands by providing meaningful benefits, delivering results, and creating a sense of belonging in a like-minded community.

Principle Six: Cultivate Partners to Extend Your Brand Reach and Influence

Collaboration is essential. A truly breakthrough nonprofit brand values strategic alliances that offer access to new expertise, relationships, and assets. By joining with others, these high-performing organizations create win-win partnerships that reach new audiences and build loyal communities around the cause.

Principle Seven: Leverage Your Brand for Alternative Revenue and Value

Charities can generate alternative revenue streams by mixing entrepreneurship, service delivery, savvy marketing, and creative fund raising. Increasingly, nonprofits are applying for-profit business concepts to address social and community challenges. The more innovative are using their brands to market their core competencies, develop new products, create aligned businesses, and forge licensing deals and merchandise—allowing them to cultivate new funding streams, drive greater awareness, and realize new value for their cause.

BREAKTHROUGH NONPROFIT BRANDS

There are thousands of worthwhile causes, served by millions of nonprofit groups. This diversity is reflected by the case studies in this book (see Table 1.2). The organizations profiled address a variety of social issues, serve diverse constituents, represent a spectrum of geographic areas, range broadly in size, and run the gamut from storied organizations to those that were founded relatively recently. Yet, they share one distinctive trait: Each excels in living many of the seven highlighted principles.

TABLE 1.2   BREAKTHROUGH NONPROFIT BRAND CASE STUDIES

	Organization	Subsector	Revenue, 2008	Year Established
1.	American Heart Association	Health	$ 681 m	1911
2.	College Forward	Education and youth	$ 900 k	2003
3.	Food Bank For New York City	Human and social services	$ 60.4 m	1983
4.	Goodwill Industries International	Human and social services	$ 3.3 b	1902
5.	Memorial Healthworks! Kids, Museum	Education and youth	$ 600 k	2000
6.	Inspiration Corporation	Human and social services	$ 3.5 m	1989
7.	Kids Help Phone	Human and social services	$ 12.2 m (Canadian)	1989
8.	NatureBridge	Environmental education	$ 12 m	1971
9.	Stratford Shakespeare Festival	Arts and culture	$ 57 m (Canadian)	1953
10.	Susan G. Komen for the Cure	Health	$ 350 m	1982
11.	U.S. Fund for UNICEF	International development	$ 486 m	1945

Summary

- A brand is a collection of perceptions about an organization, formed by its every communication, action, and interaction.

- Branding is the strategic work of discovering a focused, compelling big idea that conveys what an organization stands for that is unique and differentiated—and relevant to its core constituents.

- Effective brands create an emotional and personal connection that brings people together around shared interests, values, and aspirations and inspires action.

- Breakthrough nonprofit brands (BNBs) are strategically focused and thoughtfully built.

- Breakthrough nonprofit brands are well owned, well understood, and celebrated. They walk and talk differently than traditional nonprofit brands. They share ownership of the organization's essence and put their constituents at the center of their brand.

- An organization wins mindshare, loyalty, and resources by authentically conveying personal relevance, demonstrating social impact, and identifying reasons for belonging. Breakthrough nonprofit brands thrive by appealing to the head, heart, and hands.

CHAPTER 2

Principle One: Discover the Authentic Meaning of Your Brand

"We spent two years defining the meaning of our brand and focus on child-hood survival. We used the new focus as an energy force, as a guide to everything we did."[1]

—Caryl M. Stern, President and CEO,
United States Fund for UNICEF

"We wanted to grow. . . . That required a hard look at ourselves to understand the limitations of our current brand."[2]

—Lisa Fielder, Co-Founder and Executive Director,
College Forward

UNICEF's Brand Journey

As the focus group seated itself around the table, there was a strong current of anticipation and curiosity in the room. The U.S. Fund for UNICEF had brought the group together to analyze current perceptions of the organization and test emerging messages. This was a core part of the U.S. Fund for UNICEF's market research, aimed at enhancing its donor connection.

"We asked them to name the attributes of other organizations," explained Jay Aldous, chief marketing and communications officer for the U.S. Fund for UNICEF. "They used powerful and compelling words to describe our rivals, demonstrating their passion and understanding of these groups' work. Then, the facilitator asked, 'What do you think about UNICEF?' Silence."[3]

It was a profound moment. People tried desperately to find something to say about the iconic 60-year-old organization. Finally, someone ventured a response, and others followed. While the comments were positive, they were rooted in nostalgia: UNICEF's founding in the post–World War II era, the Trick-or-Treat for UNICEF program, holiday cards, and UNICEF ambassadors like Audrey Hepburn and Danny Kaye. Few, if any, participants talked about the organization's present-day work or its relevance to their lives. There was little understanding about the modern UNICEF brand, who it served, and what it stood for.

A Rescue from Sameness

The focus group video provided critical ammunition for those who wanted to refresh the brand. "We edited the video to provide highlights and some of the worst moments and shared it with our colleagues. Yes, it was painful," explained Kim Pucci, director of marketing at the U.S. Fund for UNICEF at the time. "Yet, it created the sense of urgency essential to rally the organization around the need for change. We needed to rethink the UNICEF brand—to succinctly define who it was and for what it stood in a manner that was relevant to our core constituents and supporters."

"It was hard for everyone. We said, okay, folks, we all take great pride in the organization. We regularly boast about our high aided awareness and how we are second only to the Red Cross in that area," recalled Jay. "But if no one understands what we actually do, how can we build greater commitment? Awareness alone is not enough to achieve our mission."

Board Chair Anthony Pantaleoni reinforced Jay's assessment. "We were not using our equity, our brand. We realized that while many people had heard of UNICEF, few knew what UNICEF did. Most people knew UNICEF had something to do with children, but that was it. This was limiting our ability to grow our donor base and positively help children around the world."

Exposing Deep Roots

"Our branding journey took us back to our DNA," explained Jay. "We were founded as the United Nations International Children's Emergency Fund as a response to the devastation in Europe after World War II. We were leaders in the child survival and the child rights movement. The U.S. Fund for UNICEF works to advocate for the world's children, increase awareness among the U.S. public of children's needs, and raise funds in support of UNICEF's work."

James P. Grant, the third executive director of UNICEF, who headed the group from 1980 to 1995, was a visionary global leader. His tireless advocacy launched the worldwide child survival revolution. Under his leadership, UNICEF improved the lives of the world's most disadvantaged—children in the developing world. The organization confronted what Grant called "the silent emergency," focusing on low-cost interventions and services under the banner of the Child Survival and Development Revolution.

"UNICEF wouldn't be the organization it is today if it wasn't for Jim Grant," noted Kim Pucci. "At the time, his vision was that every child in the world would be immunized. He was literally laughed at for his audacity." In 1979, fewer than 5 percent of children around the world were immunized. By 2006, that number had reached nearly 80 percent. When Grant passed away in 1995, then First Lady Hillary Rodham Clinton remarked, "James Grant saved more lives in the past 15 years than any other person in the world." His reputation reflected UNICEF's leadership in child survival.

Also central to the U.S. Fund for UNICEF's brand was the role grassroots volunteers played in driving fund raising and advocacy initiatives. They contributed successful ideas like Trick-or-Treat for UNICEF and the holiday card program, and they provided decades of support in propelling these major sources of revenue. Yet, with engagement waning, the formal volunteer service program was disbanded in the late 1990s, leaving staff to run programs once driven by volunteers. Concurrently, UNICEF's leadership in the child survival and development movement was losing focus and momentum.

"We're now coming back to our roots," explained Jay. "Looking at our track record, we knew UNICEF was the indisputable expert on child survival and had decades-long relationships with countries, governments, and other NGOs. UNICEF worked as a quarterback to help set health care agendas in numerous developing countries. We needed to use our brand to invite the public back and enable them to participate on their terms. We wanted their engagement with us, knowing there would be a richness of new ideas we could embrace."

The U.S. Fund for UNICEF knew it could elevate its work in the global child survival movement. To seize that opportunity, it had to take its brand to the next level—moving from basic awareness to deeper brand engagement. Its cause had to become clearer, sharper, and more resonant with the times.

COLLEGE FORWARD'S BRAND JOURNEY

Like many nascent nonprofits, College Forward spent its early years focused almost exclusively on delivering services. "We were driven by the mission," explained College Forward co-founder, Executive Director Lisa Fielder. "Thinking about our brand was not a consideration. Then we got to a point where that just had to change if we were going to build on the programming and expand our impact that was such a focus for us."[4]

Founded in 2003 under the name Admission Control, College Forward believes access to higher education is the right of every young Texan. Its mission is to facilitate the transition to college for motivated, economically disadvantaged students by providing services that make the college application process not only possible but also exciting and successful. The two-year high school program includes after-school coaching focused on all facets of the college application and enrollment process, as well as extensive auxiliary services such as a summer college road trip and parent education classes. Once students head off to college, they enter College Forward's College Persistence Program, which serves as academic and social support that provides virtual advice to students as they earn bachelor's degrees. College Forward has realized remarkable results since its founding—99.5 percent of its students have been accepted to college, and the vast majority are on track to graduate.

An unwavering commitment led to success with its first class and confidence in the organization's ability. "We worked with our first class of students for two years with the sole focus of getting them into college," Lisa recalled. "I don't think anyone was more surprised than us when they actually did it." College Forward did what they had set out to do.

Nurturing Growth

Its early success was contagious. By 2005, the organization realized both a need and an opportunity to expand its reach across the entire Austin, Texas, region. Preparing for such an exponential leap required a hard look at the organization and the limitations of its then-current brand. "We really hadn't clearly defined and articulated what we stood for. That was fine at first, but to grow, we needed to consciously establish a brand that reflected who we were and presented it in a memorable and compelling way," noted Associate Director Emily Steinberg. "We were using our mission as the litmus test for everything we did but hadn't clearly aligned our brand with that mission. This was limiting our ability to expand our work and assist more students."

At the heart of the challenge were the organization's name, logo, and the lack of a brand that was clearly expressed or well understood—even among internal staff. The Admission Control name was a major barrier (Figure 2.1). The original logo, a ClipArt spaceship, tied into the Admission Control name but had no correlation to the organization's mission or values. "Our focus was on the students, and we didn't give our

ADMISSION CONTROL
We launch futures!

FIGURE 2.1   Admission Control

logo or overall brand much thought. It seemed good enough at first, but it didn't take long to realize that it was truly doing us a disservice," Lisa explained.

"I had to spend so much time explaining who we were and what we did," Emily added. "Even worse, for the first year and a half, our grant applications would get turned down. We never got past the first stage of review. Our name was a huge stumbling block. It was just wrong." On a weekly basis, people asked if the organization was a space program—a reasonable assumption given its name, logo, and Texas location. The final straw came when a family member called and hung up, perhaps because he thought he had reached NASA. That certainly was not the message the organization wanted to convey. Yet, as a relatively young organization, how could it completely overhaul its brand without creating confusion or diverting scarce resources from its burgeoning programs?

An Overview of Principle One

Identifying the brand's true meaning is the first step in building a break-through nonprofit brand. Branding meaning answers the question "What do you stand for?" It goes beyond a static identity and describes the singular overarching idea that sets it apart and is meaningful to its supporters.

Brand meaning is the mission and values in action, relevant for the organization's current circumstances and the marketplace realities. A brand meaning is viewed inwardly as daily inspiration for employees and outwardly as an invitation for supporters to be actively engaged with the organization. A powerful brand meaning is a combination of what the organization is today and a portion of what they aspire to be in the future.

To build a breakthrough brand, a nonprofit uses the three-dimensional BNB value proposition model to define its brand meaning. It can be used to create a new brand or analyze the strategic options for established brands.

The BNB has rational, emotional, and engagement dimensions. It reflects the organization's rational unique leadership position that attracts the "heads" of core constituents. It appeals to their "hearts" by forging an emotional and personal connection with them, standing for a cause—something bigger than the organization and its programs. It connects to

TABLE 2.1   ARTICULATING AUTHENTIC BRAND MEANING: FROM BASE TO BREAKTHROUGH CONTINUUM

	Base	Build	Breakthrough
How	Conduct basic research to discover the rational portion of brand meaning: Convince supporters' "heads"	Additional research to discover emotional portion of brand meaning: Touch supporters' "hearts"	Engage with "hands" of supporters: Seek their participation to refine brand meaning
What	Construct position statement or message to succinctly articulate brand meaning	Identify organization attributes to articulate brand meaning across words and actions	Establish brand promise, communicate it, and fulfill it for those who engage with organization
Why	Ensures constituents understand rational description of organization leadership position	Connects constituents to emotional social cause that they believe in	Provides call to action or invitation for constituents to be part of a community
Who	Senior leadership team drives internal process of discovering and communicating brand meaning	Competitors assessed to help target brand meaning	External constituents engaged in researching, defining, and refining brand meaning
Where	Tangible articulation via explicit brand meaning statement or position	Tangible and intangible articulation in key messages and activities	Consistent articulation across all organization says and does internally and externally
When	During times of change – see lists that follow		

their "hands" by creating a sense of belonging, offering multiple means of engagement. By differentiating itself in each of these dimensions, a non-profit builds a breakthrough brand meaning. (See Table 2.1.)

Once an organization uncovers and articulates its unique brand meaning, it uses it as a compass and driving force; all that the organization does stems from it. Brand meaning becomes the organization's central operating principle that serves as a framework and filter for its daily actions. A strong brand meaning bridges a nonprofit's organizational strategies and its identity in the marketplace. It provides deep rationale for those who serve and support the organization and its mission.

When to Evaluate Your Brand

Before considering the how-to success factors for Principle one—discovering your authentic brand meaning—it is important to first understand when and why organizations may embark on a new branding journey. A brand is a long-term investment, not a one-time purchase. Continual micro adjustments ensure that the brand stays relevant and introduce the innovation needed for ongoing impact. However, organizational changes and the evolving marketplace require your brand to get regular check-ins, occasional tune-ups, and sometimes a complete refuel so it remains fresh and continues to foster constituent allegiance. (See Figure 2.7 following the summary.)

If you have experienced any of the following, reassess your brand and the alignment between your brand and your organizational strategies.

Internal Organizational Changes

- Significant organizational growth[5]
- Change of strategic direction that results in a new organizational mission
- Broadening geographic or demographic reach
- Mission drift through the expansion of services into new areas
- Merger of two or more organizations
- Declining revenues or membership base

External Marketplace Forces

- Evolving constituent needs or cultural trends
- Entry of new organization to marketplace with similar mission
- Failure, significant misstep, or mission shift of a major competitor
- Change in technology that threatens programs or creates new opportunities
- Major and far-reaching social and/or economic shifts

Determining the Type of Brand Work Needed

Once you have determined that attention should be paid to the brand, consider that not all brand work is created equal. Your organizational goals and the state of the current brand will determine the level and type of effort required to find your brand's authentic meaning. Review the types below and assess your situation.

Creation: Creating a new organization requires establishing a brand. This is an exciting opportunity to clearly define the organization's authentic meaning, making it personally and emotionally relevant to constituents it seeks to engage.

BNB examples: Healthworks! and College Forward.

Revitalization: This is the most common type of branding work. It can be as simple as clarifying the brand meaning or as involved as focusing all of the organization's efforts or expanding the brand meaning.

Refinement: It is an evolutionary approach that does not alter the core of the brand but recognizes some weaknesses that need to be overcome and/or additional strengths that can be harnessed.

BNB examples: Kids Help Phone, Stratford Shakespeare Festival, and Goodwill Industries.

Focus: Focus involves placing greater emphasis on certain aspects of an organization's work so those areas occupy a stronger position in the minds of its core constituents. The issue becomes what to give up or de-emphasize in order to better position the organization and serve its beneficiaries.

BNB example: U.S. Fund for UNICEF.

Expansion: Expanding the brand involves retaining all the existing characteristics but adding new qualities that strengthen and enhance the original brand meaning. Work in this arena increases the value proposition and relevance of the organization.

BNB examples: Food Bank For New York City, Inspiration Corporation, and NatureBridge.

Reposition: A much more radical approach than the previous ones, this involves changing what the brand stands for. The organization might be moving in a completely new direction as a result of a number of factors, including having successfully solved the original cause issue or because of new information or marketplace competition.

BNB examples: The American Heart Association and Susan G. Komen for the Cure.

How-To Success Factors

A BNB doesn't assume its brand is resonating with key audiences. It is willing to take a brave and honest look at current perceptions of the organization and ask, "What is breaking through? What do we do better than any other organization? Where are we falling down? How can we align our strengths and engagement strategies to become a life-changing force in the world?" By candidly answering these questions, a nonprofit can begin to discover, communicate, and align with its authentic brand meaning.

A breakthrough nonprofit brand uses three steps to guide the creation of its brand meaning.

1. *Research:* Conduct internally and externally via a competitive analysis of the issue and supporting organizations and finally gather feedback from core stakeholders.

2. *Define brand meaning:* Taking findings from its research, a BNB begins to define the desired meaning of its brand by using the three-dimensional value proposition model to attract the heads of constituents, appeal to their hearts, and acquire their hands in direct support.

3. *Refine brand meaning:* Based on these processes, BNBs refine what the organization stands for via simple, clear brand meaning statements that are revealed in messages and in actions.

Discovery Research: Reveal Current Meaning

The branding meaning journey begins with research to analyze and determine current attitudes and perceptions of the organization. This will inform the process of discovering the singular, overriding idea that conveys what the brand meaning stands for. The depth of research required will be determined by the level and type of brand work needed—see Determining the Type of Brand Work Needed (previously discussed) and our case study stories that follow.

1. Internal evaluation—What do you currently do best? What can you do best in the future?

2. External evaluation—How are you different from other organizations? What distinctive space can you own?

3. Core constituent understanding—What do your key audiences and stakeholders value?

Internal Evaluation—What Do You Do Best?   *Review current mission, vision, and values statements:* Examine these foundational documents to determine if your organization's current activities and communications are aligned. Based on your current guiding principles and activities, what does the organization claim to value most strongly and own as a leadership position?

Evaluate organizational DNA and history: Revisit your organization's heritage. Why were you founded? In what ways, if any, is the original idea still relevant today? In what ways is your work unique and compelling? What have you achieved to help you stand out and own a leadership position?

Review current program, beneficiary, and capital assets: Organizations need to determine their core assets—their strongest and most impactful programs, the largest group being served, the physical and capital assets that could provide a competitive advantage. What are your strengths in these areas? What areas could be built on to help you articulate a unique brand meaning? What can your organization do best—and in ways that no other organization can?

Audit current communications material and media coverage: A review of current communications material helps identify the consistency and impact of messages and images. How are you appealing to constituents? Which communications have elicited the strongest response, and why? What criticism, if any, have you heard over the years? Candidly assess what is working and what is not, from an objective point of view; using outside volunteers can be especially helpful for this task. Several BNBs used communication committee members or board members with such backgrounds. Look at media coverage, blogs, and/or write-ups by other organizations to determine what messages are presented.

External Evaluation—How Are You Unique and Different? What Distinctive Space Can You Own?   *Research the competition:* Analyze competitors to see what they are doing by reviewing their mission and vision statements, annual reports, and newsletters to determine their positioning and approach to communications. Chart key competitors according to marketplace position/key message statement, core services and programs, critical partnerships, and communications vehicles. The U.S. Fund for UNICEF looked at organizations such as Save the Children, CARE, and Doctors without Borders to identify the features and attributes that were important to their key constituents and ownable by the U.S. Fund for UNICEF.

Analyze the external marketplace: Examine trends that may be relevant to your cause. For example, review newspaper articles from the past year, social media trends, and statistics to identify an increase or decrease in the need for and/or availability of various services. Look for a confluence of market opportunity, legitimate need (unmet or emerging beneficiary need/interest), and existing momentum (your organization's assets, reputation, programs, and services align in this area).

Core Constituent Understanding—What Do Your Key Audiences Value?

Identify your target audiences: To understand how to connect with your supporters, first you need to know who they are. Nonprofit organizations have two types of constituents: (1) the beneficiaries, or the person whose life is being changed through your work, and (2) the supporters, or volunteers, members, partners, funders, staff, and others who drive your programs forward. Their support is vital to the ongoing success of your organization, and they need to be satisfied by their engagement with you. You should focus your brand research first and foremost on your supporters, although it also is key to understand how they connect with your primary beneficiaries. Narrowing your focus to core constituents in both categories will yield the greatest results.

You can determine your core constituents based on a combination of the following factors:

- *Demographic:* This includes factors such as age, geographic location, marital status, ethnicity, education, and socioeconomic status. For example, College Forward uses demographics—age and location— to target its beneficiaries. Students and educational institutions are its core constituents.

- *Psychographic:* This approach divides potential constituents into groups according to their psychological and behavioral characteristics. Psychographics provides insights into the lifestyles, behavior, and attitudes of individuals, allowing organizations to build more specific and engaging products, services, programs, and messages. As we will see later in the chapter, the U.S. Fund for UNICEF used this approach to deftly target core constituents. The BNBs are using sophisticated research and analysis to change the game.

Survey members of your constituent community: Look to constituents inside and outside the organization to gain insights into what is most meaningful to them. What issues are most important to them, and why? What engenders their pride? What is meaningful and relevant to them? How do they spend their time? What motivates their involvement? Then, gauge their perceptions of your organization. How does your nonprofit stand out? What makes you relevant to them? How would they describe you to a friend? After all, BNBs know it's not what they say about themselves, it's what their core constituents say that matters. What will compel these critical audiences to choose your brand to engage with and support?

This research may be simple or complex. The simplest includes small gatherings of a select group of current supporters. If more resources are available, consider surveying several groups of supporters, from those who are highly involved, to those who periodically give small donations but aren't otherwise engaged, to former or lapsed supporters. To reach a larger sample, it may help to engage a research firm. Listening to core constituents can involve a range of techniques, including:

- *Surveys:* While paper surveys are always an option, technology can play an important part in connecting with stakeholders both internally and externally. Tools like SurveyMonkey (www.surveymonkey .com) make it easy and fast to survey a broad range of stakeholders at a low cost.

- *Focus groups:* Bring together groups of supporters and ask them for responses to specific questions that are harder to explore in multiple-choice or survey form. Responses may be more candid if an outside party, ideally a trained facilitator, leads the groups.

- *One-on-one interviews:* A small number of strategically selected major supporters and influencers are often interviewed one-on-one to gain insights and strengthen relationships.

1. What is your first thought associated with the organization?

2. What is its mission?

3. Whom does it serve? How?

4. What words and images come to mind when you think of it?

5. What social impacts has it achieved?

6. What are its strengths? Its weaknesses?

7. What is most valuable about the organization's work? What makes it unique?

8. What have been your most positive or powerful experiences with the organization? What, if anything, has disappointed you?

9. Which of the following messages are most meaningful to you? Why? Which are less impactful? [Include your organization's messages for review.]

10. What organizations come to mind when you think of [name the issue your organization addresses]?
    a. Why? What are the strengths of each? What key words and images do you associate with each?
    b. Do you support them? How and why? Or why not?

Define: Focus Desired Brand Meaning

Defining the desired brand is the second step in discovering a brand's authentic meaning. Focus is critical. To be truly effective, nonprofits cannot be everything to everyone. A BNB identifies the unique meaning of its brand—the singular, overriding idea that conveys what the organization stands for—in ways that are particularly relevant and meaningful to core constituents. At this stage, organizations must take the deep research from the preceding steps and cull the most important revelations to truly hone in on the authentic brand meaning. BNBs incorporate three critical dimensions within brand meaning—head, heart, and hands.

Breakthrough Nonprofit Three-Dimensional Brand Meaning An organization can begin refining its brand meaning by using the three-dimensional BNB value proposition model (see Figure 2.2).

FIGURE 2.2   **Three-Dimensional Brand Meaning**

- *Base:* Convince the Head—Provide a rational explanation of what the organization stands for, the powerful idea that is focused, relevant, and sets it apart.

- *Build:* Touch the Heart—Layer on the emotional and personal cause constituents care about and believe in, one that inspires action.

- *Breakthrough:* Engage the Hands—Give constituents opportunities to engage and join a community of supporters and champions to help make a difference.

Base: Convince the Head—Rational Explanation of What the Organization Stands For   Using the results of the research, define the rational position that sums up your organization's unique leadership position. Think of the acronym FRUD to guide you in this exploration:

- *Focus:* What you do better than anyone else that delivers on your mission and values?

- *Relevance:* How does your organization address your core constituents and their needs today and tomorrow?

- *Uniqueness:* What are the ways you are distinctive in terms of your assets, history, resources, beneficiary group, alliances, geography, capabilities, and/or knowledge?

- *Differentiated position:* What are the differences between your organization and others working on the same issue?

Honestly and openly identifying these answers from your research should help define that authentic, rational brand meaning for any organization—in a concise way—that is difficult for constituents to argue with and easy for them to understand and rationally agree with. A logical and crisp brand meaning is a powerful focus for decision making. As Kim Pucci of the U.S. Fund for UNICEF stressed, "Determine your line in the sand. You can't please everyone, and you can't be everything. An organization that doesn't focus will dilute its relevance in the attempt to appeal to everyone."

Build: Touch the Heart—Emotional Cause Constituents Care About A BNB serves a higher purpose and defines its brand meaning to tap into the larger cause it supports and the broad social outcomes it wants to achieve. Take the rational summary you've created, and ensure the emotion and passion are incorporated appropriately. This can help ensure the brand meaning acts as a magnet for those who are passionate about the issue. Research around your target audience should help draw the lines between your organization and the deeper cause that tugs at their heartstrings.

The biggest mistake nonprofits make is that they are often so busy doing their work and raising resources that they prioritize the organization before the cause. As the U.S. Fund for UNICEF's Jay Aldous explained, "At the end of the day, our supporters don't care about UNICEF per se. What they care about is the issue, and how their support can help us advance the cause. If your focus is on selling the organization, it is truly the kiss of death."

To ensure their brand is linked to a relevant cause, nonprofits must identify, understand, and get to know their target audience inside and out. "A brand has to convey a universal emotion, as well as a specific and appealing idea that your community of supporters can relate to," reinforced Lisa Fielder of College Forward. By connecting to a cause, nonprofits serve as a mirror for constituents, capitalizing on the fact that people want to be part of something that is a reflection of their concerns, hopes, and values.

Breakthrough: Engage the Hands—Opportunity to Engage with Community All people share a strong, basic need to belong to something that reflects their individual values and commitments. Maslow's hierarchy of needs suggests that belonging follows only food and shelter in importance. Yet, too many nonprofits stop at showcasing their commitment to a broader cause and tangible outcomes. These will not break through unless they provide a clear and compelling call to action and preview of what potential supporters can expect when they interact with the organization. Take the rational and emotional brand meaning described previously, and then ensure that it is actionable.

More than ever before, supporters are insisting that nonprofits share power and give them opportunities to engage on their terms. Constituents don't want to be treated as passive cash cows. They need to feel invited to join in and know how being part of the organization can make a difference in the issue.

A BNB gives its supporters myriad avenues to engage in its cause. This hands-on invitation can create communities that not only believe in the cause but also become fiercely loyal supporters, making unsolicited donations, volunteering, and promoting the organization as if it were their own—because it is.

Refine: Articulate Brand Meaning

Now that all the work has been done to research and define brand meaning, organizations must put it into succinct words. It is critical to refine and articulate brand meaning simply and clearly and then repeat it through communications and actions. A BNB translates its brand meaning into appropriate internal and external messages. Doing so will help ensure consistency and also help to provide a summary for deeper market testing or future tweaking.

- Develop—Concise statement or message that articulates brand meaning and is communicated regularly and consistently.
- Establish—Attributes that align with brand meaning and showcase your brand's personality through words and actions.
- Reveal—Communicate a promise or benefit to constituents who engage with your brand.

Develop—Concise Statement That Articulates Brand Meaning

Develop concise position statement or message: Articulate the brand meaning through a compelling message that is repeated consistently across your organization's communications. Brand meaning is often articulated through a tagline, goal statement, or simply a primary word or phrase owned by an organization.

Establish—Attributes That Align with Brand Meaning

Establish brand meaning attributes that showcase personality: Identify the words you would use to describe the character of your organization if it were a person. Your brand meaning's attributes will dictate the tone of voice for all communications and activities, ensuring consistent and predictable messages that reinforce the brand meaning and what makes your organization unique.

Reveal—Promise or Benefit to Constituents

Reveal your promise: Answer the question of what one can expect when one interacts with the organization. It describes the benefits of engaging with your organization and helps to drive the brand meaning. While a call to action is critical to convey primarily, the promise or benefit should not be forgotten secondarily.

ENLIST PROFESSIONAL HELP

If resources allow, consultants are valuable partners in helping nonprofits discover the authentic meaning of their brands, and distill relevant communications messages. Another route is to explore pro-bono or "low-bono" (extremely reduced rate) services from experienced volunteers, including: experts who may have a personal connection to the issue; consultants/agencies that are relatively new or may be trying to build their portfolios; retired professionals from groups such as SCORE; or marketing and communications executives from corporate partners.

U.S. Fund for UNICEF Digs Deep for Brand Meaning

Through a revolutionized brand, the U.S. Fund for UNICEF today invites its supporters into a cause: putting an end to the preventable deaths of 24,000 children each and every day (2010 numbers). Sadly, the majority of these children lose their lives to situations most U.S. Fund for UNICEF supporters rarely face themselves: malnutrition, unsafe drinking water, or the lack of a five-cent vaccine.

Having saved more children's lives than any other humanitarian organization, UNICEF articulates this leadership in child survival through its new brand meaning and supporting tagline: *Whatever it takes to save a child* (Figure 2.3). Brilliantly executed, the brand issues a call to action—*Believe in Zero*—rallying supporters to help UNICEF reduce child mortality from 24,000 preventable deaths each day to zero. "Literally, there is a daily holocaust that goes largely unrecognized," said Director of Marketing Kim Pucci. "We're asking our supporters to '*Believe in Zero*' by joining with the organization that does '*whatever it takes*' to reach a day when the number of children dying from preventable causes is zero. That's the new heart and soul of the U.S. Fund for UNICEF."

"Our focused brand organized what we do in a highly memorable way," said Jay Aldous. What follows is the story of how the U.S. Fund for UNICEF discovered the true meaning of its brand.

UNICEF Connects with the Head via Research to Find Rational Brand Meaning

"Our initial focus group clearly demonstrated the lack of clarity about what UNICEF stood for," explained Chief Marketing and Communications Officer Jay Aldous. "Further research showed that our top-of-mind awareness among the general public was low. While we had grown our fund raising, other like organizations were achieving higher growth and greater impact. We knew we had to change to stay relevant and continue to deliver results."

Finding the unique meaning of its brand involved significant introspection and external research. Aldous continued, "We looked at other organizations doing similar work to pinpoint our differences. We discovered UNICEF's unique brand was its leadership in saving children's lives.

Lucy Liu, UNICEF Ambassador, actress

24,000

CHILDREN DIE EVERY DAY FROM PREVENTABLE CAUSES.
I BELIEVE THAT NUMBER SHOULD BE

ZERO.

And that's why I support UNICEF. UNICEF has saved more children's lives than any humanitarian organization in the world. In fact, right now, UNICEF is in more than 150 countries, providing children with life-

Believe in zero.
~~24,000~~
unicefusa.org

unicef ✪
united states fund

saving medicine; food; clean, safe water; education; and protection from violence and exploitation. No child should ever die from a preventable cause. Every day 24,000 do. Help UNICEF get that number to zero.

FIGURE 2.3   UNICEF BELIEVE IN ZERO AD

UNICEF had been responsible for saving more children's lives than any other humanitarian organization."

Other organizations provided similar interventions, such as basic survival aids like water, medicine, and vaccinations. Yet, UNICEF's approach made it unique. It married its unsurpassed global reach and expertise with access, innovation, influence, efficiency, and resolve to truly do *whatever it takes* to save the life of a child. Its connection to the United Nations provided additional credibility and influence in its work. The organization had stopped wars to immunize children, it had reached remote locations to provide supplies essential for survival, and it had extraordinary supply systems that ensured efficient, broad-reaching delivery. Again and again, the organization proved its ability to overcome obstacles like politics, ideology, war, and poverty to give children the best hope for survival. The final piece of brand work involved additional research into the organization's core and prospective supporters. The team wanted to better understand their interests, values, and concerns and how UNICEF's work was addressing or could address them. This was a new way of thinking for the U.S. Fund for UNICEF and required additional expertise.

One major advantage for nonprofit organizations is their ability to access highly skilled volunteers and professional services at greatly reduced cost. Jennifer Dorian, a former colleague of the U.S. Fund for UNICEF's Kim Pucci and senior vice president, Strategy and Brand Development, at Turner Broadcasting System, Inc. (TNT and TBS), joined the U.S. Fund for UNICEF's marketing committee, an advisory group of industry thought leaders. Jennifer provided advice, mentoring, and connections. "When Kim called, she was interested in gaining a better understanding of their target audience and how to position the brand. UNICEF was an organization I really believed in, and I jumped in with both feet," Jennifer explained.

Before Jennifer got involved, the U.S. Fund for UNICEF had conducted research with its own donors, garnering useful information. Yet, it didn't understand prospective supporters and what would motivate their commitment to UNICEF. To resolve this, the team analyzed current and prospective supporters from a psychographic and demographic perspective. The process used to segment and understand donor motivation was identical to the one used to determine viewer motivations at TNT and TBS.

There is often skepticism in nonprofit organizations when new research is started. People ask, "Don't we already know this? How is this going to help? Can we afford to spend the money?" But once the process identified significant new insights, the U.S. Fund for UNICEF staff was reenergized.

"The research identified a core supporter community we called 'empathetic globals,' who care about the developing world and feel very strongly that people and the government should do much more to help those in need. When these empathetic globals were asked which attribute of a charitable organization was most important to them in deciding to donate, 'providing basic and essential survival needs' was number one. And UNICEF, among all of the other international aid groups, was the organization most associated with this attribute," explained Kim.

"Joining the empathetics was a secondary group we called 'free spirits,' younger, secular givers who listed international causes among their top concerns. This group was also committed to supporting an organization that provided basic and essential survival needs—work that UNICEF was uniquely providing." With this research, the U.S. Fund for UNICEF developed a profile of an empathetic global named Jackie and a free spirit named Paul to help the organization better understand who they were, what motivated their support, how to reach them, and with what messages. The U.S. Fund for UNICEF has combined these segments into a group known as compassionate global givers.[6]

UNICEF: SEGMENTING DONORS FOR GREATER IMPACT

Meet Jackie, an empathetic globally focused giver (key characteristics of hypothetical donor):

- Jackie is a 48-year-old ad executive with a husband and two teenage children; they live in Connecticut.
- She has a liberal philosophy and feels society has a responsibility to address the ills of the developing world.
- She cares about children and makes them her top priority to help others.
- Spirituality plays a strong role in her life.
- Having achieved financial flexibility, she feels she can afford to give back.
- A concerned global citizen who wants to save children's lives, she has a number of international organizations on her radar, including UNICEF.
- She reads the *New York Times* and *Real Simple,* listens to NPR, and watches CNN, PBS, Bravo, and old films on Turner Classic Movies.

Meet Paul, a free-spirited secular giver:

- Paul is a 35-year-old, unmarried computer programmer living in Seattle.

- A free spirit, he feels there is no right or wrong way to live.

- He has extremely liberal views and believes it's society's responsibility to help others in need.

- International causes are among his top concerns, but he also cares about the environment and animal rights.

- Paul reads the news on CNN.com and enjoys blogging. He reads *National Geographic,* watches HBO and Animal Planet, and listens to alternative rock.

- He wants to pay off his debts but will still do whatever he can to help address issues affecting the developing world, and UNICEF is on his radar.

This constituent segmentation was critical in helping to hone the organization's brand, voice, and message. These two groups represented 34 percent of UNICEF donors. Trigger givers, those motivated to support international aid work in emergency or crisis situations, added 28 percent, giving the organization a possible donor universe of 62 percent of the U.S. giving public.

"With the research in hand, the next job was to convince everyone we should focus," revealed Jennifer. "The same is true in the corporate sector. To have the biggest impact, we can't be all things to all people. We had to concede certain groups and focus the organization's brand, messaging, and efforts on our best prospects."

UNICEF Touches the Heart by Communicating Its Cause

Sometimes the simplest things have the most dramatic impact. In early 2008, the U.S. Fund for UNICEF invited Jennifer Dorian to join its senior leadership retreat. She took a risk and wore a T-shirt from a small nonprofit. It featured two siblings from Darfur and the word *hope.* Jennifer challenged retreat participants to build the same level of emotion into the messaging they were developing. "If we're serious about ending needless child deaths, it can't be about us," explained Jennifer. "We needed to build a bigger tent, act as a catalyst working with others on the ground to achieve the greatest impact."

The U.S. Fund for UNICEF had built the rational story, but to effectively compete, it needed to add emotional, personal elements. The organization wanted to move beyond just the head and infuse the heart. The senior leadership team, led by President and CEO Caryl M. Stern, recognized the power of the cause—ending the preventable deaths of thousands of children daily—and its new rallying cry: *Whatever it takes to save a child.*

"For me, it was about the privilege of saving children's lives, not the job of saving lives," Caryl noted. "We needed to inspire others to join us to make this happen." Caryl presented the Believe in Zero concept in the summer of 2008 at a meeting with the organization's volunteers, key individual donors, and corporate supporters. Caryl's speech was electrifying, and when she said, "Believe in Zero—join us," the room exploded with energy. The concept galvanized the group around the compelling goal at the heart of the brand. "We had 300 people chanting, 'I believe in Zero.' The U.S. Fund for UNICEF had never spoken with one voice and one message. It felt like a revival meeting, not an annual nonprofit conference," Stern recalled.

"There's a balance between humility, confidence, and leadership," elucidated Caryl, who intuitively understood the power of a well-defined brand to provide clear direction. Its renewed brand energized the organization to re-create everything it did. "It helped all of us to think on a scale and at a level we never thought of," said Jay Aldous. "It's not 'what' but 'how' we do it now," added Kim Pucci. "'Whatever it takes to save a child' emphasizes how UNICEF goes to the ends of the earth, against all possible odds, to save children's lives." The UNICEF newly defined brand was infused throughout the organization, from its operating structure to its financial dealings, and from its physical environment to its programs. Subsequently, the mission, vision, and values were updated to reflect the brand meaning.

The U.S. Fund for UNICEF has developed a full complement of guidelines, communications tools, training programs, and stories to provide the visual and verbal identity for the new brand. Thanks to the U.S. Fund's generosity in sharing its story with others, its brand communications framework is provided here.

BRAND PLATFORM: U.S. FUND FOR UNICEF

Brand meaning: UNICEF is *the* authority on child survival.

Believe in Zero: whatever it takes to save a child

Brand position statement: For those Compassionate Global Givers who care about the plight of the world's children, UNICEF does whatever it takes to save a child, and has saved more young lives than any other organization in the world. Only UNICEF has the influence, perspective, momentum, and reach to tackle the whole range of interrelated issues that are causing children to die.

UNICEF personality and voice: Wisdom, dignity, ingenuity, optimism and determination, leadership and collaboration.

Brand promise statement: Because Compassionate Global Givers (CGG) are looking to build a better world, they are committed to the survival and well-being of the world's children. When CGGs join with UNICEF, they feel confident in the knowledge that UNICEF offers the best hope for reaching that goal.

Mission: The U.S. Fund for UNICEF saves and protects the lives of children by supporting UNICEF's work through fund raising, advocacy, and education in the United States. Our mission is to work toward the day when zero children die from preventable causes by doing whatever it takes to give them the basics for a healthy childhood.

Vision: Mobilize the U.S. Fund constituency of individuals, corporations, volunteers, campus groups, civic leaders, legislators, celebrities, and the media to actively work on behalf of children worldwide by providing financial resources for services, raising awareness for UNICEF's cause, and advocating for the survival and well-being of every child.

Values: UNICEF's reach, expertise, access and influence, innovation, efficiency, and resolve mandate we will do whatever it takes to save a child.

UNICEF Engages the Hands by Encouraging Participation

The U.S. Fund for UNICEF began its transformation from a predominantly transactional megaphone approach—send us a donation because it's the end of the year and you can get a tax deduction—to an engagement model inviting supporters to "help us do whatever it takes to put an end to the preventable deaths of children." The organization determined it would create a brand meaning based on its strengths and then build a community around it. This new mantra was a clear demonstration of its single-minded focus on children's services and volunteerism.

"This required a complete shift in mind-set. It wasn't just about coming up with new, clearer messaging; it was going to take a totally different approach to branding. We needed to move from whatever it takes to get a donation to whatever it takes to save a child; from giving to joining; from donors to members; from an emotional reaction to shared values," Jay remarked with conviction. Its new brand platform helped shift its orientation from a monologue with UNICEF at the center to a dialogue around a higher purpose.

Moving from a transactional to an engagement model has been core to the brand. "We're widening the banks of the river," Jay explained. "In the past, the river was very narrow and the banks very high, meaning we totally controlled our brand and interactions with others. Our new reality is making much more room for participation, driven by and for our community of supporters. We let people join on their own terms and support the issue in creative ways that we might not have come up with on our own."

There are a growing number of tangible examples of this change in action. The Tap Project, founded in 2007 in New York City, is a dynamic consumer engagement effort created by adman David Droga. It involves a simple concept: Restaurants ask their patrons to donate $1 or more for the tap water they usually enjoy free. All funds raised support UNICEF's efforts to bring clean and accessible water to millions of children around the world. Communities have embraced the program across the United States and Canada. "It's customized locally, and no two are alike. Tap's energy is huge and delightful. It was a refreshing change for us," Jay noted, pun intended! (See Figure 2.4.)

Letting others utilize UNICEF's brand in a highly decentralized way was unheard of. Yet the power of the new brand, *Whatever it takes to save a child*, permitted experimentation and new ideas, especially from others outside the organization. Tap (www.TapProject.org) embodied a change in the way UNICEF engaged, communicated, and raised funds. Today, more than 20 cities and five corporations have signed on as Tap partners, raising awareness of critical water issues in developing countries. But more

FIGURE 2.4   UNICEF Tap Project

importantly, 60 million days of clean and safe drinking water have been provided to children in need.

COLLEGE FORWARD BRIDGES THE GAP

Like many small nonprofit organizations, College Forward (then Admission Control) started small and grew organically, without any plans for brand development. Mounting success in students' college acceptance led to growing interest in the program from funders and the community in central Texas. "We became convinced a more precise brand meaning would help us as we approached more donors and engaged more partners to expand the schools involved in the program," explained Lisa Fielder. "Formal brand messaging, proactively managed, would reaffirm our credibility and build trust with current and potential supporters." What follows is the story of how College Forward discovered the true meaning of its brand.

College Forward Realizes the Need for Brand Work

A combination of pure serendipity and passionate commitment brought Emily Steinberg to College Forward. While researching AmeriCorps opportunities, she stumbled upon glowing reviews of Admission Control in Austin, Texas. "I was so impressed with the clear metrics and evaluation outcomes. I wanted to be part of a start-up, work with passionate staff, and contribute to a measurable, quantitative goal," explained Emily of her decision to join the organization in 2004 through AmeriCorps VISTA, the national service program designed to fight poverty.

Not long after Emily joined the organization, she began experiencing challenges in communicating its mission and expertise to those outside the organization. "When I talked about us to new people, including funders, it required a lengthy explanation. It was clear we needed to change," recalled Emily, who at the time was responsible for grant writing. "While Lisa understood this challenge, it took my best persuasive skills to convince her we needed to rethink our brand."

Lisa Fielder, co-founder and executive director, had reservations. She felt a connection to the original branding and, like any good nonprofit leader, worried about the cost associated with developing a completely new brand. From a purely practical perspective, she considered it something that would be nice to have, not something the organization needed to have.

At the time, Lisa didn't fully understand what a brand was and what it could do for the organization. "Brand was a hard thing for me to get my head around. I knew that it included our logo. I now understand that it's our reputation in the community and what we want people to think of and do when they hear our name," she explained. The organization's mission had always been its driver, yet it was not reflected in the Admission Control name or logo. Lisa knew that to grow, the organization had to rethink how it presented itself to its community. "We had to look at our brand not just as an add-on that made us look pretty," she added, "but something that explained to our supporters what we stood for, drove how we acted, and articulated what we were working to achieve. It also needs to invite people to join us and inspire action."

With everyone on board, the group began an 18-month branding journey with support from the Cartis Group, a local advertising firm. "We benefited from outside experts who helped us research and define our brand and develop communications to powerfully express it. In addition to our mission, our already deeply entrenched traditions and values were foundational pieces of this work," explained Lisa. The organization had a head-start on its branding work with a solid understanding of the unique space it owned.

Research doesn't have to be expensive or complicated to be effective. Engaging with core constituents and then actively listening to them was a key step toward revealing how the organization was different and meaningful to supporters. Directed by the agency, the organization's staff worked to uncover the core meaning of the brand. "We held a focus group of staff members and used dictionaries searching for words associated with our work," Emily remembered. "Staff has a key voice in defining an organization's brand through their daily work. It's important to consult them and consider their views on branding."

From there, the organization reached out to its core supporters. "We have a clearly defined group of constituents and wanted their input and thoughts," explained Emily. "We have a complex community that includes Texas colleges and universities, school districts, state agencies, and other community-based organizations. Teachers, students, parents, donors, and volunteers are also important constituents. We involved them in our research, incorporated their good thinking, and secured their buy-in in the process. We kept it simple by using an online survey tool to test words, images, and messaging, as well as potential new names. What we heard was that folks were very supportive of two words—*college* and *forward*," stated Emily.

"Our research really helped us articulate what we were best at and what was important to our core audience, "added Lisa. "It gave us the confidence to build on our success of getting students into college, which we know is such an important community need."

College Forward Connects with the Head by Shifting the Message

"What we discovered from our research was the need to articulate and focus on our success in getting students in college," stated Emily. "With our commitment to measurable results, we can speak with confidence that this is how we stand out. Since doing our branding work, our outcomes research continues to tangibly demonstrate our accomplishments."

"Brand meaning needs to define who you are and what you stand for. It also has to have aspirational elements to it. Our rebrand coincided with what might be called an organizational recalibration," Lisa Fielder reflected on her brand journey. "We needed a better name and more exciting visuals. But equally important was our shift in focus from admission to college. We realized gaining admission was the easy part. What was apparent was that persisting through college was a challenge we needed to address. We identified an urgent need to work on parent engagement, financial aid and literacy, career exploration, study skills, and other 'soft' skills. College persistence was becoming as important as college admission. Our new branding reflected this broader role for the organization.

"The new name affirmed our focus on college and advancing students forward," Lisa said. The adopted logo (Figure 2.5) represents, among other things, both the challenge and the possibility of working through the complicated and often confusing college application process. The bright green color was chosen to symbolize growth, change, and renewal. More broadly, noted Lisa, "We're innovative and don't always approach things in a methodical way, even though we always deliver good work."

The organization has a very strong culture, intensely focused on students' success, and the mission talks about making the process exciting and

FIGURE 2.5   College Forward Logo

rewarding. The organization strives to ensure that students have fun in the midst of hard work. The redefined brand captures that culture of positive, fun energy and is reflected in the new positioning.

The organization is changing the lives of motivated, economically disadvantaged young people in Texas by providing services that make college access and persistence not only possible but also exciting and rewarding. The extraordinary achievements are driven by a commitment to collaboration, a passionate belief in the value of and the right to an education for young people, and a desire to make real, lasting change.

Why is this important? Access to higher education is still largely stratified on the basis of income and social status.[7] "So much potential is being lost by not giving all students a chance at a college education," Lisa said with passion. "For example, according to the most recent data available, less than half of students who enroll at Texas universities earn a diploma in six years. For Hispanic students in Texas, graduation rates are much lower—only 44 percent of Hispanic students who enroll in college ever graduate, including transfers. Of course, this doesn't account for the fact that Hispanic students are far less likely to enroll in college in the first place.[8] This resonates with us at College Forward because almost two-thirds of College Forward students are Hispanic."[9]

How is College Forward making a difference?

- Virtually all of their students have been accepted to college—more than 99 percent thus far.

- Ninety-two percent of their students enroll in college immediately following high school graduation.

- Eighty-four percent of their students attend four-year colleges and universities; this is particularly impressive, considering that about half of all Texas college students attend community or junior colleges— a group that disproportionately includes low-income and first-generation students.

- To date, 77 percent of their students are still enrolled in college and making progress toward a degree, and many of the rest are actively working with the persistence program to reenroll. As mentioned before, in Texas, less than half of students who go to college—without accounting for income or social status—end up graduating.

College Forward Touches the Heart through Purpose with Passion

"Getting disadvantaged but motivated students into college is really a higher calling," stated Lisa. "We believe that access to higher education is the right of every young Texan. We are intentionally appealing to a sense of justice. We focused on college access and college persistence to better align with the national movement to increase college-going rates of under-represented students. This cause is at the heart of our brand and very much incorporated into all that we say and do and how we engage stakeholders."

College Forward's marketing communications material evolved to reflect the new brand meaning, putting students front and center and incorporating designs and graphics emphasizing fun. The organization's personality shines through, as it reflects innovation, success, and fun. "The graphics are exciting and lighthearted, just like our events, our people, newsletters," explained Emily Steinberg. "Everything we publish or host reaffirms the connection between our organization's cause and the students we serve. We have a really strong brand because it demonstrates our organizational ethos so well."

Added Lisa, "Our brand is not just a way to communicate; it's what we do, how we live and breathe within our organization and engage our stakeholders at every touch point."

College Forward Engages the Hands through Expanded Involvement

The desire to grow into a regional organization was the key driver in the brand discovery process, which paid off with dramatic results. Within a year, the organization expanded the number of Texas high schools and students in the program. "In the first three classes from 2003 to 2006, we served only students in Hays County, south of Austin. Then in 2006 and 2007, coinciding with our rebranding, we added new junior classes at four new high schools in three school districts across Central Texas. This increased our total program enrollment from 103 to 325; we recruited 222 new junior students in 2006 and 2007, an almost fivefold increase from our new-student enrollment the year prior," explained Emily Steinberg, with justified pride. (See Figure 2.6.)

FIGURE 2.6   Americorp staff from the College Forward Program

"Our new branding was instrumental in facilitating more involvement in our program," explained Lisa. "When supporters and partners join, they are confident that College Forward will deliver an extraordinary impact on the lives of students. They know our promise is to assist motivated students to successfully enter and graduate from college. Through their support, we are empowering students to have a brighter future—for themselves and for the benefit of the communities where they will live and work."

The newly defined brand better enabled it to engage students, volunteers, and staff as brand ambassadors. Key supporters now wear College Forward T-shirts, share stories, and employ proven fund-raising tactics to expand involvement. As a small organization with limited resources, College Forward uses the revised brand as a rallying flag—it provides a straightforward way to consistently communicate with current constituents and potential supporters.

It has invited greater engagement, which has strengthened financial support and social outcomes. "As soon as we defined our brand, the impact was almost immediate. Award letters started coming in saying, 'Congratulations, you've won,'" explained Emily. "Even with the same mission, services, and focus, we were getting completely different responses to our work with the clarified brand."

"We are very focused on social change and have the very specific benchmark of increasing our students' attainment of bachelor's degrees by 25 percent over the rate of demographically similar students. I truly believe our rebranding has been central to helping us achieve critically important goals," Lisa said. The organization's dynamic, dedicated cofounder, Lisa can be truly proud of the 2006 rebrand. College Forward's revenues grew from just over $200,000 in 2006 to almost $1.8 million in 2010. It has served more than 1,400 students, partnered with universities nationwide, and received numerous awards, including the Star of Texas Award, Bank of America's Neighborhood Builder Award, and recognition from the U.S. Congress for the excellence of their AmeriCorps VISTA project. The organization has a remarkable 99.5 percent success rate with its students being accepted to college, 85 percent to four-year institutions.[10]

Numbers alone never tell the full story of an organization's extraordinary impact. Bernard Blanchard, superintendent of the Del Valle Independent School District and supporter of College Forward's largest school site, sums it up by saying, "College Forward is one of the best things that ever happened to this high school."[11]

PRINCIPLE ONE: SUMMARY

- A breakthrough nonprofit brand (BNB) discovers its authentic brand meaning—the singular, overriding idea that conveys what the organization stands for. Built from a strong mission and values, an organization's brand meaning uses the three-dimensional BNB value proposition and seeks to provide a rational description of the organization's leadership position; create an emotional and personal connection that brings people together around cause; and engage people in a like-minded community and inspire action.

- Defining and articulating an organization's brand follows a process:
  - *Discovery research* to find the brand meaning. Brand research can include the following:
    - Internal evaluation—Based on mission and values, what can you be best at? What assets does the organization have, such as unique

programs, beneficiary group served, or physical and capital assets that could provide a competitive advantage?

- External evaluation—Based on marketplace and community trends and needs, what are the needs that can be filled by the organization and create a unique position?
- Core constituent understanding—Based on target audience identification, what is meaningful and relevant to them?

- *Define the brand meaning* using the BNB value proposition model of head, heart, and hands to develop a more compelling road map to constituent engagement.
  - *Base: Convince the head*—Rationally explain what the organization stands for to gain a crisp and distinct focus that is relevant, unique, and differentiated.
  - *Build: Touch the heart*—Layer on a cause that is bigger than the organization and focuses on the outcomes it seeks to achieve.
  - *Breakthrough: Engage the hands*—Invite current and potential supporters to lend a hand to deeply engage with the community through many means.

- *Refine the brand meaning:* Articulate the brand idea through concise brand statements and messages that simply and clearly state what it stands for (see Figure 2.7).
  - Develop—Concise position statement or message that articulates brand meaning and is communicated regularly and consistently.
  - Establish—Attributes that align with the brand meaning and showcase a brand's personality through words and actions.
  - Reveal—Communicate a promise or benefit to constituents who engage with your brand.

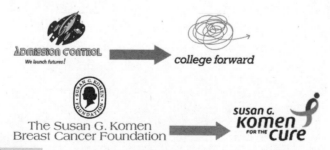

FIGURE 2.7   **Examples of Shift in Brand Meaning**

CHAPTER 3

Principle Two: Embed Brand Meaning across the Organization

"Our new brand meaning became the driver for our organizational development. We added new areas, aligned activities, and made investments in staff and programs to have the greatest impact. This work didn't happen overnight, but we began to put the pieces in place to strengthen what we stood for in the community."[1]

—Lucy Cabrera, President and CEO,
Food Bank For New York City

"The American Heart Association (AHA) identified 'what we stand for,' but that alone wasn't enough. To change perceptions about the AHA and have the impact we wanted, we needed to use this as the focus and framework for our internal and external strategies, so the whole organization could rally behind it."[2]

—Kathy Rogers, Executive Vice President,
Consumer Health, American Heart Association

THE AMERICAN HEART ASSOCIATION'S BRAND JOURNEY

In February 2004, a flicker of red sparked hope across the country. Six years later, that red flicker had grown into a full-blown blaze of energy and passion as women banded together to wipe out heart disease.

The American Heart Association's Go Red for Women campaign was a simple and emotional rallying cry that extended the power of the American Heart Association (AHA) brand meaning. With its iconic little red dress, the program brought the issue of women and heart disease—the number one killer of women—to American society. Determined to change attitudes and inspire action, the AHA set out to leverage its research in a way that was fresh and highly accessible for a broad consumer audience. As the long-standing authority and go-to resource for the latest, most credible science on heart disease, the American Heart Association had gained the public's trust, but it needed to gain their hearts as well.

As a public-facing effort, Go Red stimulated massive community engagement, expanded the organization's beneficiary audience, attracted new channels of support, and garnered extensive media coverage. *BusinessWeek* hailed National Wear Red Day, a national awareness day and corporate fund-raiser associated with Go Red for Women, as having "marketing hustle worthy of a new car rollout."

"It was remarkable the way the organization rallied around the Go Red initiative," observed Kathy Rogers, executive vice president, Consumer Health, American Heart Association. "We integrated and aligned the program right across the organization. Every department was involved—from communications to fund-raising to government relations to educational outreach."

Refashioning the Structure for Transformational Change

Go Red for Women was the first in what has become a series of four cause programs relating to heart health. Each embodies the AHA's brand meaning, best communicated through its new tagline, Learn and Live. This more emotional, consumer-oriented approach represented an important shift from the 2004 tagline, Fighting Heart Disease and Stroke, which was more internally focused, clinical, and passive. Driven by a big, bold commitment to reduce coronary heart and stroke risk and disease by 25 percent by 2010, the organization made major changes to its strategies, operational structure, and systems, while simultaneously changing the way it was perceived in the country. (For the American Heart Association's 2020 commitments, see Appendix.)

"We had a strong brand meaning grounded in our science and research. People listened to what we had to say because of it. It was our funded research, for example, which led to the establishment of CPR and to the understanding of dietary fat and cholesterol as risk factors for heart disease," explained Gordon McCullough, chief operating officer. "While we were proud of our reputation, we knew we had to reach more people with stronger, more compelling educational information to increase our impact and decrease deaths from cardiovascular disease."

The changing information marketplace meant competing with online resources such as www.WebMD.com and www.mayoclinic.com, where patients could access information easily in real time. The American Heart Association knew it needed to move its messages more rapidly from research to physicians to patients. Studies showed that Americans were not concerned with how they received information, as long as it was presented in a way that was easily accessible and meaningful and provided tangible ways to have an impact on their health. "We committed to changing the way our content was presented and how Americans—our true customers—received it," Gordon reiterated. "Our mission remained the same, but how we achieved it had to change."

The organization first identified the need for an immense realignment of its operations in the mid–1990s. At that time, the national office of the AHA acted as a service center for 52 affiliates across the country. "We viewed our 'customer' as the field offices and were very successful at disseminating plans for our local groups," explained Gordon. "We created education material and programs and rolled them out through our local affiliate channels—often unsure of and without control over the execution and impact."

In a remarkable move made possible through strong national leadership and the field's commitment to the cause, the AHA consolidated its local affiliate offices from 52 to 15. It also centralized as one incorporated entity, which now has eight offices. This streamlining enabled the AHA to facilitate more efficient decision making, ensure more consistent content distribution, and put the resources saved through operational efficiencies to work in service of the mission. It was a bold move.

The changes laid the groundwork for greater impact and stronger, more passionate bonds with supporters, staff, and volunteers, unifying them around an operationally integrated organization with strategic systemwide thinking.

"Our more focused strategies, structure, and systems made Go Red and other initiatives possible," explained Kathy. "As a result, our new programs have succeeded in reaching more people with critical messages, raising our profile, and growing our community support. The white coat, which represents the clinical, scientific aspect of the organization, will always be critically important. The red dress, as the symbol of the women and heart disease cause, helped add the passion and emotion to Go Red to resonate with women. It took time, but we successfully married the white coat with the red dress!" This case study will identify many of the best practices that allowed the shift to happen so successfully, which was key to the AHA's ability to integrate its brand meaning into every aspect of its organization.

FOOD BANK FOR NEW YORK CITY'S BRAND JOURNEY

"For our first 20 years, the Food Bank For New York City was a very mission-driven and highly cost-effective and efficient organization," explained longtime President and CEO Lucy Cabrera, who has received numerous awards for her work in public service. "The organization was established in 1983. By 2002, we had built a strong infrastructure to achieve solid efficiencies. We were doing great work, serving more than 1,000 food assistance programs like food pantries and soup kitchens across New York City. Yet, we were not visible or well known except to the community we served. Conversations with people outside the organization always required extensive explanations of who we were, and our name at the time—Food for Survival—was confusing. While there was an external lack of awareness, the demand for our services was growing, and government support was declining. We knew we had to change."

Lucy explained, "What our board and senior leadership realized was that being efficient and effective in delivery of our mission was not enough to build a strong and sustainable organization. Despite our hard work, we were constantly battling for support, and the ups and downs of the economy left us vulnerable. We sought to provide stability for the organization and encourage people to remember the Food Bank during both good and hard times."

Adding to Our Plate

These challenges led to an opportunity, driving the organization to become more externally facing by viewing its constituents as broader than just food assistance programs. The Food Bank realized that to be successful, it would need to rally New York's citizens, government, media, and corporate partners behind a common cause. "We decided to look at our brand meaning and strengthen it to stand out, create unique value, and build deeper relationships and loyal communities," recalled Lucy.

In 2002, an in-depth branding process revealed a gap between internal and external perceptions of the organization. Internally, efficiency and pride in New York City were strong brand attributes. Yet externally, there was a lack of understanding of what a food bank was, despite the growing need for its services. So the organization's leadership switched gears and committed to building its marketing and fund raising activities. It realized that raising broader awareness and understanding was essential for sustaining its critical services and recognized that its brand revitalization would be key to their success.

This involved shifting the brand meaning from food delivery to the higher-order, more compelling cause of addressing hunger and food poverty for New York City systemwide (see Figure 3.1). The subtle but powerful change required taking a more methodical approach to the Food Bank's already strong programs, while also aligning them with

FIGURE 3.1   The new logo for Food Bank For New York City

communications outreach, fund development activities, and building a supporting organizational structure.

"We wanted to be bigger and bolder. There was intense conviction driving the change. We knew talking about the expanded brand meaning wasn't going to be enough. To propel the transformation, it had to be reflected in our programs, operations, and external activities," Lucy said with passion.

"Building a stronger identity for the Food Bank and inviting more people to join us became a driving force behind our strategic plan. We strengthened existing programs, expanded our staff, and reinforced our existing, integrated approach to running the organization," explained Lucy. "The focus on our brand meaning rallied and inspired staff. Externally, we now have literally hundreds of new partners and friends who have united with us over the past seven years. The results have been remarkable—doubling fund-raising revenue, raising significant awareness of the issue, and reinforcing the Food Bank as the go-to hunger-relief organization in New York City. But the process took time. In fact, we continue to evolve to most effectively implement our brand meaning."

DEVELOPING ALIGNED BRAND EXTENSIONS AND SUBBRANDS

Once an organization has a clear and compelling brand meaning, it can create sub brands to reach new stakeholder segments.

It is important to ask some basic questions to determine if brand extensions or subbrands like AHA "Go Red" are right for your organization. For example, would a brand extension:

1. Create opportunities not available through the master brand alone, such as new sponsorships or other forms of fund-raising?

2. Open doors to new communities through more varied communications or by giving the organization a broader or more targeted voice?

3. Eliminate confusion among supporter communities due to lack of awareness of the master organizational brand?

FIGURE 3.2   Go Red

4. Reduce the risks inherent in focusing new or evolved strategies around the master brand itself—for example, the risk of alienating traditional audiences or stakeholder segments?

If you answered yes to these questions, then it may make sense for you to consider a brand extension effort—but not before your overall brand meaning is well integrated into the fabric of your organization.

AN OVERVIEW OF PRINCIPLE TWO

A clearly defined brand meaning is a vital management tool that makes the business strategy clearer, more motivating, and more attractive to the organization's key stakeholders. It drives the focus for strategy and then acts as a filter for daily actions. It provides deep meaning for those who serve and support it.

Building a truly breakthrough nonprofit brand (BNB) requires that an organization align and integrate its internal strategies, programs, structures, and information-sharing systems to bring the brand meaning to life. Once you have identified and crisply articulated your brand's meaning (see Chapter 2), the real power comes from fitting it into the everyday working realities of your organization. A breakthrough nonprofit brand is shaped as much by the way it operates and acts as by what it says.

What does it take to effectively align and integrate brand meaning across the organization? To successfully navigate any organizational change requires sensitivity, transparent communications, discipline, and commitment. It is challenging work, yet the payoff, as demonstrated by the American Heart Association and the Food Bank For New York City, can be extraordinary. As those case studies illustrate, while there is no single approach, there is a common framework for success, as shown in Table 3.1.

How-To Success Factors

Integrating brand meaning into strategic plans, structures, and processes is hard work that can require a real transformation in the way the organization is run—and judged. Even if the changes promise greater efficiencies and impact, reorganizing programs and internal structures can make valued staff and volunteers feel threatened or undervalued. It can challenge traditional funding patterns and ruffle the feathers of some long-standing donors. Aligning programs and activities may require choosing between competing priorities, making tough and sometimes unpopular decisions about what stays and what goes. Yet, to move beyond the base level, you can't be all things to all people, which inevitably erodes and confuses brand meaning.

The chances of success increase when a nonprofit adopts a continuum of three key strategies for embedding its brand meaning across the organization, starting at the base, moving up to build the brand meaning, and breaking through at the final level.

1. *Base:* Align—Focus mission-based programs, communication outreach, and development activities to drive brand meaning.

2. *Build:* Integrate—Ensure brand meaning is integrated in organizational structure and HR systems.

3. *Breakthrough:* Institutionalize—Embed processes in systems to facilitate effective organizational implementation of the brand meaning.

Base: Align Strategies and Activities

The first key is to adapt existing strategies and adopt new ones that put the brand meaning at the center of everything your organization does. Brand meaning is reinforced through strategic focus and relentless repetition.

TABLE 3.1   EMBEDDING BRAND MEANING ACROSS THE
ORGANIZATION: CONTINUUM FROM BASE
TO BREAKTHROUGH

	Base	Build	Breakthrough
What	Align: Focus mission-based programs, communication outreach, and development activities to drive your brand meaning	Integrate: Ensure brand meaning is integrated in your organization structure and HR systems	Institutionalize: Embed processes in systems to facilitate effective organizational implementation of your brand meaning
Who	Senior leadership team informs and drives strategy development and prioritization	Cross-functional teams are empowered to develop, prioritize, and implement strategies	Partners, vendors, and key third parties begin to drive strategy as an extension of the internal organization
When	During or directly following strategic planning period	During strategic planning period and critical evaluation period	Continuous cycle of strategy assessment, structure evaluation, and measurement systems
Where	At executive level and home office or organization headquarters	Across organization, including field offices, satellites, and/or formal volunteer groups	Across organization as well as with key partners, vendors, and third parties
Why	To control how brand meaning is brought to life consistently through core strategies	To set up structure that best allows brand meaning to be proactively integrated into relevant activities	To create systems that ensure brand meaning is automatically central in activities as second nature
How	Use brand meaning as focus, filter, and framework for strategy and program decisions	Empower the right people in the appropriate positions to bring brand meaning to life	Develop decision-making processes, internal communications, and success metrics

Strategy Alignment   Aligning all activities behind the brand meaning is critical (see Figure 3.3). To be most effective, mission-based services, communications outreach efforts, and fund development activities must be aligned, send the same message, and work toward the same end. If one

Use brand meaning to align strategies around a consistent focus, ensure the structure is in place to support their execution, and create the systems for communicating, reporting on, and measuring against them.

FIGURE 3.3   **Brand Meaning Strategies**

piece is out of sync, value will be left on the table, and results will be far less than what they could be. As the following case studies of the American Heart Association and the Food Bank For New York City demonstrate, cross–functional integration is essential.

PROGRAM CONTINUITY

Utilize your brand meaning as a strategy filter to identify any gaps in services, communications, funding, or organizational support. These gaps could offer powerful opportunities for growth and innovation. Before investing in those areas, fully analyze the potential risks and rewards to determine where those options rank among other organizational priorities.

Keep: Programs, communications, and other efforts that are consistent with the brand meaning should continue. Maintain the current level of funding, staff, and other resources these initiatives receive.

Expand: The most highly aligned efforts should be bolstered; communications and fund-raising should spotlight those initiatives, and organizational structures and processes should be created to ensure their long-term sustainability.

Eliminate: Any efforts that are not aligned with the brand meaning should be discontinued. Some programs or materials may be cut immediately. For others, outline a plan to gradually reduce funding levels and the focus the programs receive until they are eventually terminated, which could mean transitioning some worthwhile efforts to another nonprofit or a government agency.

Rational Trade-Offs   Every organization knows that to evolve and grow, new programs must be added. However, nonprofits rarely have the luxury of additional dollars. Therefore, choices and sometimes hard decisions must be made. Trade-offs are usually necessary to align program strategy with an organization's brand meaning. When considering new activities, a BNB uses brand meaning as the lens for determining when to say yes and when to say, "No, thank you." Brand meaning helps determine not only the best programs and services to continue and expand but also which to terminate.

In considering strategic trade-offs through a brand lens, don't forget finance. In a BNB, finance plays a critical role in determining the costs and potential revenue sources involved with various approaches. Engaging in an ongoing dialogue with the financial team is essential to anticipate and preempt potential concerns. It also is a smart way to proactively build support for the new investments in people, processes, and facilities that are needed to support the change effort.

FINANCE ALIGNS WITH BRAND MEANING

Ed Lloyd, U.S. Fund for UNICEF's CFO, weighs in on the power of finance to support brand meaning:

1. The CFO's role is to help the organization find the resources to enable people to do their jobs. As brand meaning shifts, organizational resources also need to shift to advance the mission.

2. Working collaboratively with colleagues across the organization, the CFO builds trust. The finance team can shed new light on the organization's needs and can help frame more responsive solutions.

3. Understand that infusing brand meaning into an organization is a 360° investment in:
   - People: Talent drives the numbers, so to invest in a nonprofit's financial health, you have to invest in its people.
   - Facility: The physical spaces a nonprofit occupies and the tools it uses must be efficient and effective for the purposes articulated by its brand meaning.
   - Services: Align with and reinforce the brand meaning.
   - Communications: Build awareness, understanding, and engagement around the brand meaning.

Build: Integrate into Structural Support

As the power tool for the organization, brand meaning creates the clarity needed to focus strategy and direct organizational staffing and structure. To build the brand meaning requires it to be incorporated into the organizational and people structure to unify and rally staff, volunteers, and the board.

Brand Meaning Leadership　The discovery of brand meaning typically represents a turning point for any organization. Transformational change often is needed to align internal structures and processes with brand meaning and to devote the necessary resources to executing newly focused strategies.

The key to any structural reorganization is strong leadership—often in the form of true change agents. Most staff and volunteers are hungry to be part of a passionate, compelling cause. Yet, they may not see why they need to change to bring the brand meaning to life. Every organization needs someone to show the way. Leaders model the change and act as energizers, enablers, and communicators. Open and honest about the challenges involved with integrating brand meaning into the organization, they continually refocus others on the larger vision. Leaders can be found across your organization—at every level and in every department—championing a broader vision, inspiring new understanding, and building consensus.

The leaders of the BNBs profiled in this book have varied backgrounds. Some hold MBAs or PhDs, and some don't. Several can claim more than 25 years of experience in the nonprofit world; some are comparatively new to nonprofit leadership, hailing from professions as diverse as law enforcement, architecture, and technology. Yet, they all are, first and foremost, passionate about and committed to their causes and organizations. They have been open to a range of creative ways to deliver on their brand meaning, knowing it will power extraordinary results.

What if your senior leadership doesn't share this passion? Look to your board, individual coaches, or outside consultants to help make the case. Consider approaching other nonprofits you admire or nonprofit professional organizations for counsel. Put together an internal team with representatives from across the organization who can serve as an exploratory committee to determine whether brand work is needed and what the potential benefits might be. There are many potential sources of leadership that can influence perceptions around the need to weave the brand meaning more fully into the fabric of the organization—and that can help make the case for change.

Powerful People Placement   Refocusing on the brand meaning requires not only the right leadership but also the right people in the right positions organization-wide. Brand strategies often call for specific capabilities and experience, which is sometimes different from what is currently available internally. BNBs identify the most effective staffing models and redesign their organizational charts to get the right people into the right jobs. This may mean some combination of new hires, new training, or redeployment of existing players to beef up priority functions; expansion or enhancement

of select departments; collaboration or integration of formerly discon-
nected areas; or a revisioning of reporting structures.

For example, the AHA engaged in a significant restructure to support
programs such as Go Red, which served to extend its brand meaning.
What started with a few key people in the Corporate Relations Department when Go Red launched eventually grew into an entirely new department: Cause Initiatives and Integrated Marketing. This burgeoning team
implements the cause activities that bring the Go Red brand extension to
life and liaises with development as it sells corporate sponsorships and with
communications around internal and external cause messages. Most of the
new department was composed of existing staff who were empowered to
take on this new challenge by building and leading integrated teams.

Similarly, the Food Bank For New York City realized it needed more
staff to support its expanded services in external relations (development,
marketing, and communications), government relations, and research. It
hired leaders in each area and empowered them to build the team.

Cross-Functional Teams   Traditionally, many nonprofits have taken a
compartmentalized approach to management. A BNB breaks down silos,
knowing that the component parts of an organization work best in relationship with each other, not in isolation. Creating a cross-functional team is one
way to unify and align activities. Groups or committees should be made up
of employees from each of the organization's functional areas, including
communications (marketing, PR, events, etc.), fund-raising (individual, corporate, government, etc.), program staff (direct services, advocacy, education,
etc.) and administration (human resources, finance, IT). This approach helps
ensure that everyone has a clear, shared understanding of the organization's
overarching focus, which fosters a stronger, more cohesive brand.

Once integration starts to succeed, there's often a snowball effect.
Others begin to move beyond their narrow area to collaborate in new
ways that help drive the bigger idea. A BNB develops a deep-seated in-
tolerance for self-serving attitudes. It uses its brand meaning to eliminate
turf wars by outlining areas of ownership, sharing objectives, and establishing clear, often shared metrics. When the brainpower, energy, and commitment of the entire organization are focused on the bigger purpose
underlying any given project, it produces tremendous value—greater efficiency and innovation—for the organization and all its stakeholders.

A CHECKLIST FOR CREATING HIGH-PERFORMING CROSS-FUNCTIONAL TEAMS

☐ Select a cross section of functions within the organization to ensure a mix of skills, perspectives, and expertise. Forge new relationships and break down silos by choosing team members who do not typically collaborate day to day.

☐ Clarify the team's short-term objectives, including how, when, and which outcomes will be measured. (As its initial work progresses, the team also should develop longer-term objectives for each key functional area, with metrics tailored to each department and/or strategy.)

☐ Even if it feels simplistic, make time for process questions and housekeeping. For example, identify the roles and responsibilities of all team members, including a team lead or facilitator, who will draft meeting agendas and serve as a primary point of contact, and a scribe, who will keep meeting notes and other records. Determine regular meeting and/or check-in times, and consider creating an e-mail group list, shared server, or intranet site to streamline communications.

☐ Use the knowledge and job functions of the entire team to determine strategies for advancing brand meaning objectives across the organization. As new strategies are being considered, encourage active input. For example, make a practice of explicitly asking each team member for input from the perspective of their department—particularly those team members who tend to be more reserved.

☐ Develop a concrete work plan, including key actions and timelines. Identify areas of crossover or similar activities that could be combined for greater impact.

☐ Provide team members with access to training in skills essential for integrating the brand meaning into the organization; this may include level-set sessions on best practices in branding or teamwork skills such as active listening and facilitation.

☐ Periodically evaluate the team's process and processes, and engage in course corrections and future-focused planning.

Breakthrough: Institutionalize via Systems and Processes

Some nonprofits may feel that they have a strong, clear brand meaning and do not understand why it does not move the organization forward. Too often, the goals and focus are driven from the top and never appropriately integrated organization-wide. To truly break through, the brand meaning must be operationalized—put into day-to-day practice.

Shared Agendas and Decision-Making Frameworks   To operationalize brand meaning, it is critical to articulate inspiring yet achievable goals supported by shared action plans. Although inclusion of a range of internal stakeholders is critical, leadership needs to build agreement while avoiding the paralysis of endless discussion. Spelling out a clear decision-making process in advance is particularly important in nonprofit organizations with large staffs or high staff turnover or where volunteers play major roles, since institutional memory can be very short. Establishing a framework up front reduces the number of hours spent on meetings and debates, as well as the amount of confusion and miscommunication that can accompany any change process. The failure to articulate clear decision-making frameworks can result in lessening organization impact, increased costs, distraction from the core mission, and ultimately the burnout of staff and volunteers.

Internal Communications   The brand meaning must be relentlessly communicated through every internal touch point to promote consistent execution across departments. This may include relatively simple communications, such as e-mail, intranet content, and internal handbooks and policy guidelines, to more in-depth contact such as staff outings and retreats, where the brand message becomes a focal point for the entire organization. You also could create training programs that present the rationale for proposed shifts, outline the new focus, and illustrate how each functional area plays a role in living the goals and mission associated with the new brand meaning.

One relatively straightforward yet often overlooked way to integrate the brand meaning into an organization's structure is to revise the job descriptions and performance goals against which staff are measured. Even the best teams and most disciplined cross-functional integration won't realize their full potential without a realistic outline of roles and responsibilities. If staff view brand work as an add-on, it will be difficult to sustain momentum as multiple competing priorities vie for attention. Instead, roles need to be redefined so that the brand meaning is at the heart of *what* everyone does and *how* they do it. In some cases, this may mean eliminating less vital responsibilities or creating new positions—options that should become clear when every job description is revisited with the organization's higher purpose in mind.

Success Metrics   Measurement both drives and documents the return on an investment in brand meaning integration. It reveals the progress and the wins in greater awareness, community support, and achievement of mission that can come from a crisp, effective articulation of brand meaning. A brand measurement plan based on metrics deemed useful by the organization should be developed. Metrics should focus on quantitative measures that include hard numbers such as increase in media coverage, fundraising growth, and number of people who participate or were served. Qualitative measures that are more subjective can also be included, such as strengthened relationships and more positive feelings toward the organization.

Metrics are vital to sustain motivation to drive internal brand alignment. In this way, measurement allows a positive cycle to continue. When an organization undergoes its next strategic planning process, measurement against its current goals will be critical to determine what stays, what gets greater focus, and what goes.

THE AMERICAN HEART ASSOCIATION REMAINS FRESH AND INVITING

The American Heart Association (AHA) has remained relevant by evolving its brand meaning—the focused idea that conveys what the organization stands for, presents its unique and differentiated position, and is relevant to its core constituents and the times. In the mid-1990s the AHA went through an unparalleled structural change that allowed it to operate more efficiently and better infuse its brand meaning into every aspect of its organization. This case study identifies many of the best practices that allowed the shift to happen so successfully.

The AHA Builds Structural Supports

The consolidation of the AHA is the largest merger of any organization—for-profit or nonprofit—in the history of the state of New York, where the AHA is incorporated. Its success is a remarkable achievement made possible by an inclusive process that engaged hundreds of volunteers and staff at the leadership and field levels. Together they determined how to improve the efficiency and impact of the American Heart Association.

"We were as open as possible on the front end," explained Gordon McCullough. "We engaged with each affiliate to get their input and buy-in on moving toward a more public-facing organization, since we thought it was the best way to support our mission. The process was transparent and data-driven, and we did not back away from tough discussions. We met with our local constituencies where they were, explaining the value of freeing up resources and the efficiencies that could occur."

Listening, being open, and communicating to the point of overcommunicating were success factors. Those conversations generated so much excitement that the vote to consolidate the affiliate offices and create one corporate operating structure was almost unanimous, with only 2 nay votes out of 450. The growing sense of urgency around brand meaning as a higher cause pushed local staff and volunteers to look beyond self-interest and serve the greater good.

Once the proposal was approved, to widespread delight, the AHA began to introduce the new structure immediately. Within nine months, 52 affiliate offices were consolidated into 15 regional offices (now 8). This streamlining enabled the redeployment of 150 staff to frontline mission and fund-raising work, increasing the AHA's impact. For the first time, a national executive management team was assembled, including the CEO and EVPs responsible for key functional areas. This team, which worked alongside the regional heads, dramatically reduced the number of decision makers, which increased efficiency.

The AHA Focuses Strategies and Aligns Activities

With a restructured organization and clear decision-making framework in place, the AHA was ready to bring its brand meaning to life through new national educational programs. "Making decisions about where to focus limited resources is always challenging," explained Kathy Rogers, executive vice president, Consumer Markets, American Heart Association. "We are an organization that cares about the people affected by cardiovascular disease and stroke. It is a broad issue, covering everything from nutrition to hypertension to childhood obesity to heart failure and everything in between. Our constituents are diverse, and all are equally passionate. They have a strong voice, and we have to balance the broad range of their needs."

The organization-wide goal to reduce coronary heart disease, stroke, and key risk factors by 25 percent by 2010 was central in determining programmatic priorities. "The goal perfectly reflected our brand meaning, and it changed where we put our resources," Kathy continued. "We were driven to dial up high-impact programs, which allowed us to measure outcomes and connect on a more emotional level with consumers."

One area of concern was women and heart health. The Take Wellness to Heart campaign was launched in 1997 to raise awareness of the issue. Although it failed to take hold at that time with consumers, valuable lessons were learned. In response, the AHA launched The Passion Project to take an integrated approach that incorporated PR, media awareness, and advocacy efforts around the issue of heart disease and women.

To strengthen this work and to achieve a goal of raising $75 million in corporate sponsor dollars in three years, in 2003 the American Heart Association called Carol Cone, the founder of Cone, Inc., a strategy and communications agency recognized as leaders in cause branding. At Cone, a team led by Carol Cone, Kristian Darigan Merenda, and Anne Erhard conducted significant primary and secondary research to identify a strategic direction around heart health that the AHA could own. The process reaffirmed the critical link between the AHA's brand meaning strength, corporate support for the issue, and public interest in women and heart health.

Heart disease is the leading cause of death for women. Yet, the American Heart Association's own research showed that only 13 percent of women considered it to be their greatest health risk. The research team believed the cause of heart disease in women should be a focused, relevant, and unique differentiator for the AHA. The team wanted to focus on a legitimate health need that could attract both media and large-scale corporate interest. Additionally, it sought to select an area where the AHA's existing assets could be used to defray start-up costs associated with a new program.

To confirm this early assessment, additional research was conducted. With data in hand, the Cone team recommended creating an integrated cause branding program focused on women's heart health. The effort would serve as an extension of the overarching, or master, American Heart Association brand. The color red and the red dress icon were used to identify the brand extension, named Go Red for Women.

To drive its message to target audiences, the team added core PR and marketing activities, such as the creation and distribution of Web content, collateral, and red-dress pins. The AHA promoted a series of annual fundraising activities such as local luncheons, a national corporate awareness day and fund-raiser (Wear Red Day), and corporate sponsorships and promotions. Perhaps most important, it focused its mission-based services, such as consumer education and professional outreach, around the cause. The goal was for Go Red to become a simple, emotional rallying cry that would engage others in bringing the issue of women and heart health to the American public.

Building Further Structural Supports for Go Red for Women

"It was a big idea and had all the elements we were looking for—passion, relevance, impact—and was a national cause that could be implemented on the grassroots level. There was an opportunity to attract new corporate partners and community support, which would get the message out and make an impact on women and generate revenue for the work of the AHA," enthused Kathy Rogers. "I was sold. My job was to rally the organization around the idea and put the structure and processes in place to implement it—all in under 10 months!" (See Figure 3.4.)

"As a highly integrated program, we needed to bring together our science, medical, fund-raising, and field teams to get buy-in," recalled Kathy. "And it couldn't be about me 'telling people.' It had to be a true engagement process." Because Kathy understood the AHA and where the sensitiveness might be, she spent a lot of time talking and listening to organizational insiders. Her approach was to meet with key people one-on-one, explain how the program could benefit their work, and invite their input. "I didn't want to appear to be just driving a previously determined agenda. I wanted to listen, hear other ideas, and allow for everyone to own the program and make it better based on their expertise," she added.

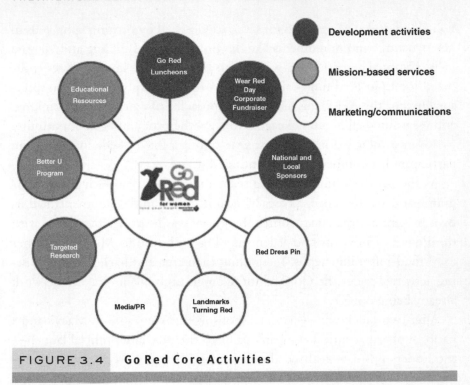

Development activities

Mission-based services

Marketing/communications

Go Red Luncheons

Educational Resources

Wear Red Day Corporate Fundraiser

Better U Program

National and Local Sponsors

Targeted Research

Red Dress Pin

Media/PR

Landmarks Turning Red

FIGURE 3.4   **Go Red Core Activities**

"People in every department offered great suggestions that made the program bigger and bolder."

"We're a data-driven organization, so the research we conducted helped to make the case internally," Kathy explained. The executive staff and volunteer team could see the program made sense. To gain broader consensus, a cross-functional team met weekly leading up to the launch and continued during the first year of the program. One of the biggest tasks was to integrate Go Red across functional areas for the biggest impact. "This required people to think in new ways," Kathy observed. "My role was to help and encourage people to think differently. Internal champions for various aspects of the strategy helped keep the lines of communication open and the vision in focus."

"We created a cross-functional approach to the program," explained Kathy. "For example, we worked with the science journal on an article on women and heart health for the February issue. Our advocacy team held a Go Red luncheon on Capitol Hill with the Congressional Heart and Stroke Coalition and the Congressional Caucus on Women's Issues. Our volunteers and staff arranged for cities to Go Red by turning lights reds in key structures and monuments like the Empire State Building and Niagara Falls. National activities also went local. For example, local affiliates organized local Go Red fund-raising luncheons and then secured local sponsorship. For the AHA, this integrated approach was a new way of thinking, and we wanted all of our colleagues to view the program as an opportunity to advance their work." The first year, about a third of the local affiliates participated, a number that has continued to grow.

As the initiative unfolded, the team discovered that each major programmatic area (science, advocacy, health care, and development) had its own programs targeted at women. February was heart health month, with the Power of Love around Valentine's Day, Choose to Move, and other local fund-raiser luncheons. Integrating each area and harnessing its existing activities under the Go Red for Women umbrella leveraged the work already being done.

After two quick wins—national sponsorships were sold to Macy's and a national pharmaceutical company prior to the program's official launch— the leadership team realized the new cause brand would need an infrastructure beyond the scope of Rogers's corporate relations team to provide significant support. Staff, resources, and priorities were shifted, ultimately creating the Cause Initiatives and Integrated Marketing Department, which was tasked with delivering on the overall cause program and on sponsor expectations. Rogers was the clear choice to lead the new group, and she quickly began building a team of talented internal staff and new hires—which today boasts 15 staff who work on the cause programs, with a total of 40 in the consumer health area overall.

The team worked with their sponsors to reach consumers where they are. Efforts included advertising, celebrity spokespersons, product promotions, and social media tie-ins. Rogers and her team worked very closely with the head of development (specifically corporate relations), as well as communications, to push the cause forward, solidify relationships with its key sponsors, and keep up the momentum—ultimately shattering the three-year, $75 million goal. To date, the cause has raised over $200 million in revenue. More than a million women have joined the movement, and over 1.9 million women have taken the Go Red heart check-up. Awareness of heart disease as the number one killer of women is at 54 percent, and awareness of the Go Red for Women brand is at 62 percent.[3]

AHA Embeds Brand Meaning into Its Systems and Processes

The integrated initiative spanned departments and represented a marked cultural shift for the organization. This required relentless repetition of communications to ensure that the new approach pervaded the whole organization. Internal educational systems were put in place, from training across departments at the national center to a train-the-trainer model that would ensure that the Go Red brand meaning and goals were conveyed to the local staff critical to its implementation. Today, the education system has grown into a full-fledged AHA University, which includes required and elective courses on cause branding as one of several organizational strategies presented.

To succeed, the cross-functional model also meant revisions to existing policies and procedures, including changes to the corporate relations guidelines to allow nimbler decision making and to facilitate new types of partnerships. Macy's was one of the first companies to commit to a three-year partnership, delivering both financial resources and a distribution and promotional channel in the form of its network of 1,000 stores from coast to coast. Most recently, Merck joined as a partner at the highest level, bringing the ability to provide critical information about women's heart health to practicing doctors, many of whom are not fully cognizant of the latest guidelines for women. Branding guidelines were also updated so internal staff and partners would consistently use the new Go Red brand extension and its accompanying logo and messages.

Measurement was critical. Regular recalibration of strategies helped the organizational shift to achieve the return on investment (ROI) so many of its adherents suspected it would deliver. National fund-raising, awareness, and impact goals for Go Red flowed from the national office and were amplified by corresponding local goals. Metrics were added, against which staff, departments, and positions would be judged.

As a focused, compelling brand extension, Go Red for Women has been instrumental in achieving the AHA's goals. It has increased fund-raising, engaged more partners, and created greater awareness and action on the prevention and treatment of heart disease in women. Based on a cost-benefit analysis and key learning from Go Red—as well as external marketplace trends—three additional brand extensions have been built. Those cause platforms are childhood obesity, partnering with the Clinton Foundation (Alliance for a Healthier Generation); physical inactivity in adults (Start); and stroke in African Americans (Power to End Stroke). All use the same approach, and all have resulted in powerful internal collaboration, effective and targeted messaging, and the growth of external funding partners.

Food Bank For New York City Delivers Food and Beyond

"It's remarkable how New Yorkers have rallied around the Food Bank For New York City," marveled Lucy Cabrera, president and CEO, "and our efforts to end hunger and increase access to affordable, nutritious food for low-income citizens." Remarkable, yes. But it was no accident. Any effective shift in brand meaning requires tremendous effort and the deep integration of the brand meaning into the organization's structures, programs, and systems. And it's just that kind of dogged determination that enabled the Food Bank to bring its brand meaning to life.

Food Bank For New York City Builds Structural Supports

The Food Bank needed to shift in its new brand meaning from one focused on food delivery to the issue of food poverty and hunger in New York City. It began by strengthening key functional areas and specifically by expanding its external relations team. "I had been doing most of the fund-raising myself, supported by a marketing and fund-raising team of two," Lucy explained. "So we added a vice president of external relations who had strong skills and the ability to raise our profile by connecting with New Yorkers more broadly."

Paralleling this change was the addition of a government relations team and expansion of the organization's research work. "Completing my doctorate strengthened my understanding of the value of research. It illuminates hidden dimensions of important social issues and can be a valuable tool in advancing the dialogue," Lucy added. To increase its impact, the organization expanded its research efforts and added an advocacy and government relations group to take that research and put it into actionable public policy.

As a result, the Food Bank has become a go-to resource for government officials, media, and others seeking timely, reliable information on the issue of food poverty in the city. "Public officials and media rely on our data because of its quality," noted Lisa Jakobsberg, vice president, Marketing and Business Partnerships. "That area of the organization has grown significantly, strengthening our reputation in the community and increasing support for our work."

To expand its community influence, the Food Bank For New York City added a series of volunteer advisory committees. "We knew there were people beyond our current board and volunteers who could help us. We wanted to cultivate additional advocates, and the results have proven the effectiveness of this approach," explained Lucy.

While the organization strengthened its outward-facing work, it also expanded its support of its internal constituencies. "Our goal is to build the capacity of our network, not just provide them with food," Lucy reported. "If we're going to assume a leadership role in ending food poverty and hunger in New York City, we have to offer a comprehensive range of programs and knowledge. So, we deliver training for our organization at our annual conference. We provide nutrition education in public schools, lead workshops for emergency food programs, and conduct food stamp prescreening and outreach. We operate a senior food program, a soup kitchen, and a food pantry and coordinate one of the largest free tax-assistance programs in the country."

The Food Bank Aligns Strategies

Once new staff were in place on the external relations team, it was critical to develop an identity that clearly reflected the organization's brand meaning. Its original name was Food for Survival, and its tagline was New York City's Food Bank. "Before the name change, every conversation started with 'What is food for survival?' We'd have to spend time clarifying what we did—and even worse, everyone thought we were a government agency," Lucy said. "As we undertook the rebranding, it suddenly dawned on me to flip the name and use Food Bank For New York City. It emphasized we were *for* New York City. There was real pride in that word and we played it up by purposefully capitalizing the *F* in *for*."

"The name was changed, a new logo developed, and the color orange added to emphasize the fresh, outward-facing nature of our organization," recalled Gregory Boroff, then vice president, External Relations, who played a leadership role in the rebranding process. "External relations was central in communicating our broader brand meaning and connecting us with the public in new ways."

The organization undertook a major revamping of its marketing and communications collateral. "Our material was bare-bones," Gregory explained. "Our annual reports were clinical looking. They provided only basic and financial information. There were no stories, no compelling images, and no effort to bring the organization to life.

"Very few New Yorkers knew we existed, let alone what we did. Once we clarified our messaging and brand meaning, the next step was awareness building," Gregory continued. "We had few resources for advertising but big dreams. Lucy challenged our team to get the billboard in Times Square for the Food Bank." (See Figure 3.5.) "It seemed unlikely until we mentioned it to one of our new corporate partners. They agreed to give us their space. There we were—for the first time—front and center in the busiest place in the city. It galvanized our staff when they saw the impact of

FIGURE 3.5   Food Bank Times Square Billboard

our brand work. They went to Times Square to chronicle that milestone—it generated so much pride."

Another key to the new branding initiative was its strong engagement strategy and emphasis on being *for* New York. "We invited people to join us. We wanted to mobilize individuals, government, business, media, and other organizations, to cultivate a sense of ownership so they would work with us to address the issue of hunger," stated Gregory. "We now have deep and broad relationships with a range of companies of all sizes. Part of our brand strategy was to grow their involvement in ways that are meaningful to them and the Food Bank. So we invested in strengthening our corporate partnership program."

Media engagement was also a top priority. The Food Bank worked closely with a number of outlets, building long-term relationships that resulted in extensive coverage. "Awareness is vital in fund-raising, and those initiatives started to see a noticeable lift. Our growing profile and our hunger and food poverty advocacy work led the Robin Hood Foundation to provide us with a challenge grant of $1 million in December 2008. We expected it would take us a year to match it. Through creatively using online tools combined with more traditional avenues like direct mail, we hit the target in the first month. It was a true testament to the breakthrough nature of our brand."

Embedding Systems for Efficacy

"At the Food Bank, all programs are aligned with our marketing and communications outreach and our fund development activities," said Gregory. "I have worked for organizations where fund-raising was in a corner on its own and marketing engaged in totally different activities, and neither area connected with the programming. When I joined the Food Bank, a crucial consideration for me was the deep internal integration that already existed between various functions. Lucy's vision was remarkable. She understood the value of bringing marketing and fund-raising together and aligning them with the work of our frontline programs. It seems obvious, but too few organizations do it!"

"Silos is a bad word in my mind and yet much more common in the nonprofit sector than you might expect," Lucy observed. "We operate as one organization and ingrain this approach in the leadership team. Each part is critical to the whole; I want everyone to feel they are part of the solution.

"The Food Bank is made up of about 175 individuals who are all needed to make it work," Lucy added for emphasis. "From me as president, right down to the folks who pull the pallet of food in the warehouse just outside of my office, we all are working to address the issue of food poverty. We have common focus, common commitment. There is a shared understanding that without everyone in the organization, we can't achieve our overarching goals. I've seen organizations where there is tremendous internal competition between areas because they don't have a common sense of direction. They fight over limited resources so they can advance a goal their area is working on. It is demoralizing and, in the end, minimizes outcomes."

Breaking down silos is especially important for organizations with more than one location. The Food Bank For New York City has operations spanning across the city and touching each of the five boroughs. So the Food Bank can't just preach integration. It purposefully practices it. "We reinforce the importance of every job in the effective operations of the organization by having administrative staff volunteer in our on-the-ground operations. It's our policy," Lucy revealed (see Figure 3.6). "The 'walk a mile in my shoes' approach can make a big difference to interdepartmental communication and teamwork. Senior directors of specific programs send out all-staff e-mails asking for volunteers."

FIGURE 3.6   **Food Bank For New York City Van can be Seen Travelling Throughout the City**

"Working across functions is tenaciously championed and modeled by senior leadership," affirmed Lisa Jakobsberg. "It puts a smile on my face to watch our webmaster collaborating with our major gifts officer to ensure alignment with current communications messages."

Cross-Functionality Helps "NYC Goes Orange"

The use of integrated teams has grown, particularly for special projects. For example, the Food Bank created a cross-functional team for NYC Goes Orange, the organization's brand extension that is an integrated program-matic, fund-raising, and marketing campaign. "We set up the initiative in 2005 to bring all of our external programs, activities, and events under one umbrella for efficiency and greater impact. The team is made up of some-one from every area of the organization—we recently added government relations staff," Lisa reported with enthusiasm. "Our teams are very passion-ate and methodical about ensuring joint goals are met. We involve great, quality people who bring different expertise, experiences, and thinking to the table. Everyone is valued and has a role in the initiative's success."

Each fall, NYC Goes Orange becomes the focal point for the Food Bank's activities. Lisa explained how it works: "Every aspect of the organi-zation is involved, and NYC Goes Orange drives our direct mail program, fall newsletter, and marketing efforts. Our government relations team uses it to connect with officials in a fun and meaningful way. We use it to release new research and reach out to teachers through our nutrition education program, CookShop. Our fund-raising and business partnerships have strengthened and grown through this larger, more comprehensive approach. We have more than 300 corporate and media partners, many of which are small and mid-size organizations. It's an effective and easy way for them to get involved and receive the benefit of the larger awareness effort. For smaller organizations, for example, they accept donations dur-ing the campaign and provide Go Orange buttons to donors. The organi-zation and the whole city join together in standing up for hunger relief."

"In addition to its external success, the initiative has been a great internal team builder," Lisa concluded. "Each year at the end of the campaign, we do a seven- to eight-minute wrap-up video that we share internally and externally. People love to actually see themselves as part of the broader effort."

The Food Bank Continues to Evolve

"As the organization continues to evolve, we continually ask, is this the strongest structure for living our brand meaning, for delivering results?" noted Lisa. "Lucy engages in broad discussion with staff to get our input and buy-in at many points, and, as a result, we've made some pretty significant structural changes."

For example, in 2007 the Food Bank came together with a like-minded organization, FoodChange Inc. They officially merged in early 2009. "It was the right thing for hunger in New York City," explained Lucy. "It was an efficient and effective way to strengthen our work. They had strong programs, funding, and a solid reputation, although they were facing some financial difficulties. Rather than building those assets from scratch ourselves, it was an opportunity to buy and renovate to realize our vision."

Reflecting its strong commitment to accountability and transparency, the Food Bank engaged in significant due diligence, regular staff communications, and open discussion. The merger has saved in operating costs, which is being put back into achieving the mission.

"Over the past seven years, we've grown and strengthened our emphasis on our role in eliminating food poverty and hunger in New York City," Lucy reported with pride. "We have strong measures in place to evaluate impact and help us identify ways to move the program forward."

CAUTIONARY ADVICE TO POWERFUL BRAND MEANING EXECUTION

Beware of these challenges to focus your brand meaning:

- *Efficiency pressure:* Nonprofits are constantly challenged with proving the efficiencies of their operations. Operating via focused brand meaning may initially cost more but ultimately should deliver greater results. Create metrics for each strategy to credibly assess and prove its worth.

- *Mission drift:* The desire to raise funds can often lead to chasing money for money's sake, leading organizations to engage in disparate, unrelated activities. Establish a clear fund-raising direction that aligns with your focused brand meaning.

- *Individual agendas:* Making tough decisions about what to do and not do isn't always popular. Some employees may push program ideas that would benefit your community but don't fully reflect your brand meaning. Communicate how decisions will be made and the reason for individual choices. Recognize and reward staff based on their pursuit of aligned activities.

- *Compromises and inconsistencies:* It can be a slippery slope, with compromises eroding the power of brand meaning over time. Be courageous and doggedly consistent in the way brand meaning is used as a filter for decision making.

PRINCIPLE TWO: SUMMARY

- BNBs achieve exceptional results not just by what they say, but by what they do. They adapt and execute strategies to achieve their brand meaning by focusing all of their work, filtering which activities and programs to employ, and creating frameworks for strategic planning, decision making, and future innovation to filter which activities and programs to employ.

- *Base: Align*—Focus mission-based programs, communication outreach and development activities to drive brand meaning.
  - Filter programs to determine what is essential and what should be expanded, explored, or eliminated.
  - Integrate and align all mission-based programs, marketing and communications outreach, and development activities.
  - Determine outcome measures.

- *Build: Integrate*—Leverage your brand meaning in your organizational structure and HR systems.
  - Determine skills and competencies needed, based on strategic brand direction.
  - Develop organizational structure.
  - Create cross-functional teams.

- *Breakthrough: Institutionalize*—Embed processes in systems to facilitate effective organizational implementation of the brand meaning.
  - Create a decision-making process.
  - Solidify the internal communication structure.
  - Outline success measures.

CHAPTER 4

Principle Three: Rally Internal Brand Ambassadors

"Our belief is that our brand is about relationships, treating people—our guests, our supporters, our volunteers, and each other—with respect and dignity. The Marketing or Development Department does not own our brand; the whole organization is involved. We are a community that doesn't just think this way. We act on it. Constantly."[1]

—John Pfeiffer, Executive Director & CEO, Inspiration Corporation

"Our team embodies and represents our brand meaning every day. We help them understand it and be inspired by it. It motivates them to do great work. They have become a community of champions who communicate and live our brand meaning through their action and work."[2]

—Reg Wagle, Memorial HealthWorks!

INSPIRATION CORPORATION'S BRAND JOURNEY

You'd be hard-pressed to find an employee or volunteer who doesn't know and value the story of Inspiration Corporation's beginning. Founder Lisa Nigro grew up in a family that knew financial hardship. She talks movingly about how challenging it was, especially because of the lack of respect her family was shown due to the fact that they didn't have a lot of money.

Fast-forward to the late 1980s, when she served as a member of the Chicago Police Department's drug enforcement team in a tough area on Chicago's west side. She saw firsthand that many of the residents suffered from mistrust and disrespect. Lisa wanted to do something that would create a level playing field, to build a place where they could go and be treated with the dignity we all deserve as human beings. She believed strongly in the importance of treating people like individuals and of providing an environment where those who need help can become self-reliant on their own terms.

Yet, Lisa couldn't find space or the support to launch her concept. Never one to give up, she borrowed her nephew's red Radio Flyer wagon and filled it with coffee and sandwiches. She pulled the wagon around the Uptown neighborhood, offering quality food to the homeless men and women she encountered. Lisa chose Uptown because so many homeless people lived there and it was within walking distance of her. Over time, Lisa expanded beyond the red wagon that became a symbol of her work. First, she and a growing handful of supporters turned a van into a kitchen on wheels. Then, she converted an entire bus into a traveling cafe.

Lisa provided good-quality, wholesome food, the kind of meal she would make for her own family and a sharp contrast to the sparse, industrial fare typically available to low-income families. She cooked eggs Benedict with hollandaise sauce, omelets, and French toast, serving each portion on dinnerware she would later take home to wash. All meals were provided with a dash of hope and a warm welcome. Her work captured the attention of the neighborhood—and of the Chicago media. It wasn't long before she received a phone call from a building owner offering her a six-month lease on a local storefront for just $1. The cafe moved into the new space and became a restaurant where homeless men and women could sit down, order off a menu, and be served with dignity.

Inside-Out Branding

"Lisa established a very strong brand and brand meaning values that remain at the heart of Inspiration Corporation," explained John Pfeiffer, current executive director and CEO. "Our staff brings the brand meaning to life every day through their work and their commitment to advance our cause. They are at the core of our brand management."

This philosophy was front and center during the organization's two mergers, the first in 2003 and the second in 2005. The expansion allowed Inspiration Cafe to better address the needs of its patrons through case management, supportive services, housing, and a restaurant skills training program called Cafe Too. "When we considered a merger, we knew the benefits for the community we served would be enormous," explained John. "The organizations fit well, with a similar approach and mind-set toward serving homeless people. Our fundamental brand values clicked, and we realized we could have a greater impact if we joined forces. Yet, we needed the staff of both organizations to believe that, too."

Leadership recognized that the success or failure of most mergers is determined by the attitudes and actions of people on the front lines. Through countless daily interactions and decisions, staff either resists change or opens up to new possibilities, so it is vital to address their concerns and enlist their genuine support from the start. How was Inspiration Cafe able to navigate two major mergers to emerge as a BNB? As we will see, the answer lies in its distinctive culture and ability to rally internal brand champions and ambassadors.

MEMORIAL HEALTHWORKS! BRAND JOURNEY

It is more than a little unusual for a hospital to run a children's museum. But that's exactly how Memorial HealthWorks! Kids' Museum was started. Memorial Health System and Memorial Health Foundation's vision is to inspire South Bend, Indiana, to be the healthiest community in the nation. The organization created a nontraditional learning space to motivate kids in the South Bend community to make healthy life choices and provide them with the information and tools to do just that. "If we just wanted to be about curing people once they are sick or injured, we could just sit back and wait for them to come in and do what we have to do. But if we want to be a healthier community, we need to get to children about choices, because so much of what affects our lives is about the choices we make," explained Diane Stover, Memorial's vice president, Marketing and Innovation, and chief experience officer. Since its opening in early 2000, the museum has been "infectiously contaminating kids of all ages" with its positive vision and engaging programs.

Memorial is recognized nationally as a leader in providing high-quality care. It is also seen as an innovator, offering new methods of delivering health care and building healthy communities. As President and CEO Phil Newbold noted, "Most hospitals have health in their mission and vision. But they really mean that they take good care of sick people. We find new ways to keep our community healthy, to prevent illness and injuries. We are committed to innovation and invest continually in the health model. That is what our brand stands for, and we don't just talk about it, we authentically live it."[3] HealthWorks! reflects the innovation at the heart of the Health System's brand meaning.

While setting up a museum was completely unknown terrain for Memorial Hospital, that didn't stop it from moving forward and advancing its cause. The team of staff, community leaders and supporters visited dozens of facilities across the country, gleaning best practices and making important connections. Soon, its vision became reality with the creation of HealthWorks! It is a one-of-a-kind place that blends the best of children's museums and health education centers with Memorial's own creative spin.

The Untraditional Museum

In everything from distinctive and humorous titles for staff and volunteers to colorfully tie-dyed uniforms to a colorful kid-friendly logo (see Figure 4.1), HealthWorks!'s focus is on connecting with kids in a fun and inspiring way so they feel important and comfortable learning and talking about health and their bodies. This engaging, irreverent approach to

FIGURE 4.1   Healthworks! Logo

serious topics isn't what most students and teachers expect from the average field trip.

Surprise is everywhere. Students enter the museum through a shower of bubbles. Once inside, they cluster around their guide—or High Flying Kid Motivator—who prompts them forward swaying a makeshift underpants flag, made with boxer shorts. Examples of popular programs include HealthWorks! Double Dare, a game show–style activity that encourages learning through energetic competition, and Scrubbadubbaveggethinker-cising, where activities provide a close-up look at a third grader's daily health decisions.

"We educate kids by making them laugh, grossing them out, and encouraging lots of participation and cheering. Everything we do is a bold statement around who we are and our educational philosophy," enthused Sarah Seales, one of the museum's High Flying Kid Motivators. "We know if the kids are relaxed and enjoying themselves in a positive environment, our messages and activities are going to stick with them more, but it's very unmuseum-like. We go to great lengths to inspire students to be open to learning new ideas about their bodies."

As Chief Infection Agent, Rebecca Zakowski leads HealthWorks! efforts at "spreading the epidemic" through program and replication development. "The 'infectiously contaminating' language has become our creed and is symbolic of everything we do," she explained. "We work hard so that our students catch the bug. When they leave, they spread it like an epidemic."

How has HealthWorks! been able to create a brand meaning so powerful that it breaks through to communities far outside its organizational walls? They have been able to tap the power inherent in a community of internal brand ambassadors.

An Overview of Principle Three

Breakthrough nonprofit brands (BNBs) know that brands are built from the inside out. Motivated, loyal, and creative employees, volunteers, and boards drive nonprofit organizations. They are the front line that represents the brand's meaning.

Too often, nonprofits focus on branding as an external marketing function and neglect to appreciate that potential supporters are frequently introduced to the brand meaning through contact with internal constituents. If internal team members don't understand and reflect the brand meaning, it's hard for those on the outside to get it. At the base level, employees and volunteers must continuously communicate and act in ways that reinforce a brand's positive attributes. They must build an emotional connection with the organization's supporters by enabling them to genuinely experience the brand meaning.

To break through, it is essential to embed your brand meaning into operations as seen in Principle Two, but also to build your brand meaning into your organizational culture. Ensure that all of your internal constituents understand what your group stands for, and equip them with the tools to express it in everything they do. A BNB creates a sense of belonging, the feeling of being a community with shared commitment, common beliefs, and unique rituals. It continuously infuses brand meaning into the organization until it becomes a palpable part of the environment and culture.

To achieve this strong degree of buy-in, you need to create a comprehensive internal brand engagement strategy. This isn't about a new program; it's about helping staff and volunteers deeply connect with a shared set of values that can advance a cause and encouraging them to express those qualities in their everyday behavior.

Building a strong internal brand requires more than an e-mail message and a set of brand guidelines. You can't take a top-down, command-and-control approach; it's much more efficient and effective to rally brand ambassadors across the organization. Employees need to be educated around brand meaning and messaging, motivated to live shared values, and encouraged to behave in a way that reflects the brand meaning. It must be bolstered by the right communication tools, a senior team and brand champions that model behaviors, and an effort to bring on employees and volunteers who truly match the organization's personality. With this consistent focus, the internal team can build bridges with potential supporters outside the nonprofit's walls (see Table 4.1).

How-To Success Factors

A BNB inspires staff and volunteers to live the brand. They follow a continuum that moves the brand meaning from base to build to breakthrough.

TABLE 4.1   INSIDE-OUT BRANDING CONTINUUM—FROM BASE TO BREAKTHROUGH

	Base	Build	Breakthrough
How	Explain and educate: Communicate brand meaning and key messages to internal stakeholders	Engage and empower: Give staff and volunteers the power to "live" the brand meaning via daily actions and interactions	Energize and motivate: Instill a sense of pride and build an internal community to further drive the brand meaning externally
What	Practical internal communications tools and templates	Hiring systems, regular meetings, and internal practices	Celebrations, rituals, rewards, and recognition
Why	Ensure external audiences are consistently receiving the right messages	Increase retention, efficiency, and overall morale to drive funding and mission goals	Inspire external pride in organization and reputation desired by modeling it internally
Who	Leadership models communications and actions desired and communicates broadly internally	Staff at all levels engaged in brand strategy, evolutions and model it cross-functionally	Internal stakeholders rally external stakeholders to share in brand meaning together
When	In select formats and time periods (trainings, rollouts, etc.)	Across multiple formats (performance standards, reviews, standing and specialized meetings)	Present across all interactions
Where	Headquarters and key operating facilities	Across online and offline internal interactions	Across interactions between internal and external stakeholders

Base: Explain and Educate—Communicate the brand meaning and key messages to internal stakeholders.

Build: Engage and Empower—Give staff and volunteers the power to "live" the brand meaning via daily actions and interactions.

Breakthrough: Energize and Motivate—Instill a sense of pride and build an internal community to further drive the brand meaning externally.

Base: Explain and Educate

A BNB ensures that the internal team—including staff, volunteers, and board members—has a complete understanding of and ability to express the brand meaning. A strong brand requires the type of deep understanding that enables people to clearly and authentically live their commitment. Simple tools and guidelines are sometimes all people need to connect with the brand meaning and express it easily, effectively, and consistently.

Communicate Consistently and Transparently People need to understand what the brand is about and what difference it's going to make. Tell them as much as you can about brand strategy, how decisions were made (including internal and external factors), how brand meaning differentiates the organization, and how your brand meaning evolution represents a shift from past to present to future, and so forth. By being transparent, you instill trust, new understanding, and room for open communication—and once people are inspired, they find ways to deliver amazing results. Employees serve as natural brand ambassadors for their organizations. Failure to adequately share the brand meaning with them squanders a powerful, cost-effective, and credible channel for reaching external stakeholders.

Authentically Lead by Example   Not only are senior executives critical to driving the branding process, they need to become real evangelists for the brand internally, not just externally. Their verbal and behavior cues are key to internal stakeholders identifying the links between the organizational culture and the brand meaning. No amount of investment will deliver the full benefits of a strong brand unless leaders themselves explain it and encourage others to infuse it throughout the organization. They may do this by communicating consistent messages in internal and external speeches, demonstrating an understanding of how all areas within an organization drive the mission and funding goals, displaying a clear sense of pride in the organization, and visibly helping to boost morale and internal reputation. Senior management drives internal brand alignment by demonstrating the strategic importance of their commitment to brand goals and values.

Provide Practical Tools and Resources   It's important to recognize that most people can't make the leap alone. Staff and volunteers may need support in determining what to do next as they learn about brand strategy. Give them practical tools, such as clear style and communications guidelines, presentation templates, and other tools that make it easier to use revised brand elements accurately and consistently. Also, identify a point of contact for questions or input. As part of your communications efforts, always ask what other resources your internal constituents would like or need to best support them. Offering practical tips and tools shouldn't be about policing the brand; rather, it's about creating a culture where everyone is buoyed in their efforts to bring the brand meaning to life in their day-to-day work throughout the entire organization.

BRAND GUIDELINES CHECKLIST

An organization may include the following in their brand and communications guidelines to consistently communicate brand strategy to staff.

- ☐ Mission, vision, and values
- ☐ Brand meaning, as described through personality, promise, position statements
- ☐ Communications goals and guidelines
- ☐ Overview of the organization's key constituents: donor audience, beneficiaries, supporters
- ☐ Key messages, including the elevator speech, as well as words or phrases to avoid
- ☐ Founding story
- ☐ Illustrative stories of the brand meaning in action—stakeholder stories that humanize the organization through inspiring tales of service
- ☐ Voice and tone guidelines
- ☐ Logo usage guidelines
- ☐ Typography guidelines
- ☐ Photography, illustration, and color use guidelines and samples
- ☐ Templates: print collateral, stationery, PowerPoint presentations, e-mail signatures, voice-mail messages
- ☐ Contact list for approvals and assistance
- ☐ Frequently asked questions

Marketing Material Hub for Consistency and Ease   Some organizations may go a step beyond brand and communications guidelines, and create a virtual marketing and branding hub to house critical tools, templates, and key messages. The American Heart Association (AHA) created an online marketing hub with branding guidelines, photographs, and templates for collateral materials such as brochures and flyers. The hub provides a readily accessible tool for staff in offices across the country; it is a green solution that ensures consistency and saves time and money. For example, if a local AHA affiliate is doing a Jump Rope for Heart event, it doesn't need to invest in creating materials from scratch—it just logs on to the hub.

> **TIPS FROM BNB FOOD BANK FOR NEW YORK CITY—*TOOLS OF THE TRADE***
>
> To support brand meaning awareness and consistency among its internal community, the Food Bank For New York City created a pocket-messaging guide. The 28-page booklet equips staff and volunteers with key messages about food poverty in New York City, the Food Bank's comprehensive approach to the issue, and ways others can help. "All staff and volunteers are provided with the clear, easy-to-read messages to ensure we're all speaking with a coherent voice and providing consistent and accurate information," explained Lisa Jakobsberg, vice president, Marketing and Business Partnerships. "It's a simple tool, but it really works well and helps our internal stakeholders nurture the brand."

Build: Engage and Empower

A BNB generates greater employee commitment to the organization and competes more effectively for talent. Having an employer brand requires leaders to actively engage employees and effectively manage the employment experience, using the strategies that follow.

Create an Employer Brand   The 2008 economic reset inspired widespread reflection. Many are reconsidering the degree to which their work aligns with their values, creating a rich opportunity for nonprofits to attract exceptional employees. How can you compete effectively for a share of this growing talent pool? It is critical to build an employer brand.

An employer brand entails what people feel and say about working at the organization. An organization should stress the importance of connecting its communications with its culture and brand meaning to elevate its reputation and attract the best and brightest. Proactive opportunities to develop and strengthen an organization's employer brand include internal focus groups and exit interviews for departing employees. These actions can help determine areas for organizational improvement. Key learnings should be translated into human resource refinements and clear job descriptions that list qualifications as well as expected behaviors and how they align with the brand meaning.

Hire for Skills and Beyond   As one of the nonprofit leaders interviewed for this book emphasized, "The nonprofit sector requires workers at all levels who have exceptional energy and drive, as well as exceptional people and emotional skills." In addition to those qualities, nonprofits typically see greater performance and employee commitment if they hire for the right fit.

Potential employees should be assessed for both performance capabilities and cultural fit. While it is critical to seek employees with the skills qualifications, also look for employees and volunteers who match your values and culture—who, before even starting, are aligned and in sync with the organization, what it stands for, and the values that drive its work. It's almost always easier to help an employee who gets the brand meaning to gain new skills than to deal with a highly skilled employee whose behaviors and attitudes are out of step with the culture. Of course, the ideal mix involves high-performing employees who naturally embody the brand essence. You can get a better sense of such fit by using the following checklist.

- ☐ Get referrals from current staff members.
- ☐ Have board and staff members participate in the interview process to ensure cultural and values fit, not just skills alignment.
- ☐ Require candidates to make presentations on real-time content to give interviewers a sense of the candidate's approach to relevant issues.

- ❐ Ask nontraditional questions and present hypothetical scenarios to get a sense of a candidate's personality and how the person would fit with the organization's culture.

- ❐ Take candidates on a tour of the facility and see how they interact with other staff and the organization's beneficiaries.

- ❐ Request references from places where the candidate has volunteered, as well as more traditional contacts.

Breakthrough: Energize and Motivate

Strong internal brand management cannot be a license to stagnate. Entropy is the enemy of a BNB. Organizations need to constantly strive to keep the brand meaning fresh for staff and volunteers, following the principles outlined here.

Build a Sense of Community   BNBs like Inspiration Corporation and HealthWorks! create internal communities where people bond around mutual commitments. They unify stakeholders from across the organization around the shared brand meaning, while empowering them to live the brand meaning in ways most relevant to their day-to-day work. Ensure all staff (including operations, marketing, communications, and others) as well as key volunteers have chances to deeply experience the programs and services of the organization and potentially even meet or observe beneficiaries. Only then will internal stakeholders really be able to articulate the magic of your organization's brand meaning.

"Nonprofits aren't privately owned. They're owned by the community, and that includes the one they create internally," stated John Pfeiffer emphatically. "We work really hard to make sure employees feel the organization is theirs and to create a true sense of ownership."

Develop New Rituals, Stories, and Symbols   People don't work for money alone. Most of us want to contribute to something bigger than ourselves and feel allegiance to the people around us. Whether formal or informal, rituals at the workplace can go a long way in creating a team out of a seemingly random group of coworkers and strengthening the bond between employees and the organization.

FROM THE INSIDE TO THE OUTSIDE

To bring their brands to life for their employees, BNBs employ a variety of stories and iconic symbols. They also encourage internal constituents to incorporate iconic elements into their communication work.

- *The creation story:* The creation story recounts the who, why, what, when, where, and how behind the founding of an organization. Retelling this history provides important insights into the organization's belief system and conveys a sense of purpose and belonging.

- *Storytelling:* Storytelling is a classic form of experience sharing designed to foster a sense of solidarity and provide ongoing sources of inspiration. Continually capture and retell stories of your organization's work and of its values and brand meaning in action: UNICEF has created a storybook filled with stories of how its staff did whatever it took to save the life of a child. Karen Skalitzky, a long-time volunteer with Inspiration Corporation, wrote a book of great sensitivity and power, *A Recipe for Hope: Stories of Transformation by People Struggling with Homelessness.* The book shares first-person accounts of the struggles and triumphs of some of the people who have walked through the doors of Inspiration Corporation. Its moving chapters are punctuated with recipes from Chicago's chefs, including some who work for Inspiration Corporation, creating a sense of connection to the broader community. Copies of the book are found throughout the Cafe.

- *The founder bio:* Organizational founders are catalysts, determined risk takers, and visionaries who want nothing less than to change the world. Along the way, they help others believe anything's possible. Nancy Brinker of Susan G. Komen for the Cure, Lisa Fielder of College Forward, and Lisa Nigro of Inspiration Cafe are all examples of leaders who dedicated their lives to creating solutions to serious community challenges. Their presence can be highly motivating, and their stories are worth sharing.

- *A creed:* A creed is a statement of belief or faith. Great nonprofit brands define their beliefs and how those beliefs support the brand meaning and mission. While faith-based organizations are

(*continued*)

(*continued*)

the most likely to use a creed to anchor their work, a belief statement can prove a touchstone for any organization. For example, Inspiration Corporation's creed is: "Inspiration Corporation inspires change and enriches our community by providing people who are affected by homelessness and poverty with essential social services that create choices and enable our participants to lead happier and more fulfilling lives."

- *A rallying cry:* Many nonprofits deftly use language to channel energy and enhance cohesion. HealthWorks! uses "Infectiously contaminating kids of all ages, everywhere." At Komen, "For the Cure" unites an army in pink around the goal of eradicating cancer. Similarly, at the U.S. Fund for UNICEF, the rallying cry has become "Believe in Zero."

- *Sacred words:* The words used to describe a brand need to be infused with meaning and power. For example, at HealthWorks! innovation is not a cliché, but one of the few things considered sacred by that irreverent organization. For Inspiration Corporation, trust and respect are not an empty tagline, but a sacred promise to the community it services. At each organization, sacred words embody the brand personality, values, and culture.

- *Symbols:* Lisa Nigro's little red Radio Flyer wagon has become emblematic of Inspiration Corporation's brand promise. Her wagon still hangs at Inspiration Cafe, and a replica can be found at its sister, the Living Room Cafe. "It reminds us of our founding story and reflects our humble roots. It explains who we are and defines the organization to the inside and outside world," explained Diane Pascal of Inspiration Corporation.

- *Colors:* One of the most useful and powerful design tools you have, colors create a point of differentiation and capture the attention of staff and volunteers. Many nonprofits use colors as an instantly recognizable and universal symbol of their cause—think pink and breast cancer, red and heart disease, orange and food insecurity. Go Red for Women has rallied the American Heart Association around the color red, and New York City Goes Orange uses that color as a symbol of support for the Food Bank For New York City. "People around here wear orange with pride," explained one Food Bank staff member. "It's like a uniform that sets us apart and brings us together all at once."

> - *Branded gear and uniforms:* Distinguish staff and volunteers through clothing and uniforms that convey the organization's personality and culture. At HealthWorks! tie-dyed clothing unites the team around a sense of fun and shared purpose.

Celebrate Success   Take the time to celebrate. It isn't always a priority. Everyone is busy; there are fires to fight and a never-ending to-do list. It is easy to find reasons not to recognize smaller milestones, and with so much important work yet to be done, it might not feel right to savor success. But every organization should do so. It's one of the main reasons people work at nonprofits. We are all motivated by the feeling of shared achievement.

A BNB creates opportunities to spotlight extraordinary effort, putting particular emphasis on activities that bring the brand meaning to life. By thanking people for their effort and linking the celebration back to the brand, the brand meaning becomes part of the fabric of the organization. By offering more acknowledgment of the team than the individual accomplishments, you create a culture where people more readily collaborate to advance mutual interests and aspirations.

To forge a strong internal community, nonprofits need a clear sense of organizational purpose, shared values, employees that match the organization's brand DNA, and common symbols and rituals that build the brand from the inside out.

INSPIRATION CORPORATION INSPIRES FROM THE INSIDE OUT

Inspiration by name, inspiration by nature! All of the BNBs profiled here are inspirational leaders, but only one actually has *inspiration* as part of its name. Chicago-based nonprofit Inspiration Corporation lives and breathes its brand meaning every day. As a catalyst for self-reliance, its staff works in what its mission describes as "an atmosphere of dignity and respect, helping people who are affected by homelessness and poverty by improving their lives and increasing self-sufficiency." Inspiration Corporation advances those goals by providing social services, employment training, and housing.

Just as important, it has created a strong internal culture that reflects the brand meaning and benefits the entire organization.

Base: Explain and Educate

A BNB embraces internal branding as a strategic priority. Its leadership models the organization's values, repeating and reinforcing the brand meaning through word and deed. "We started with a great brand that is kept alive through our leadership," explained Diane Pascal of Inspiration Corporation. "People like John Pfeiffer, Lisa Nigro, and our board members live it every day through their actions and words."

"We bring the brand meaning to life not only by modeling what it means but also by being clear about what we don't do," stated John. "While we have a unique service approach that no other homeless service agency follows, many other groups offer services we don't. We regularly refer our guests to these other organizations. This not only helps people get the additional support they need, it reinforces what we stand for to our clients, staff and volunteers." Yet, Inspiration Cafe, as it was then called, also remained open to expanding services in ways that aligned with its brand meaning.

Merger Impacts Internal Brand   The Living Room Cafe and The Employment Project both served Chicagoans affected by homelessness and poverty. "Before we merged, we worked side by side with them serving Chicago's homeless population. There was very strong brand alignment, which is critical if you truly hope to become one seamless group," John explained.

"A lot of time and care went into the two mergers," explained Shannon Stewart, Inspiration Corporation's COO and the former executive director of The Employment Project. "We explained to staff that by saving on administrative and fund-raising costs, Inspiration Corporation would focus more resources on our mission: leading homeless men and women toward self-sufficiency. We worked hard to ensure all staff and volunteers felt not only informed but also involved and that they felt personally important to the success of the merged organizations. We communicated widely, organized joint staff merger committees, and promised no jobs would be lost."

"The merger was a great example of keeping our internal team informed and engaged in the process," affirmed Diane. "Staff participated in committees that dealt with every aspect of the merger. No question was off-limits, and our leadership was always approachable."

The merger provided an opportunity to communicate the heart of the brand meaning. By keeping brand meaning front and center, Inspiration Corporation has forged one integrated organization that provides holistic services to better meet the needs of its guests and participants. "It took time, but the mergers have given us the confidence to expand in ways that draw on the combined strengths of both organizations," added Diane. "More importantly, because the merger was well executed, it has given our supporters the confidence to give us the resources to continue expanding. For example, Inspiration Corporation has added more than 120 units of supportive housing and is planning to open a second restaurant. These changes have strengthened our brand meaning. We have stayed true to the brand essence while keeping it fresh and infusing new energy."

Providing Practical Tools   The two mergers solidified the need to include "inspiration" in the combined organizational name. "We were known as Inspiration Cafe but changed to our official name Inspiration Corporation," explained John. "We had support from Northwestern's Kellogg School of Management to adapt our messaging and visuals and build a brand style guide. They helped us understand the importance of using one name to avoid confusion. We decided to keep our name and update the logo while keeping the recognizable elements, but we added a tagline, *Catalyst for self-reliance*. It is unmistakable and has become a rallying cry that articulates our unique brand. Since our name is more aspirational than descriptive, staff can use the tagline to communicate quickly and effectively what we do" (see Figure 4.2).

FIGURE 4.2   **Inspiration Cafe**

"We have formulated our key messages, but we don't have a formal written branding strategy. We focus on consistency and activating the brand meaning by living it," observed Diane. "Nothing brings it to life more than experiencing it. As we've grown in size, we have maintained a seamless experience for our clients, many of whom touch different programs and parts of our organization. We want our staff to understand and experience that, too. We've developed a quarterly cross-volunteering program that requires staff to work in another program. We're very intentional and ensure everyone rotates. People volunteer to serve a meal, do mock interviews in our employment program, and then help organize a clothing closet. It builds understanding and respect for everyone's role. It keeps us feeling like a team."

Build: Engage and Empowers

"Successful brands are built by people," explained Inspiration Corporation Executive Director and CEO John Pfeiffer. "For us, it starts with those closest to the organization—our employees, board, and volunteers. They are our ambassadors and reflect our brand in the workplace and community."

John joked, "I would describe it as the opposite of a command-and-control culture, although some days I wish it weren't." The involvement of staff at all levels makes perfect sense. After all, Inspiration Corporation is built around a commitment to dignity and respect for its clients. To be credible and enduring, those brand values need to emanate from a deep respect for the organization's staff. (See Figure 4.3.)

Ensuring Fit   "We have very low turnover and are viewed as an employer of choice in the social service sector," John observed.[4] "The external brand meaning helps to attract strong candidates. Our focus is to ensure we get the right people on board." Diane agreed: "I had worked in the private sector and for other nonprofit organizations. Inspiration Corporation has a strong external reputation, and I was drawn by it and the ability to work directly with end beneficiaries."

"The interview process provides opportunities to see how a candidate aligns with the brand meaning," stated John. "During the interview, we ask nontraditional situational questions to determine if someone can cope with the pressure of working with people who have multiple life barriers. We select on skills, attitude, and personality."

NEWS FROM CAFE TOO

Some may know me, some may not; I am the former Head Server at Cafe Too. In December when our General Manager, Kate Weichmann, returned home to Australia, I was promoted to Front-of-House Manager. Kate did an amazing job leading us through those early years and will be greatly missed. Thank you for everything Kate!

Cafe Too's success has grown through believing in and staying true to our values. This is something that personally is near and dear to me; good food, great service, good prices, great purpose. Some things never change!

I will work to expand our internet presence by utilizing social media tools such as Facebook and Yelp!. These tools allow us to interact with our customers in new ways, and they give our "customers opportunities to let us know all of the good (and not so good) things we are doing. I plan to utilize these marketing and communication tools to the fullest extent.

I would like to take this opportunity to thank everyone involved for giving me the opportunity to help shape the future of Cafe Too. Here's to another four years, and "Come see us at Cafe Too!"

Tony Reinert Front-of-House Manager & Cafe Too Alumnus

FIGURE 4.3   Cafe Too

"When I'm involved in interviews, I incorporate opportunities to see how candidates directly interact with our guests in the Cafe," explained Lisa Nigro, the founder of Inspiration Corporation. "Our founding values— respect, dignity, and individuality—are such an important part of who we are. Almost everyone shares those values intellectually, but the real test is whether they consistently act on those values in demanding, real-world situations. Having great academic credentials can be impressive, but that doesn't guarantee success in an organization like Inspiration Corporation. Candidates have to embody the right attitude and attributes for our culture."

What are some other ways to tell if a candidate's natural behavior and values fit closely with your organization's brand meaning? "Engage employees in interviews, even if they think they don't have the time," advised Diane. "Other staff has a sixth sense about whether someone will fit in. And it takes a lot less time to participate in an interview than to train someone and maybe have to pick up the slack and then start all over again if they don't work out."

The Risk of a Wrong Hire   Employees who don't fit the organization's brand meaning can have a significant impact on an organization. Inspiration Corporation went through a rough patch in the mid-1990s when it hired an executive director who was highly qualified but didn't fit well with the organization.

"It was a very challenging time," recalled Lisa. "The organization was close to shutting its doors. Changes were made that led to mission drift and that eroded financial support. The culture was shifting, too. No one felt welcomed. Even I didn't feel comfortable coming to the Cafe. But amazingly, our board and volunteers raised $10,000 from their own resources to keep it going. It was humbling to see this happen," she recounted earnestly. Inspiration Corporation is authentic and genuine because it changes lives. But like all organizations, it needed the right leadership to keep that brand promise alive.

Volunteers and Beneficiaries as Brand Stewards   "Volunteers are cherished assets. We value their input and thinking, not just their manual labor," affirmed Diane. "Many volunteers are also core donors. They come in to cook or serve and get a firsthand experience of meeting our guests and seeing the program's impact. We have a special gift for engaging our volunteers as stakeholders and building an organization that is a community owned by all who come here, whether they're volunteers, staff, or participants."

Beneficiaries are equal brand stewards. "They feel welcome when they come. Our goal is to give them a sense of ownership. They take pride in being part of us," John reported. "They know our brand values as well as anyone, and what they say about us and how they interact with us sets a tone. They appreciate who we are. We provide them the tools to reclaim their self-sufficiency without sacrificing their individuality. We have had some recipients of our services transition to become employees. When they sign on, they've already worked side by side with our staff and volunteers and can express our brand culture, values, and messages."

Breakthrough: Energize and Motivate

"It's hard work being in direct service support," John admitted. "Every day, our staff works with a series of people who have multiple challenges but relatively weak personal support networks. It's motivating and draining all at once. We thank our staff all the time and share stories to remind them of the higher purpose behind our work."

"Stories have become a big part of our culture, and we regularly share accounts of our successes," explained Diane. "They convey the true value of our work and demonstrate the brand meaning in action. Our founding story is extremely powerful, yet we also try to amplify other great stories that reveal the importance of our work today. We often don't hear from people who have made it. But we recently had one of our guests return. He had really struggled with a learning disability and many other challenges. He came in for breakfast with his daughters. He'd gotten a job, an apartment and he'd reconnected with his children. I know he's so proud of them and of what he had achieved."

"It was a glorious moment," recalled John with pride. "When you first start interacting with guests, it can feel like an unequal transaction. When they get on their feet, they really feel like a peer, and that's rewarding for staff. Sharing those stories is an opportunity for staff and volunteers to reflect. They get a sense of satisfaction about their work and what's possible. [The guests] help us understand who we are and what we stand for."

Creating New Rituals   Monthly staff meetings are viewed as a major commitment the staff makes to one another. Those meetings provide an important venue for sharing updates, previewing future plans, relating success stories, and celebrating achievements with staff and volunteers. A peer award program has become a valued part of the meeting.

"The award came about organically," Diane recalled. "Someone got a fuzzy eagle wearing an American flag hat as a promotional item. It looks cheesy but reflected our commitment to independence. Half jokingly, staff started to present the award to one another for some outstanding achievement or even their regular ongoing work. It was simple, but there was a lot of meaning and emotion behind it. Since staff help drive the organization, it became institutionalized fairly quickly. We're intentional about recognizing success, and the American Furry Eagle award reflects our shared commitment."

Celebrating a Treasured Symbol of Origins   Today, the combined organization serves 3,000 individuals a year, with 50 full-time staff, 1,500 volunteers, and three locations, with a fourth to open in 2011. While the nonprofit has grown, the little red wagon serves as a reminder of how and why the work began more than 20 years ago.

"Lisa Nigro established the brand personality, values, and culture of the organization through her words and actions. As the founder and an on-going leader, she set a tone that is found in every aspect of our brand values and internal community," John explained. "The red wagon can be seen in both of our cafes that serve people who are homeless or at risk and symbol-izes the importance of respect and dignity, as evidenced by her commit-ment to this organization. Lisa put everything she had—her heart, soul, and financial resources—into making it a success. In fact, she only recently paid off the personal debt she incurred to establish Inspiration Corporation twenty years ago."

In 2009, the 81st Academy Awards was upstaged by a commercial that showcased Lisa's story and her little red wagon in an ad about the Inspira-tion Cafe that was underwritten by Frito-Lay. "After reading thousands of inspiring stories, our team felt that Lisa Nigro's journey exemplifies the purpose of Frito-Lay True North snacks: giving life extraordinary mean-ing," said Regan Ebert, vice president, Frito-Lay North America.

"The True North snack recognition built morale and an esprit de corps," added John. While some organizations might have circulated an e-mail, in a sign of the culture, "we had a big party and everyone joined the celebration."

VIEW LISA NIGRO'S OSCAR COMMERCIAL

Inspiration Corporation founder Lisa Nigro was featured in a com-mercial during the 2009 Oscars! Lisa's story was selected from 2,300 submitted in a national contest. See it at www.youtube.com/watch?v=C3AOzj7mVNQ.

MEMORIAL HEALTHWORKS! LIVES AND BREATHES ITS ORGANIZATIONAL DNA

When you give your people a cause to work for and a sense of direction in which to take that cause, you infuse your organization with a powerful sense of purpose. "At HealthWorks! we all understand and believe in the bigger cause," noted Conductor of Creative Chaos Laura Garvey. "We have a laser focus on the mission. By working together, we know that the whole is much greater than the sum of the individual parts."

Base: Explain and Educate

HealthWorks! leads by example and drives the broad dissemination of its model through collaboration with other nonprofits. It licenses the HealthWorks! approach to programs, camps, and activities. With the help of this proactive outreach, nearly a million people have experienced its irresistible health edutainment through field trips, community outreach programs, birthday parties, special events, and general admission visits.

In 2006, HealthWorks! began to attract attention outside Indiana. It was contacted by other children's museums and hospitals in such far-flung locales as Everett, Washington; High Point, North Carolina; and Tupelo, Mississippi. A purpose-built strategy to replicate and license the museum idea was developed, and Chief Infection Agent Rebecca Zakowski was empowered to work with interested organizations to bring the Health-Works! brand meaning to life in other communities.

The first full-scale HealthWorks! replica facility opened in northern Mississippi in January 2009. The new facility, HealthWorks! North Mississippi, was developed through a partnership between Memorial Health System and North Mississippi Medical Center. It capitalizes on learning from the original HealthWorks! Staff members at the two facilities are in close contact, sharing their learning and creative ideas, yet operating independently and retaining their own distinct characters. "The value of having two laboratories for experimentation drives amazing and even unexpected learning synergies," said Reg Wagle.

Providing Tangible Guidelines   As HealthWorks! grew, the need for more explicit tools and templates became clear. "Writing the replication manual has forced us to put into words who we are, what we stand for, and how we operate," Rebecca explained. "We wrote the handbook using the HealthWorks! voice to get across our personality and culture. We shared our titles, gave examples of how to keep fun at the core. It's easy to think that all that is needed are the exhibits and facility. But those aren't the most important parts. It's the innovation, connections, and focus on kids that are central. Writing the manual has been a great discipline and has reminded everyone involved about what we do and how far we've come."

As HealthWorks! implements its replication strategy and opens similar health models across the United States, it is committed to protecting and strengthening the overarching HealthWorks! brand while allowing local input and innovation. "The HealthWorks! brand meaning is our mission, vision, and values in action," explained Rebecca. "But we don't believe that innovation stops and starts with us. Our goal is to provide the skeleton. We encourage new sites to add flesh to the bones according to their local need, skills, and circumstances. We're excited to learn from them as they implement their HealthWorks! and build innovative new ways to program. We love sharing fresh, new ideas. It keeps us energized and enthusiastic."

Build: Engage and Empower

Most organizations don't think they have an employer brand, but they do. "We try to be aware of the way our people experience our organization," explained Reg Wagle, senior vice president, Memorial Health Foundation, who oversees HealthWorks! "We want to be a great place to work, but we can't just say we're cool or a fun place to be—even if we believe it ourselves. We can't just tell people to feel passionate. We have to act on it so they feel it, too." That is why HealthWorks! empowers its staff by giving them what they need to excel: respect, tools to succeed, and opportunities to be innovative.

Infusing Brand Meaning into HR Practices   HealthWorks! goes out of its way in its use of job titles to express the innovation that drives the brand. HealthWorks! staff titles include Conductor of Creative Chaos (aka general manager), Detail Diva (administrative support), High Flying Kid Motivator (school program instructor), Captain of the Universe, and even Happy Handler of Hubbub. Staff developed the job titles because they believe they are an important part of the museum's persona and reflect the culture and meaning of its brand.

"It makes sense that attracting and retaining people who share the same values as your organization makes it easier to authentically live the brand meaning," observed Reg. "When the entire team is truly on board, it catapults the group to a higher level. The shared focus naturally results in a higher level of loyalty and efficacy."

"When we hire, we look for a sparkle in the eye and an energy that matches that of the museum staff. First, we ask why they want to work here. Even more than an intellectual interest in health and science, we want to hear enthusiasm and passion for the organization's approach, for our brand meaning," explains High Flying Kid Motivator Sarah Seales. "We go beyond the resume and standard interview. We ask candidates for a three-minute audition on a topic of their choice. We've seen everything from the art of pencil sharpening to the execution of graceful cartwheels. It's a moment of truth. Can they connect with us in a fun, entertaining, and engaging way? These characteristics are so critical to who we are and what we stand for that they determine who we hire. This focus helps us make better choices. We're seeking community members, not just employees or volunteers."

Empowering Employees and Leading by Example   The culture at HealthWorks! is highly supportive, with employees actively encouraged to take risks. "We're given lots of leeway to experiment with new things. Nothing is a mistake as long as you learn from it," explained Rebecca. "That makes us willing to experiment. It encourages us to live the value of innovation—tied to accountability for learning and improvement. I've worked in other places where that principle has been expressed but not lived. Not here."

Rebecca continued, "The organization is dedicated to inspiring, motivating, and charging up the staff. Reg is really passionate and gives a renewed sense of purpose when he talks to us. He and Phil Newbold, our CEO, always talk about the mission and goals."

Open and flexible, Reg models creative thinking and innovation. "He will frequently ask us, 'What's trying to happen here?' Instead of trying to force what you think should happen, that question makes us step back and see the bigger picture. He says it so often, a lot of us have picked up the habit of asking this to each other when someone is stuck," Rebecca reported. "He's also willing to roll up his sleeves. So if you see something needs to get done, you know you'd better be doing it. There isn't a strict hierarchy, so we're all responsible for everything, not just what's in our job descriptions. The organization listens to everyone's opinion and makes you feel like it counts. He inspires us in such an authentic and genuine way."

"We're enabled and motivated to do our best and to allow the magic to happen," Sarah added. "We have the freedom to experiment, fail, and learn. In fact, some of the best ideas have come from those that initially failed. Reg makes everyone feel the job is important. Everyone is valued and made to feel their role is critical to our success. You might be working at the admission desk, which isn't exactly glamorous. But he'll say, 'You know, you are the first person our guests see, and you set the tone for their experience. I really appreciate the way you manage to stay upbeat and focused. It makes people want to come back, and that helps us all succeed.' His only agenda is to help you grow, and he provides such positive energy."

Breakthrough: Energize and Motivate

Memorial HealthWorks! *Infectiously contaminating kids of all ages, everywhere, to learn, have fun, and make great life choices. . . . Let the epidemic begin!*

"This is our rallying cry," explained Sarah. "Whenever we say it to new staff or volunteers, it instantly conveys our spirit and our purpose. It strongly reflects our culture and brand personality, and the notion of an epidemic suggests a really big, long-term vision."

Visually Representing the Brand through Symbols   "One of the ways we connect with each other and the HealthWorks! spirit is through the uniforms we wear to distinguish ourselves. We all wear tie-dye shirts," explained Rebecca. "That might sound simple, but it has become a big part of our personality. You wouldn't believe how often I find myself mentioning the tie-dye to friends and relatives outside the organization. It's so much more than just the shirt. Tie-dye is especially symbolic of the culture—it's crazy, colorful, and irreverent. They're a symbol of inclusiveness; since we've been empowered to choose uniforms that make us feel comfortable, they are about thinking different—no polyester nightmare here!"

Coming Together as a Community of Education Fanatics   A purpose-driven culture makes it easier to build a strong, cohesive, and focused internal community. "Our team is united behind inspiring kids," explained Rebecca. "We have a strong sense of camaraderie and a shared commitment to working for the greater good of the organization. Our leadership drives this innovative approach to connecting with children."

"Building an internal community has come naturally because that infectious spirit is not only motivating for the kids who visit, but for us, too. We're a group of people who show up to work because we love what we do," observed Sarah. Through a relentless focus on its brand meaning, HealthWorks! has forged a strong internal community that comes together around shared goals and is exceptionally loyal to one other and the organization. "When we develop a great new program or have an exceptional day, we feel it's a shared victory," Rebecca continued. "Symbols like the bubble entrance are a daily reminder of our shared commitment to infect kids with a passion for making healthy choices" (see Figure 4.4).

Reg Wagle, senior vice president, Memorial Health Foundation, the museum's major funder, explained, "While the facility is important, HealthWorks! is more than a place. It's a reflection of who we are, how the organization lives innovation and puts our brand values into action every day."

HealthWorks! employees have forged a culture of community. "The kids love coming here, but we love it just as much," Rebecca admitted. "We don't see ourselves as museum employees, and we don't see HealthWorks! as just a traditional museum. We belong to a community of education fanatics who come to work to share our passion to inspire kids

FIGURE 4.4   **Healthworks! Inspires Kids to Make Healthy Life Choices**

to make great, healthy life choices. I get up every morning committed to doing just that!"

Adding Energy through Celebrations and New Growth As the nonprofit replicates its model and creates a nationwide network of HealthWorks! it also is infusing new energy into its existing organization, giving staff and volunteers a sense of being part of an even greater cause. "It is strengthening our sense of pride, our energy, and our commitment to the brand meaning. We're not just working to make the children in our community healthier and more capable of making great choices, we're creating a national movement," Rebecca clarified.

"We all want to be successful," Rebecca continued. "That's why we work so hard. When something remarkable happens, we take some time out to celebrate. We know these are the milestones by which we measure our lives and the organization's evolution. And when someone goes above and beyond and we all celebrate that dedication, it goes a long way in reinforcing our values and in making the workplace a lot more fun."

Principle Three: Summary

- The BNBs know their brand meaning is often introduced through contact with the internal community. From the communications and actions of staff and volunteers, the brand meaning flows to external communities.

- *Base: Educate and explain*—Communicate the brand meaning and key messages to internal stakeholders.
  - Consistently and transparently talk about brand evolution and innovation.
  - Authentically model and lead by example through behavior and words.
  - Provide practical communications and brand meaning tools and resources to ensure consistency of internal communications and make everyone an owner.
  - Publish clear brand meaning guidelines and standards that enable staff to plug and play.

- *Build: Engage and empower*—Give staff and volunteers the power to "live" the brand meaning via daily actions and interactions.

- Make the brand meaning part of the hiring, training, and feedback process.
- Free your staff to focus on their role of building and being the brand.
- *Breakthrough: Energize and motivate*—Instill a sense of pride and build an internal community to further drive the brand meaning externally.
  - Create a sense of community bonded around mutual commitments, shared values, and joint goals.
  - Develop stories, rituals, and symbols to communicate the brand meaning and bring it to life.
  - Celebrate achievements and recognize staff.
  - Create new rituals to bring people together around shared values and commitments.

CHAPTER 5

Principle Four: Develop 360° Brand Communications

"Over the past 10 years, the U.S. Fund for UNICEF has rolled out a new visual and verbal identity—from a name change to a sharpened purpose and focus, we simplified our messaging and increased our relevance. We moved from an underperforming and unfocused organization to a powerhouse of marketing, communications, and fund-raising that over the past seven years has seen our annual revenue increase by more than 600 percent."[1]

—Lisa Szarkowski, Vice President of Public Relations, U.S. Fund for UNICEF

"We're clear about what our brand stands for, and we communicate in a way that is relevant to each of our core constituents. Our strategy takes a holistic and integrated approach using multiple communications tools, including social media."[2]

—Robyn Landry, Executive Vice President, Field Health Strategies, American Heart Association

Whether a video, public service announcement (PSA), advertisement, annual report, magazine, social media messages, direct mail, or another appeal, breakthrough nonprofit brands (BNBs) use a 360° integrated approach to effectively communicate with and engage their audiences.

KIDS HELP PHONE 360°
BRAND COMMUNICATIONS

Kids Help Phone (KHP) began when a passionate group came together with a shared vision: to make Canada a better place for children. At the time, the idea that children who were being abused could be helped over the phone was new. Traditional thinking was that a child needed face-to-face interaction for effective help. Radical for its time, the founders believed that technology could be used to serve kids in need, providing them with a simple tool to connect to professional counseling support. The help could be anytime, anywhere, in confidence, and at no cost to the child. By adapting their skills, professional counselors broke new ground. Today, Kids Help Phone is internationally recognized as a leader in the delivery of phone and online counseling to kids. The organization has made a difference in the lives of hundreds of thousands of children, and it continues to break new ground in supporting children through technology-based tools.

Building and Evolving a Visual and Verbal Identity

A simple message, a compelling idea, and a promise of impact were a powerful foundation for the organization. But as a new approach to helping kids, Kids Help Phone's identity needed to articulate who they were and what they stood for. The name was chosen to instantly and clearly convey the organization's mission: Kids—Help—Phone. The original logo added to the message by depicting the intersection of a telephone and a helping hand.

As the organization evolved, so, has its brand identity. In 1996, Kids Help Phone launched a web site for teenagers to learn more about youth issues such as peer pressure, health, sexuality, violence, depression, and even suicide. In 2002, the organization revised its positioning to embrace a broader mandate to serve children experiencing all kinds of abuse, including physical, emotional, and sexual. Messaging also changed to reflect the focus on troubled and abused children. Two years later, the organization pioneered direct online counseling services.

"The kids continue to transform the service with their calls for help. Beyond the original idea of abuse, there is a growing list of issues they face in everyday life," explained Ellen Réthoré, vice president, Marketing and

Communications, at Kids Help Phone.[3] "We have children calling with more mainstream issues such as family relationships, mental health concerns, friendship questions, dating advice, and so much more. We reflected this shift with a new advertising slogan in 2004: 'Whatever the problem. Talk to us.' At the time, we revised the logo to add the speech bubble to symbolize the conversation between counselor and kid inherent in our expanded service." Recent research has evolved the logo to make the phone number and URL larger and more visible. Kids' input has also led to the addition of a brighter color scheme to enhance visibility and inject energy" (see Figure 5.1).

AMERICAN HEART ASSOCIATION 360° BRAND COMMUNICATIONS

Creating an award-winning advertising campaign or generating media coverage is no longer enough to build awareness and form relationships. The marketplace is cluttered and highly competitive. "Our competition isn't only other nonprofits, it includes anyone who is trying to reach a similar audience, talking about a similar issue using similar channels," said Executive Vice President Robyn Landry, with the American Heart Association.

Delivering the Right Message to the Right Audience through the Right Channel

The American Heart Association's communication strategy focuses on delivering the right message to the right audience through the right channel. Added Robyn, "We put the consumer in the center of all we do. We make sure we're talking to and with them. We think about where they are, how they spend their time, and what information they need. We make sure we deliver it, because without consumers our brand doesn't exist."

FIGURE 5.1   Evolution of Kids Help Phone Logo

The American Heart Association's (AHA) overarching communications and specific cause campaign messages (such as Go Red for Women) are developed to provide relevant information targeted to a defined audience's needs. Audiences are segmented based on demographic and psychographic analysis and an integrated approach that incorporates an online and off-line communication strategy. A call to action inviting supporters to join in getting messages out is a core tenet.

"The advent of social media has really changed the way we communicate and engage with our stakeholders," explained Robyn Landry (see Figure 5.2). "We embraced it, but in combination with more traditional communication tools to ensure broad reach as well as a reinforcement of messages through repetition."

FIGURE 5.2   American Heart Association, Go Red for Women

COLLEGE FORWARD 360°
BRAND COMMUNICATIONS

When only 15.9 percent of economically disadvantaged Texans have a chance to attend college every year and the state fell to 48th of 50 in high school completion rates, a champion had to emerge.[4]

College Forward answered the call and now directly addresses the state's crisis by offering cost-effective programming free of charge to deserving participants. In 2009, 99 percent of College Forward students graduated from high school and were accepted to college.

Storytelling Drives Communications

"Stories about our students' personal experiences and data-driven evidence about our effectiveness success power our communications," stated Organizational Advancement Manager Joe Valdeck, at College Forward. "We use stories extensively in the organization. They populate our web site, newsletters, and e-mail. This information demonstrates the real difference we're making in our community and in the lives of young Texans."

"At College Forward, we have always had tangible goals and quantifiable results. So often we come across organizations that excel at either data or stories, but rarely both. We believe combining them is critical in any external communications activities," added co-founder Lisa Fielder. "The stories come from the successes we demonstrate through our numbers. We encourage our students to tell their own stories, in their own voices. This is the most poignant way to convey the need for our program and the significance of the work we do."

U.S. FUND FOR UNICEF 360°
BRAND COMMUNICATIONS

"The earthquake in Haiti was catastrophic for some three million people, and nearly half are children," shared Lisa Szarkowski, vice president, Public Relations, for UNICEF. "Within minutes of the earthquake, the U.S. Fund for UNICEF had mobilized its emergency response team, led by the PR department."

Communication Plan Activated

Simultaneously, as calls to the regional headquarters in Latin America were placed, a media advisory was drafted and posted to the web site, along with an appeal for donations. Celebrity supporters were enlisted to spread the word via social media; *Larry King Live* producers were pitched for a UNICEF representative to be on the show that night. Communications to board members, major donors, volunteers, corporate partners, and other networks were sent out with news of the earthquake and an urgent appeal for funding.

Communications drive fund raising. By March 2010, $58 million had been raised to help the children of Haiti. "We followed our plan, lost no time, and put children first—never letting up," passionately stated Lisa. "We lived and breathed our brand promise—to do whatever it takes to save a child."

INSPIRATION CORPORATION 360°
BRAND COMMUNICATIONS

For Chicagoans facing homelessness and poverty, Inspiration Corporation is a convener of heroes.

"We are conscious of the need we have to fill—and the opportunity it provides to tell our story," stated Chief Executive Officer John Pfeiffer.[5] "We are working to be the go-to organization for as many people as possible who want to help. In order to communicate this, we collaborate to show we're bigger than just ourselves. Being part of a bigger purpose and broader cause movement doesn't decrease our value. It amplifies it."

Using Networks to Extend Communications and Awareness

The organization collaborates with others whenever possible to get its message out (see Figure 5.3). The organization's more than 1,500 volunteers act as communication champions. "A person who volunteers, even just once, at one of our sites has a great experience and story to tell," added John. "We know that it helps increase awareness, engagement, and fund-raising."

| FIGURE 5.3 | Inspiration Corporation Billboard Promoting its Work. |

Communication is central to building a BNB, and every principle presented has communications as a core element of success. Whether it's articulating brand meaning through positioning and promise statements, sharing brand messaging with staff, or using it to connect with external stakeholders to build and strengthen relationships, effective communications are essential.

AN OVERVIEW OF PRINCIPLE FOUR

This principle explores the role of a clear visual and verbal brand identity in the marketplace to create maximum awareness and bring an organization's brand meaning to life. It showcases the use of compelling and targeted messages, storytelling, and tools, both online and offline, to make a meaningful connection with core stakeholders. It demonstrates the value of engaging supporters and champions in cocreating communications to extend reach and impact.

The BNBs communicate through carefully considered and emergent channels. Their messages are relevant and meaningful. They target the right channels in a way that is measured, connects with their target audience, and is creative—because money is always tight.

Because of this principle's importance, and the wonderful depth and creativity of our case studies, we have opted to showcase the work of five organizations. Chosen for their representation of a variety of sizes and types of nonprofits, they present best-in-class principles and practical tactics to take a brand meaning communications program from base level to breakthrough. See Table 5.1.

How-To Success Factors

Breakthrough Nonprofit Brands build breakthrough 360° brand communications through a continuum:

- *Base:* Create a unique and strong verbal and visual identity—Develop strong identity that reflects the brand meaning.
- *Build:* Integrate online and off-line—Create compelling brand meaning communications customized for target audiences.
- *Breakthrough:* Act as a catalyst—Empower supporters to cocreate communications and drive actions.

Base: Create a Unique Verbal and Visual Brand Identity

At the base, BNBs build a clear and consistent verbal and visual identity that vibrantly reflects the brand meaning. A strong verbal and visual identity provides the distinctive outward expression of the organization's position, personality, and promise. To be effective, it must be strategically conveyed, passionately delivered, and consistently presented. Above all, an organization's identity must reveal the brand meaning in a way that is genuine and authentic so that the organization can stand behind it.

Verbal Identity   Building a strong brand identity starts with a name that articulates what an organization stands for, why it exists, and what it is trying to achieve. A strong brand name converts the brand meaning into action that makes it easy to understand, believe in, and be inspired. A brand name is often aided by a tagline and reinforced by communications reflecting an organization's personality and values.

Explained Ellen Réthoré of Kids Help Phone, "We view our name as our calling card. It is the cornerstone of our organization's brand meaning and what it stands for. Because we had a new concept for helping kids, it

TABLE 5.1 **360° BRAND COMMUNICATION CONTINUUM: FROM BASE TO BREAKTHROUGH**

	Base	Build	Breakthrough
What	Create unique verbal and visual identity: Develop strong identity that reflects the brand meaning	Integrate online and off-line communications: Create compelling brand meaning communications customized for target audiences	Act as a catalyst: Empower supporters to cocreate brand meaning communications and drive actions
Why	Build awareness and help the brand be well known	Make a meaningful connection and help the brand be well understood	Freedom within a framework; encourage the brand be adopted and well owned to extend reach
How	Identity consistently and effectively presented in all communications and materials to all of an organization's stakeholders	Segmented communications, based on target audiences, aligned with brand meaning, presented through a variety of online and off-line channels	Empower dialogue that allows supporters at all levels to amplify the message via interactive communications
Who	Responsibility held by communications staff; everyone in the organization is considered a brand steward	Responsibility for content contributions and target audience data matrixes with communications, fund raising, and services staff	Responsibility for monitoring and fueling dialogue shared by communications, fund raising, and information technology staff
Where	Developed by marketing and communications staff based on brand meaning	Developed to more heavily incorporate an external focus, based on demographic and psychographic supporter segmentation	Developed with a focus on networks and creating communications that connect to users' spheres of influence
When	Steady state; similar messages all year round	Targeted messages, with strategic push periods	Dynamic messaging, supporting overarching plan and ability to seize opportunistic events to fuel buzz

really needed to say and explain what we did. The founders did a great job of creating a simple and clear name that delivers a message and a personality, all in less than a second."

When a Name Is Inspirational   Inspiration Corporation has a name that doesn't describe what it stands for, but that has never held them back. Elucidated Diane Pascal, director, Development & External Relations, at Inspiration Corporation, "It's not too challenging having a name that doesn't describe our work specifically. In conversation, I usually follow our name quickly with a short message like 'We serve people affected by homelessness and poverty in Chicago.' In writing, we simply include a statement that explains what we do. The upside is that people really like our name because it is so uplifting and, well, inspirational."

When a Name Needs to Change   Principle One featured the story of Admission Control, now College Forward. Explained Organizational Advancement Manager Joe Vladeck, "When the decision was made to change the name, the whole organization got behind and committed to systematically moving to the new name."

To make the transition, the organization sent out a mailing to key stakeholders with a "Visual Perception Exam" card. "It showed the new name and logo and asked a multiple choice question about what it was. Each answer described some aspect of College Forward. Then the final part of the card explained it was our new logo and name and that it included all the answers. It was a cheeky and funny but simple way to launch our new brand identity," explained Joe.

The organization also used its first College Challenge annual fund-raiser, held in late 2005, to give friends and funders a sneak peek of the new identity. On July 1, 2006—the start of the fiscal year—the new College Forward web site went live. "We didn't really have any sophisticated e-marketing at the time, so there was no e-mail blast or coordinated online campaign," added Joe. "As for student marketing, many of our students had participated in focus groups and were aware that Admission Control's name was going to change. At the time, our entire staff (which was quite small) had close personal relationships with every one of our students, so it wasn't a big deal."

When a Name Adds Subbrands   A master brand is the primary name and image for an organization. A subbrand can also be created for specific suborganizations, programs, or services. These systems may be designed to work closely within the overarching identity or to stand alone. For example, nonprofits like the American Heart Association have created subbrands like Go Red for Women or Start! targeted at different audiences to create a deeper relationship and extend partnerships and support.

WHAT'S IN A NAME?

David Placek, president and CEO, Lexicon Branding, and board member, NatureBridge, shares his expertise in brand name development.

How Do You View an Organization's Name?

A name is one of the most effective marketing tools and a critical piece of an organization's intellectual property. A good name gets your attention. A great name changes your thinking. A great brand name has a purpose; it provokes, inspires, uplifts. It allows you to tell a story, deliver meaning, or make a promise.

What Are the Considerations When Changing an Organization's Name?

It's important to be objective in diagnosing the challenge and opportunity. Be confident that it is required before leaping into a name change. Here is a list of key questions to ask before undertaking a name change.

- Is there a communications problem? If yes, is it because the name is underpromoted, undermarketed, or underresourced?
- Is it confusing, and does it lack alignment with the brand meaning?
- What is the cost of making a change? Will the benefits outweigh the costs?
- Is this going to slow down an organization's momentum and growth or strengthen its future?
- Are there internal or external challenges? Does the name sound likes it's from a different age? Have you had issues where a name

(continued)

(continued)

change would assist the organization's revitalization? Do you have new competitors that require a repositioning?

- Has there been a major organizational change or transformation? Was there a merger, or is there a new vision that requires a different name to reflect and symbolize the changes?

WHEN CHANGING THE NAME, WHAT SHOULD BE CONSIDERED?

- What are the organizational mission and values?
- What should the word(s) stand for? What do you want the name to meaningfully communicate?
- What provides powerful, positive imagery that helps consumers have a clear idea of what the organization stands for when they hear the name?
- What is the role of the name in the overall communication experience? Can it change attitudes and behaviors or open up and create new markets?
- Does it provide a strong trademark that is believable and credible?

WHEN AN ORGANIZATION CHANGES ITS NAME, IT MUST:

- Be an organizational commitment and drive organizational behavior, action, and activities.
- Have an overarching strategy to change all communications and marketing material over a certain time frame. The strategy must be consistent and rigorously implemented.
- Adopt the goal of 90 people in 90 days. Focus initial efforts on internal constituents, such as staff, organizational influencers, and those in the marketplace who need to be told first. Consider how they should be approached: meeting, lunch, letter, phone call, or brochure.

Voice and Tone   When people encounter your organization, either face-to-face or through communications you put out, what kind of language, words, and tone do they perceive, and does it align with your organization's brand meaning? The best brands reflect the organization and speak with one distinctive voice—on the Web, in advertising, in speeches, and elsewhere—whether it's an organization's executive director or a frontline program worker.

Treating people with dignity and respect is core to Inspiration Corporation's brand meaning, and it shines through in the voice and messaging of the organization. "We have developed language and key words that describe our organization's mission and brand meaning, and we use them repeatedly," stated Inspiration Corporation's Diane Pascal.

"Effective communications is about allowing your audience to have their own honest response to your communications," shared Lisa Szarkowski, of the U.S. Fund for UNICEF. "Be aware of tone, and avoid self-congratulatory language like 'we are working tirelessly.' If a third party makes that observation, it's worth sharing. When it comes from the organization, it sounds self-serving."

Tagline   A tagline can be a brief, easy, and effective way to communicate your brand meaning. Having a tagline is not always essential, and a bad one can do more damage than not having one at all (see Figure 5.4). A tagline can serve as a way to quickly and inexpensively present a refreshed or revised brand meaning. The American Heart Association's tagline *Learn and Live* effectively reinforces the repositioned brand meaning; Inspiration

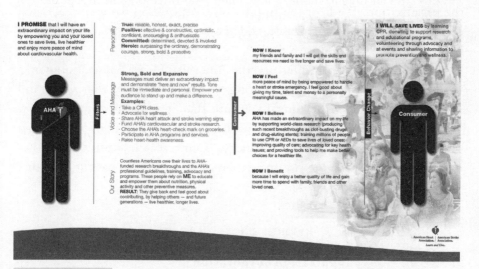

FIGURE 5.4   **Living the Promise, American Heart Association**

Corporation's tagline *Catalyst for Self-Reliance* communicates succinctly the idea behind its brand meaning. As Kids Help Phone expanded its original services, the tagline was updated to reflect its elevated brand meaning: *Being There for Kids*.

Visual Identity   A visual identity helps bring the brand meaning to life by presenting it through color, design, and symbols. It distinguishes the brand meaning in the community's mind. We live in an increasingly visual age, and great design can visually convey the powerful meaning of the brand. For this, consistent and disciplined presentation is vital.

Ensuring Logos Connect   Since the beginning, Inspiration Corporation has evolved and expanded its mandate through the merging of several organizations. The organization has had three logos to reflect its history. "Our first logo was homey and cute but became dated," explained Diane Pascal. "When we merged with the Living Room Cafe in 2003, we changed our name from Inspiration Cafe to our legal name, Inspiration Corporation. It also seemed like the right time to update our logo. The design firm that led the rework donated their time. The new logo had edgy colors and really targeted our donors. It helped us begin to differentiate from other social service agencies. When we did our second merger in 2005, we did a deep investigation as to how to build a brand identity for the organization. We kept the Inspiration Corporation name and updated our logo to keep it recognizable, added a tagline, and selected a palette of primary colors" (see Figure 5.5).

With nearly 100 years of history, the American Heart Association works to build on the power of its existing identity, regularly reviewing and refreshing the brand meaning to ensure that it remains contemporary. "About 10 years ago, we refreshed our heart and torch symbol to give it an updated look," explained Robyn Landry. "Our research consistently shows that there is a lot of equity in this symbol. The new logo gave it lines that

FIGURE 5.5   Inspiration Corporation

were cleaner and a flame that had the feel of movement. We didn't move too far away from the earlier version to avoid consumer confusion and to continue to build on what we have gained throughout the years."

Logo and Typeface A good logo and accompanying typeface gives people an initial introduction to your organization and can make people more receptive to communications with you.

Points to Remember

- Simplicity: the best logos and typefaces are elegantly simple
- Practicality: make sure it works in color and in black and white and is a size that can be as easily understood on a postage stamp as on a billboard
- Relevancy: it should not be trendy, and it should have timeless distinction
- Personality: it should imply something about the organization (e.g., progressive or conservative)
- Distinctiveness: it should offer a unique presentation of the organization

Colors Color is a powerful part of your logo and evokes emotion, expresses personality, and requires a clear vision of how the brand meaning needs to be perceived and differentiated. Colors also have a functional impact on readability and the ability to attract attention. All of this is important in designing letterhead, business cards, web site pages, print ads, and other marketing media. The ultimate goal is to own a color that facilitates recognition, acts as a rallying flag, and builds brand equity. For example, the color pink has become synonymous with breast cancer, red with heart disease, and orange with the hunger movement.

Brand Architecture Here's the architecture platform and hierarchy to guide brand meaning development.

Organizational Mandate (Foundation of All Brand Development)

- Mission
- Vision
- Values

CONSISTENT PRESENTATION

Consistently presenting the brand should be the default option. Organizational procedures should eliminate harmful or chaotic branding practices in the shortest possible time and replace them with tools and methods that ensure that the brand meaning is promoted rather than degraded. Guidelines, templates, and regular brand audits can ensure that an organization's brand meaning is being consistently portrayed to the community. This is an important internal tool and one that should be made available to external partners. An outline of branding communications guidelines is presented in Chapter 4.

Many organizations undertake periodic brand audits to determine how consistently the brand identity is portrayed from the consumer vantage point. The American Heart Association, with all its touch points nationwide, has done two brand audits during the last decade. "The audits include gathering and reviewing a range of our external communications from our field and national offices. We look for consistency, look, and feel and use the recommendations of the audit to strengthen our brand meaning unity. For example, we've made greater use of the color red, determined consistent placement of the American Heart Association trademark, and updated our branding guidelines to give better clarity for both our internal team and external partners," explained Robyn Landry. "We usually hire an outside firm to look at this with fresh eyes, but I've worked in nonprofits where our marketing committee or volunteers with marketing backgrounds have undertaken the brand audit on behalf of the organization."

Kids Help Phone conducts regular brand touch-point audits, identifying every piece of communication and reviewing whether it stays, goes, or is reviewed and revised. "This is an important best practice," explained Ellen Réthoré. "It ensures consistency and gives us a chance to see the whole spectrum of our communication material."

Brand Meaning Platform

- Position
- Personality
- Promise

Verbal Identity

- Organizational name and subbrand names
- Voice
- Tagline

Visual Identity

- Logo and typeface
- Colors
- Visual look and feel
- Images and photography

Build: Compelling and Integrated Online and Off-Line Communications

To build the brand meaning is to create and deliver a compelling communication plan that connects with target audiences, using integrated channels both online and off. "Our communications strategy is developed to purposefully build and manage our brand meaning," explained John Pfeiffer of Inspiration Corporation. "In 2007, volunteers from the Kellogg Graduate School of Management and the Taproot Foundation surveyed key stakeholders to learn what people thought of us. Because we knew what we want people to think when they hear about us, we developed a communications plan to close the gap."

Added Diane Pascal, "For example, we learned that many people knew about Inspiration Cafe—our first program—or one of the other programs named for an organization we merged with (two mergers in three years!). What they didn't know was the programs were part of Inspiration Corporation. We make a concerted effort to always refer to Inspiration Corporation when discussing our organization and to tie it back to Inspiration Cafe or another program that the audience might be familiar with. In the same way, we are now focused on appealing to the public by emphasizing that Inspiration Corporation gives participants tools to increase their self-sufficiency. With another grant from Taproot Foundation, we added a tag-line to our updated logo [*Catalyst for Self-Reliance*], and we have woven this message into our language."

Breakthrough nonprofit brands map out a brand communications strat-egy at the outset, not leaving anything to chance. "We create an integrated calendar of annual marketing and communications interdependencies and opportunities. For example, getting a media relations push in the market before the annual giving ask is received in homes has proven very effec-tive," shared Ellen Réthoré, Kids Help Phone.

The goal of any BNB is to create communication experiences that will be meaningful, memorable, and associated explicitly with the brand. This is the second step in building breakthrough brand com-munications. It starts with creating a strategic road map for the com-munications campaign. Annual objectives are listed, followed by core audiences. Who are they? How do you best communicate with them? What are their preferred communications channels? Using demo-graphic and psychographic analysis, BNBs segment stakeholders to un-derstand their needs, beliefs, and values, which help craft messages and select appropriate communications.

Know Your Audience   "We put our core constituents and supporters at the center of the brand communications, and we aim to be relevant to as many people as possible," explained the American Heart Association's Robyn Landry. "We understand our constituents and have our communi-cations meaningful and useful to them day in and day out. Our focus is to connect with them emotionally and personally to drive action."

Segment and Customize   A key element of success has been the seg-mentation of messaging to ensure the right information for the right audi-ence. "We know our broad-based messaging is important as an organization, but it's the targeted messages and content that have been essential to our success," added Robyn. "In 2005, we launched our first cause brand, Go Red for Women, targeted specifically at women. The success of the cause resulted in the addition of three other demographic- and psychographic-segmented strategies. The first was geared at childhood obesity, Alliance for Healthier Children; the second focused on stroke in

African Americans, Power to End Stroke; and the third centered on addressing inactivity in adults aged 25 to 54, Start! In particular, Start! aimed to motivate people to get active by reaching them in the workplace. We keep our messaging simple and look for every opportunity to say it, say it, and say it again."

Build Clear, Simple Messages   Keep it simple, clear, and relevant to the audience. The fundamental rule of activities tell and benefits sell holds true here. Don't get caught up in going on and on about what you do; rather, focus on what the audience wants to know and what they will derive from it.

"Over the past decade, we have sharpened our focus and simplified our messaging," shared Lisa Szarkowski of the U.S. Fund for UNICEF. "The result has transformed our ability to communicate and fundraise."

The U.S. Fund for UNICEF has a message that is simple yet complex. It is every child's birthright to be protected, cared for, and loved in order to grow to his or her full human potential. Continued Lisa, "Simple. Few would challenge this. However, the way we pursue this goal is complex. From education to advocacy, from nutrition to immunization, from providing bed nets to combating discrimination, to name a few."

"Saving children's lives is at the heart of what we do and therefore central to our messaging," summarized Lisa. "We know that 24,000 children a day die needlessly, and UNICEF does whatever it takes to save the lives of children. Whether traveling by donkey, camel, or bike, there is no lack of effort or resourcefulness spared" (see Figure 5.6).

Messages were simplified under the umbrella of ensuring each child has the right to grow to her or his full human potential. "By simplifying our mission message into its starkest terms, we emboldened all. Our staff, board, volunteers, and celebrity ambassadors are grateful for the clarity and focus this has brought to their work. All now have a uniform message. Whether a media appearance, B-roll, interview, e-mail, formal speech, or tweet, we explain that 24,000 children die of preventable causes each day, and UNICEF will do whatever it takes to get that number to zero. We have a clear mandate, a clear message. We must speak louder, be more forthright, and state the truth. We share what we are doing to change it and invite others to join us."

24,000

CHILDREN DIE EVERY DAY FROM PREVENTABLE CAUSES.
I BELIEVE THAT NUMBER SHOULD BE

ZERO.

And that's why I support UNICEF. Working in over 150 countries, UNICEF has saved more children's lives than any humanitarian organization in the world. From Haiti to Darfur to Afghanistan — UNICEF is providing children with lifesaving medicine; food; clean, safe water; education; and protection from violence and exploitation. No child should ever die from a preventable cause. Every day 24,000 do. Help UNICEF get that number to zero.

FIGURE 5.6   UNICEF, United States Fund

TOP 10 TIPS FROM OUR BNB COMMUNICATORS

1. Be clear. Decide what your brand stands for and build a simple message to describe it.

2. Be consistent. A solid brand is an investment. Resist the temptation to dilute the power of consistency.

3. Cut your word count by 30 percent. See what you can pare down.

4. Be authentic. If you want to stand out, be on message and stay relevant.

5. Be honest. Contribute something to the conversation other than just what your organization wants or needs.

6. Be yourself. Talking points are good, but be in the present and be yourself. Humans connect to humans, not talking points.

7. Be considerate of your audience. They want to be heard and have an experience, not just a transaction.

8. Be persistent. Repeat and reinforce your message—look for every chance to say it and then say it again.

9. Be audience-centric. Put your audience at the center of all you do and talk with them, not just at them.

10. Be accessible. Use understandable language and defend against using insider language or abbreviations.

Storytelling Drives Communication Messages   Great nonprofit brands are storytellers. Stories are the most potent form of communicating. They help us understand; they bring an organization to life; they convey meaning. In our overwhelming and fast-moving world, meaning trumps information. Stories provide a key way to create a memorable message that will grow with repetition and time.

"We use stories extensively and have evolved their use over time," shared the American Heart Association's Robyn Landry. "Our first paid advertising campaign in the late 1990s used personal stories comprehensively. We featured individuals impacted by heart disease and stroke from all walks of life and all races, ages, and sexes. Our research showed that most people thought of heart disease as an older person's issue. We wanted to chip away at those perceptions through storytelling and the use of targeted cause campaigns."

Throughout the years, the way the organization uses stories has evolved with the growing diversity of communications channels. "We have provided people with forums for sharing their stories through social media, which is very empowering," continued Robyn. "We engaged celebrities who have personal stories, which has generated significant media coverage. We also use personal stories in our annual report, cases for support videos, and on our web site."

Field volunteers and staff are an effective way to find the right story for the right circumstance. Social media provide many individual stories.

"We have developed mechanisms for quickly getting these stories for both immediate needs but also media requests, often looking for very specific stories based on their community or a type of heart issue," shared Robyn.

As women, we often suffer in silence. Being caretakers by nature, we don't want to worry our loved ones or draw attention to ourselves. Well, I'm here to tell you that silence almost killed me.

More than 20 years ago, I was diagnosed with something called idiopathic hypotrophic subaortic stenosis. To put it simply, I had an enlarged heart.

I was treated successfully with medication for about 16 years. One day I felt dizzy at work and started slurring my words, but I shrugged it off and said I would be fine. Six weeks later, I had a second episode and went to see a neurologist. While waiting in the exam room, I read pamphlets on the symptoms of a stroke. The doctor walked in to give me my prognosis, "It's a stroke, isn't it?" I should have known better, given our family's history of heart disease: My grandparents, my parents, and my nephew all died from heart disease.

I finally wised up and started taking control of my heart health. At a Go Red for Women luncheon earlier this year, I went for a stroke screening that showed I had 90 percent blockage in my right artery. This time, I immediately went for more testing, and my surgery was scheduled for the following day. Without that screening, I could have died.

Today, a toy ambulance sits on my desk to remind me to call 911 should I have a heart attack or another stroke. Heart disease is known as a silent killer. But sometimes it's us, and not the disease, who are guilty of the silence.[6]

Think Like a Storyteller

Storytelling forges powerful connections between an organization and its audience. The most enduring stories are built on several essential elements.

Be Authentic and Genuine   At Kids Help Phone, two sets of very personal stories are threaded through all communications, both internally and externally. "Our professional, volunteer counselors are heroes. When they share a story or a feeling, there is a hush and total quiet in the room as those listening are taken right to the heart of the important work of Kids Help Phone," shared Ellen Réthoré. "We use their stories at quarterly staff meetings, board meetings, and in fund-raising videos. They attend major fund-raising events where they are an important part of the communications component of the activity. We also have them participate in our media relations activities as experts, and they bring their points to life through the use of stories."

Stories also come from kids—heartfelt, sometimes tragic stories are found in posts to www.kidshelpphone.ca. "The 'Ask Us Online' section offers a rich source of verbatim information, representing the unsolicited, spontaneous expression of thoughts, wishes, and needs of kids across Canada," added Ellen. "We make extensive use of the stories in our print collateral, web site, and social media activities, although because of our commitment to anonymity we don't publish full names. For example, in an ad we ran in the national edition of the *Globe and Mail*, we used a quote from a child to bring to life our important work."

Humanize, Then Support with Facts   Joe Vladeck of College Forward shared: "Genuine and authentic stories really bring our brand meaning to life. Stats are important, and we use them together with stories to reinforce our brand meaning. But it's one thing to say that in 2009, 99 percent of our students enroll in college immediately after high school—and another thing for one of our students to explain why being the first member of his family to go to college is the first step toward breaking the cycle of generational poverty" (see Figure 5.7).

"We use an individual's story to illustrate how a program works, and we back it up with statistics about the program impact and success," explained John Pfeiffer of Inspiration Corporation. "We've struck a balance between real life experiences, facts, and figures that seems to work."

Deliver a Personal and Practical Benefit   Breakthrough 360° brand meaning communications show how they are improving the lives of supporters and society as a whole. The American Heart Association provides valuable information to improve an individual's cardiovascular health while lowering the number of deaths across the country from heart disease. Kids

Eiliana at her graduation from St. Mary's University

college forward

College Forward provides college preparatory and college retention services to motivated, economically-disadvantaged students in order to facilitate their transition to college and make the process exciting and rewarding. We believe that access to higher education is the right of every young Texan.

We accomplish this by providing:

- Orientation to the college experience
- Preparation for college entrance examinations
- Assistance with college applications
- Assistance securing financial aid
- College retention support

College Forward Celebrates First College Graduate!

College Forward was the answer to Eiliana Castañeda's dream of becoming an optometrist. As a junior at Hays High School in September 2004, Eiliana attended a presentation describing a program to help low-income students through the college application process. Eiliana heard the message loud and clear: if she stayed with the College Forward program and did her part, she could become the first in her family to go to college. Eiliana committed to attending after-school classes twice a week throughout her last two years of high school, and with the help of her College Coaches, she successfully applied to five colleges. She especially appreciated College Forward's help with the financial aid application. "My parents got a lot of help in the financial aid process," she says. "We were a little doubtful in how to do it, and they were right there with us."

Eiliana and her parents decided that St. Mary's University in San Antonio was the best college for her. Although she was committed to succeeding in college, the thought of leaving her family and facing the next four years on her own was overwhelming. When she realized that College Forward's Retention program was a continuation of the support she had received in high school, she knew there would be someone to help find the answers she would need to get through college.

On Saturday, May 8, Eiliana graduated from St. Mary's University. "I didn't feel the accomplishment until I received that diploma and I was on stage," she says. "When I looked at that diploma, I felt like I finally did it, it finally paid off." She adds, "I'm the eldest in my family, so I feel very grateful that I can set an example for my brother and my sister."

Now, Eiliana will continue her education by attending optometry school. And of course, she knows that College Forward will always be in her corner, supporting all the dreams to come in her future.

FIGURE 5.7   College Forward Uses Storytelling

Help Phone provides information on how to reach their counselors—24 hours a day, every day.

Use Compelling Language   Language that is active and conjures up images is an art. The American Heart Association recently revised its brand meaning statements using powerful language to bring it to life. The personality traits are described as "true, positive, committed and heroic." "The organization's philosophy is to reflect 80 percent of what the organization is now with 20 percent as aspirational," stated Robyn Landry. "Being heroic is our aspirational piece. Lives being saved through CPR speak to us being heroic. But we also want to talk about being heroic using words like *demonstrating courage, surpassing the ordinary, being strong, bold, and proactive.* All of these characteristics are reflected in both the language and images presented and help drive the identity we want to present in the marketplace."

The newly developed brand promise drives the messaging. "To have an extraordinary impact on your life by empowering you and your loved ones to save lives, live healthier, and enjoy more peace of mind about cardiovascular health." According to Robyn, the key pieces—extraordinary impact and empowering to live a healthy life—came from extensive qualitative and quantitative research.

Support with Evocative Images   Great stories are supported by photography and illustrations. They can speak volumes about who you are, what you do, and the messages you're promoting. "Visuals reach the nooks and crannies of a person's psyche, so *use them!*" emphasized Lisa Szarkowski.

Most powerful are images that feature one person or a small number of people and focus on their eyes and expressions to capture their emotions. This practice draws people in and helps them see themselves in the image. The American Heart Association makes extensive use of photography and has built up a significant photo library for organizational use. A key practice is using photography that has one strong iconic image.

"Kids Help Phone's first ever paid advertising campaign featured one powerful image of child with a short, story-like quote," explained Ellen Réthoré. "It's very different than earlier ads with heavy text dominating the space. Kid-centered photography is very impactful in bringing our message to life" (see Figure 5.8).

"We're fortunate to have a board chair who is a professional photographer and specialist in portraiture," shared John Pfeiffer of Inspiration Corporation. "We have a large supply of excellent photos that tell our story more eloquently than any words, and we use them liberally."

Tell a David and Goliath Fight   Nonprofit brands break through when they represent a noble idea that inspires and a challenge that must be vanquished. The American Heart Association stands for learning and opposes ignorance and inaction surrounding heart disease; UNICEF breathed new life into the brand meaning by harnessing the tension between what it stands for and what it's against. The highly successful campaign Believe in Zero positioned the brand meaning as an advocate of childhood survival battling for the 24,000 children who die needlessly—every day.

FIGURE 5.8   **Kids Help Phone National Advertising Campaign**

College Forward crusades for young Texans' right to have access to higher education. Explained Co-Founder and Executive Director Lisa Fielder, "We intentionally appeal to a sense of justice and the injustice that economically disadvantaged students face." Great stories have a protagonist and an antagonist, a yin and a yang that underscore a call to arms.

Move to Action   Great stories have the ability to persuade people to do something with the idea. They offer hope and aspiration and compel people to action. A straightforward call to action should prompt supporters to act now. "We declare that the unnecessary death of poor children is unacceptable. We make an unambiguous statement that we will do whatever it takes to save their lives," passionately stated Lisa Szarkowski. "We issue an invitation to like-minded people to join our movement."

The American Heart Association uses a friend-to-friend "heartfelt" strategy to personalize its message about heart disease. They've created a card with two red dress heart pins, one for the giver and one to give to a friend. This caring gesture shows concern for a friend's heart health and generates further awareness about prevention and treatment.

Make It Easy to Be a Storyteller   The U.S. Fund for UNICEF staff draws on anecdotes, reports, photographs, and video from field-based colleagues, as well as firsthand reporting to tell their story.

"A few years ago our communications team compiled a storybook of individual profiles grouped into programmatic themes," shared U.S. Fund for UNICEF's Lisa Szarkowski. "For example, there was a chapter on HIV/AIDS and, within that, the stories of individual children and mothers affected, plus the interventions UNICEF made to assist them. Our fundraisers used relevant examples of real children to tailor their outreach to donors. The database of stories, photos, and video is constantly refreshed as our staff and volunteers visit new locations."

Make the Stories Relevant   Humanizing the stories helps make them relatable to audiences. Searching for multiple layers to the stories adds richness. Lisa continued: "Perhaps 5 million children were inoculated in Ethiopia over a three-day period. What else? 50,000 Ethiopian mothers volunteered to be trained to deliver the immunizations, while funds for the program were generated through a cause-marketing program supported by thousands of Americans."

Working with Celebrities   Today, nonprofit engagement is a must-do for celebrities. Yet, the depth and authenticity of that engagement is critical for effective brand building and communications. In 1950, UNICEF pioneered the category of goodwill ambassador with entertainer Danny Kaye. Audrey Hepburn, Mia Farrow, and Lucy Liu have followed his path. Each has made a deep personal investment of hundreds of hours to learn about UNICEF, traveling the world to see the organization in action and bearing witness to the plight of children in Somalia, Darfur, and earthquake zones in Pakistan.

In some cases, the public is better able to connect with a faraway situation or population if someone familiar to them serves as a genuine storyteller. In Lisa's office is a framed photograph of Hepburn taken during a visit to Somalia. In it, she tenderly cradles a severely malnourished child who appears to be on the brink of death. Her beautiful face is uncharacteristically somber with her gaze afar. She appears anguished and outraged by the condition of the child. Her expression conveys what we might imagine ourselves to be feeling in that same situation, with the photo telling a story far more powerful than words.

These celebrities create special bonds with UNICEF supporters because they genuinely care about the organization's mission and passionately share their stories in media interviews, at special events, and in social media. "Whether speaking before politicians or college students, Mia Farrow is so credible and passionate when speaking about the people of Darfur and showing her personal photographs that people in those audiences appear awestruck," said Lisa.

Embrace and Integrate Online and Off-Line Communication Tools   To create awareness, connect with their constituents, and build relationships, BNBs work across communications channels. They recognize the value of traditional media such as TV, print ads, newsletters, radio, and media relations and embrace the power and effectiveness of social media tools to get their message out, hear from their supporters, and inspire action. Their robust strategic online campaigns are married with off-line efforts to reach supporters when, where, and how it is most relevant.

Because it has the ability to inspire deep engagement, expose supporters to peer reviews, and immerse them in highly emotional and engaging stories, BNBs view interactive media as a powerful brand-building medium. They welcome social media as a source of creativity and dialogue, not only as a vehicle to communicate messages.

"We use social networking tools like Facebook so that stakeholders can control how they relate to Inspiration Corporation," explained Diane Pascal. "We have seen firsthand how off-line and online communications can really be effective. The True North commercial about Inspiration Corporation was debuted during the 2009 Academy Awards telecast. It was transformational, thrusting Inspiration Corporation onto the national stage. While it was great to hear from people from all over the country, the real value of the commercial is that it made people in the Chicago area view us in a new light. We also use the commercial on our web site and through YouTube. It was a huge third-party endorsement that made our current stakeholders proud of their connection to Inspiration Corporation and won us many more new volunteers, donors, and advocates."

Breakthrough nonprofit brands recognize the value of print, radio, TV, events, and other more traditional forms of communications. "We know it's almost impossible to reach senior corporate executives with a viral video," reinforced Inspiration Corporation's Diane Pascal. "Or older

TABLE 5.2 360° BRAND MEANING COMMUNICATION TOOLS CONTINUUM

	Base	Build	Breakthrough
Off-line	• Newsletter • Annual report • Print collateral (e.g., organizational brochure, flyers)	• Advertising—PSA and/or paid Proactive media relations program	• Media partnerships to extend reach and impact • Networks to spread word virally • Organizational friends and celebrities spread the word Firsthand experiences with the brand meaning
Online	• Web site • E-newsletter • Prepare internally to ensure there is support and structure to facilitate social media activities	• Strategically determined social media vehicles • Establish presence on social media vehicles • Provide compelling information Monitor and listen to response	• Establish an online community • Let others drive conversation and add to dialogue • Have two-way dialogue • Build relationships to drive the discussion

audiences, for that matter, through Twitter. There is power and effectiveness in using traditional media, and we embrace all forms of communications. We work to figure out how best to deploy each." See Table 5.2.

Added Lisa Szarkowski, "In our real-time news environment, people still turn on their televisions to see events unfold. As nonprofits, we can't turn our backs on traditional media forms. However, increasingly, conventional news is a backdrop to human interaction, as people turn to each other online to share and understand what they are seeing. Whether *Good Morning America* or *The Situation Room,* these programs solicit and respond to the views of their audience in real time as standard fare—via social media. This reality can provide nonprofits with a powerful opportunity to shape discussions about issues of importance to their mission. We're still learning how to do this."

Establish Metrics, Test, and Learn Breakthrough nonprofit brands embrace hard and soft metrics, recognizing the importance of both. True professionals work hard to balance these seemingly conflicting goals. Evaluation and metrics help determine if goals are being accomplished, and learning can be incorporated into future work. A key aspect of brand communications is paying attention to brand efforts and whether they are resonating with stakeholders. Establishing goals and analyzing results seem obvious but are often missed in the flurry of demands and activities.

Great marketers know many new and good ideas are doomed to fail. But instead of being paralyzed, they build learning cultures to improve their odds of success. If something doesn't work, they celebrate the insights gleaned and focus on how to do better next time.

"Don't be afraid to try new things—and fail—especially in the world of social media," championed the American Heart Association's Robyn Landry. "Some of our greatest successes have come from trying something that's unproven. It's okay if a few things don't work along the way—just so long as you learn. The Passion Project we launched in the late 1990s didn't yield the benefits we had hoped but was the basis for moving into the world of paid advertising. All we learned was foundational as we developed our cause initiatives."

Social Media Checklist   Communications is an interactive dialogue between the organization and its constituents. The BNBs are asking not only "how can we reach our constituents?" but also "how can our constituents reach us?" In an always online culture, engaging audiences through technology can be a powerful, cost-effective tool to increase awareness, understanding, and action among current and new audiences. Like all communications tools, it is a means. Relationships are the end game.

Social media tools offer an ever-expanding platform for expression and connection. In 2010, you could share pictures on Flickr, post videos on YouTube, make friends on Facebook, or connect with colleagues through LinkedIn. Social networks have expanded reach and united people who share interests, experiences, and values. They also help tap collective intelligence and provide a platform for collaboration, networking, and information exchange on a scale never before seen.

The size and scope of social media tools is both mind-boggling and rapidly changing. For example, Facebook eclipsed MySpace as the popular meeting space for people of all ages in less than one year. No one could have predicted the popularity and rapid growth of Twitter in 2009.

This demonstrates the need to focus less on the tools and more on sophisticated planning, thoughtful use, and the right culture to leverage its full potential.

Getting Started   "Social media was a new tool for us that facilitated and strengthened our ability to communicate and build relationships with our constituents," stated the American Heart Association's Robyn Landry. "To maximize the opportunities it presented, we undertook an organization-wide project to consider where social media fits in our overall communications strategy and how best to integrate it into the organization."

Think Strategically   Breakthrough nonprofit brands place social media at the heart of their organization's overarching organizational strategy and integrate it into their communications and marketing plans.

1. Map mission goals

    Think how mission goals can be achieved through the use of social media. The American Heart Association, for example, has outlined four core mission objectives for its social media work: improve health outcomes, engage with professionals, advocate and incorporate calls to action, and fund-raise. Each mission has a specific plan to achieve through the use of social media.

2. Secure buy-in
    - *Get an executive champion:* An executive champion can be at the leadership table explaining and promoting the use of social media.
    - *Seek precedence:* Look to examples of success from other organizations to establish the credibility and potential of social media.
    - *Ensure buy-in:* Involvement across functions and throughout the organization breaks down silos and solidifies understanding and commitment.

3. Align and integrate the overall communications strategy

    Where does it fit into overall communications strategy? How is it aligned with off-line efforts? What are the goals? How do you manage it all once you have it going? The principles of good branding apply online or off.
    - *Align all communications with the brand meaning:* Reinforce your brand meaning difference and relevance.

- *Use a clear voice that personifies your brand meaning:* Use this to represent your brand values, beliefs, and character traits.
- *Invest in content that people want:* Create compelling and relevant content that people can use and will send friends to see.

4. Put processes and people in place

   "To encourage and make it easy for staff to use consistently, we've created a can-do guidelines framework. It's easy if you're new to this not to know all the things you need to think about," stated Robyn Landry of the American Heart Association. "For example, we encouraged people to think of the implications on workload of engaging people. For example, we did a Go Red casting call the first year, asking people to share how they had gone red. We got hundreds back, which was terrific, but then we had to make sure we could manage them on the backend by posting their stories and then recruiting advocates and spokespersons from the submissions. If people don't see the impact of their time and effort, they won't participate again, and, of course, worse they'll spread the word!" Simple-to-use guidelines and a checklist help staff feel comfortable within a framework."

   - *Extend impact by encouraging other areas' involvement:* The American Heart Association involves colleagues beyond the communication's department to post to Twitter, blogs, and YouTube. Social media isn't something that belongs only to the communications and marketing team," states Robyn Landry. "We wanted other people across the organization to get in the game. This was a big project so we established a cross-functional working group that meets to discuss how best to use social media. Each department identified someone who had an affinity or interest in the area. We had technology partners, science, legal—every area was represented. So rather than going to departments after we'd come up with a road map and guidelines, we had them right at the table, approving and buying into our strategy. They've become the power thinkers and power users across the organization and are champions and social media leaders in their area."
   - *Consider workload issues:* The most successful application of social media involves regular use and updating of content so people

know where to find the organization and that if they check back, there will be fresh information. Understand the work involved and determine how the organization will keep information up to date, respond to inquiries, and keep the tools active. If you're inviting feedback, an organization must listen to what's being said and be prepared to respond and implement good ideas that come your way.

Determine the Technology Application   The American Heart Association focuses on going where people already are and considers building applications only if they don't already exist. "Our strategy is to make use of the social media tools that exist and are well used by our constituents and supporters," explained Robyn. "We also look at how we can integrate social media platforms."

- *Identify where they are and what they're doing:* Find out where your constituents are hanging out and getting their news, entertainment, and information. People use technology to make life easier and more convenient, so invest in developing a presence where they already are.

- *80/20 rule:* 80 percent of all social media applications are community management, and only 20 percent are technology applications. Social media platforms such as Facebook and Twitter are tools that are means to an end—connecting with community supporters, engaging them in a dialogue, and listening and responding to their feedback is the ultimate goal. Make sure that is the focus of social media initiatives.

Move to Action   With a plan, people, and processes in place, the first step is to immerse the organization in all the social media tools. "Playing with the various tools helped us to understand what they were and how they worked," explained Robyn. The American Heart Association did an immersion session with the Institute for the Future on social media, visited social media companies, and had experts talk to them.

Cultivate Trust and Transparency

- *Don't make promises you can't keep; be transparent about activities:* If you falter, tell the truth. Transparency is a hallmark of the Internet, and while it can be powerful, it can also work against an organization if you're not careful.

- *Listen to what's being said; understand what they're doing:* Study what they are saying and what is relevant to them, and determine how to present it in an easy-to-understand and user-friendly way.

Continue to Learn   Stay ahead by keeping up with the latest social media technology, and experiment personally with new media such as YouTube, Twitter, and Facebook. Invest time following the changing landscape. Here are some important tools:

- Beth's Blog: How nonprofits can use social media to power social networks for change: www.bethkanter.org/.

- Read Beth Kanter and Alison Fine's book: *The Networked Nonprofit: Connecting with Social Media to Drive Change.*

- Use www.Go2Web20.net, an amazing visual directory to stay up to date on social media tools and Web 2.0 sites. In an always-online culture, it is increasingly important to communicate with and engage audiences where they're already plugged in.

- Read Groundswell and keep up to date with "winning in a world transformed by social technologies" at the blog at: www.forrester.com/Groundswell.

Join a Network   There are a number of Web 2.0 and social media learning communities at LinkedIn: www.linkedin.com/groups?gid=1172477&trk=myg_ugrp_ovr.

Or through the Association of Fundraising Professionals at: www.linkedin.com/groups?gid=2117896&trk=fulpro_grplogo&goback=.mid_16 94239327.

Breakthrough: Empower Supporters to Co create Communications and Drive Action

Breakthrough nonprofit brands allow supporters at all levels to amplify the importance of an organization via interactive communications and social media. Friends telling and inspiring friends, external advocates, and champions can act as third-party endorsers and communication vehicles.

"Even if the how is still evolving, one thing is clear—the future of non-profit communications must include the faces and voices of stakeholders," exclaimed UNICEF's Lisa Szarkowski. "We must allow for customization and interaction—not just prescribed formulas for support of our work."

Use Networks and Empower Dialogues   As Kids Help Phone expanded its services, the local volunteer network increased. "From 6 volunteer chapters in 2000 to 50 today, volunteers execute events and act as key communication channels in their communities," explained Ellen Réthoré, explaining the value of a network. "Through their time, influence, and affluence, Kids Help Phone's 10,000 volunteers nationwide help to identity and secure partners, host events, and communicate the organization's message of help and hope.

"Our volunteers include a network of student ambassadors who work in local high schools across Canada, as well as teachers and guidance counselors," explained Ellen. "Our partnership with educators is critical to achieving our mission. Educators trust the quality and accessibility of our service, and they encourage kids to reach out for help to qualified counselors."

Talk with and Listen to Constituents   Breakthrough nonprofit brands don't just communicate. They listen and provide opportunities to connect with those closest to help advance the mission, get their feedback, and provide them with information so they can spread the word.

"We think of our office as an open house. We host site visits for partners and funders, invite community members to our events, and engage volunteers whenever possible," explained College Forward's Joe Vladeck. "They in turn act as advocates and communicate our work."

"Because we have such an open and collaborative culture, feedback often finds us," explained Inspiration Corporation CEO John Pfeiffer. "But we also purposefully seek input from our stakeholders. We have a participants' council, use suggestion boxes, and do periodic surveys. Every five years, we reach out to all our stakeholder groups as part of our strategic planning process to seek their input on our performance, priorities, and organizational change. We frequently meet with donors to seek their input and provide information."

"We also ask our supporters what kind of communications they would like to receive. They can check off the communication vehicles they want, such as our newsletter, e-mail only," added Inspiration Corporation's Diane Pascal. "With computer database systems, it's easy to customize."

Enable Friends to Inspire Friends   "We allow for customization and interaction—not just prescribed formulas for supporting our work," shared UNICEF's Lisa Szarkowski. "Whether a young girl staging a lemonade stand to raise funds for the children of Haiti, a corporation eager to promote its good work in support of immunization programs, or a college student mobilizing his peers for a volunteer program, each needs to be able to communicate with their unique networks in compelling and personalized terms."

Many stakeholders utilize social media to engage others in an organization's mission. For example, one college student had the idea to create training for UNICEF volunteers via video on YouTube. A high-profile UNICEF supporter made use of a camera backstage during fashion week in New York to create a Believe in Zero minimovie. She asked a number of celebrity designers, models, and VIPs to explain what the organization's Believe in Zero campaign meant to them personally, and it was posted to a high-profile site for the fashion community.

"Last year, a journalist wrote about child survival," shared Lisa on the value of encouraging supporters' involvement in promoting an organization. "We asked our supporters to share their views with the journalist directly. The volume of e-mails was such that the journalist reached out to our CEO and jokingly asked if she would ask our supporters to promote his new book!"

Protect the Brand While Allowing Supporters to Make It Their Own   "The strength of the Kids Help Phone brand meaning is based in the mission," stated Ellen Réthoré. "As we developed our revised communications strategy, we engaged stakeholders in its development so they felt a sense of inclusion. We then issued key messages for use. This ensures the entire organization speaks with one voice about challenges and problems for kids in Canada and the role of Kids Help Phone in providing support and assistance. A brand meaning and graphic standards manual also helps guide our staff and volunteers to consistently represent the brand meaning across all channels. We have developed a signature base-bar, a unique element that anchors all communications so that regions or volunteers can incorporate it into their own creative work to provide consistency."

"Enthusiasm for College Forward has resulted in 1,400-plus passionate high school and college students who love what we do and want to be part of us, as well as help get our message out," explained Joe Vladeck. "It's great, but we have struggled to ensure consistency in a way that meets their needs but ensures it fits with our style guide. We've had to assume control over Facebook pages created by staff or students to ensure our brand meaning remains accurate and consistent. We're conscious of the benefit and the need to make it work. We're still resolving it."

Be Diligent, but Have Some Fun!   *CoFo* is informal internal shorthand that College Forward people commonly use. "It's a fun moniker that a student came up with and has been adopted as the 'official unofficial' nickname of College Forward. While we never use it as a nickname in serious correspondence, we do sometimes use it in e-mails internally or with friends, like this one. We've also been known to put CoFo on signs, though our usage guide might not technically allow it."

PRINCIPLE FOUR: SUMMARY

- *Base: Create a unique visual and verbal identity — Develop strong identity to reflect the brand meaning.*
  - Reflect brand meaning through compelling visual and verbal identity.
  - Develop clear guidelines to provide consistency for internal staff and external partners.
  - Ensure consistency and discipline through regular brand audits.

- *Build: Integrate online and off-line communications—Create compelling communications customized for target audiences.*
  - Know your audience: Segment and target messages through the use of psychographics and demographics.
  - Use storytelling to bring your brand meaning to life and connect the audience to the cause. This could include the founding story, brand meaning narrative, and beneficiaries and supporter stories.
  - Integrate online and off-line communication vehicles for the most effective use of resources and broadest reach.

- *Breakthrough: Act as a catalyst—Empower supporters to cocreate communications and drive actions.*
  - Use networks and empower dialogues to allow supporters at all levels to amplify the importance of the organization via interactive communications and social media.
  - Talk with and listen to constituents. Communications is an interactive dialogue between the organization and its constituents. Breakthrough nonprofit brands are not only asking, "How can we reach our constituents?" They also ask, "How can our constituents reach us?"
  - Protect the brand while allowing supporters to make it their own.

CHAPTER 6

Principle Five: Expand Your Brand by Mobilizing an External Community

"We know our organization will only be successful if we engage a community of people who join with us to make this possible. We invite them to be part of us and aim to be part of them."[1]

—ANTONI CIMOLINO, GENERAL DIRECTOR,
STRATFORD SHAKESPEARE FESTIVAL

"Our founder, Nancy Brinker, has always been clear. She didn't establish the organization to merely raise money for breast cancer, but to empower women and give them a voice around the issue of breast cancer. We mobilize individuals to join us and be champions in their communities."[2]

—KATRINA MCGHEE, SENIOR VICE PRESIDENT,
GLOBAL BUSINESS DEVELOPMENT AND
PARTNERSHIPS, SUSAN G. KOMEN FOR THE CURE

STRATFORD SHAKESPEARE FESTIVAL'S BRAND JOURNEY

It is a story worthy of a great play. The year was 1952, and the remote town of Stratford, Ontario, faced a major economic upheaval. The railway industry that had sustained the town for nearly 80 years had pulled up stakes, leaving the community to face an uncertain future. Unprepared to see his hometown wither, native-born journalist Tom Patterson came up with a creative idea: Take the Stratford name, use its beautiful setting on the Avon River, and build a world-class theater festival devoted to the works of William Shakespeare.

The concept of a knowledge economy was generations away, and many scoffed at the notion that Shakespeare could save a blue-collar town. Tom knew that mobilizing a critical mass of the right people would be essential to making his vision a reality. Tom was undeterred and soon after countless conversations, began attracting attention. Friends began talking to friends in local shops, over coffee, and along tree-lined sidewalks, fueling a small movement. With the Stratford City Council and an enthusiastic committee of community members now behind the idea, Tom traveled to New York City to recruit an artistic leader. There he ultimately convinced legendary British actor and director Sir Tyrone Guthrie to become the proposed festival's first artistic director.

Within a few months, the Stratford Shakespearean Festival of Canada Foundation was incorporated as a charitable nonprofit. As a second order of business, a giant canvas tent was erected on parklands by Stratford's Avon River. This is where construction began to create a concrete amphitheater, complete with a revolutionary thrust stage—essential to authentically present Shakespeare plays. From that venue, on the night of July 13, 1953, actor Sir Alec Guinness spoke the opening lines of *Richard III,* marking the triumphant beginning to what would become the largest classical repertory theater in North America (see Figure 6.1).

FIGURE 6.1   Stratford Shakespeare Festival Logo

Passionate Community Grows

Nearly six decades later, what started as a grassroots movement has grown well beyond the borders of Stratford and a small circle of traditional theatergoers. Stratford has connected with young people, ethnically diverse audiences, Shakespeare newbies, and others from across the globe. The combined power of their support has propelled the Stratford Shakespeare Festival from a local theater to an institution of international renown.

Annually, more than 600,000 theatergoers trek to the off-the-beaten-track town to be part of the remarkable Stratford theater experience. But why?

Shakespeare can be found almost everywhere. From Broadway to regional theater to high school plays, hundreds of productions of the bard's masterworks are staged each year. What compels more than half a million people each year to descend on a town that was once literally and metaphorically at the end of the line? The secret lies in the power of external community to building a brand.

SUSAN G. KOMEN FOR THE CURE'S BRAND JOURNEY

"Our very essence is a loosely banded community of grassroots activists who rally around a singular cause—breast cancer," asserted Katrina McGhee, senior vice president, Global Business Development and Partnerships, Susan G. Komen for the Cure. "Our founder, Nancy Brinker, was an early voice that sounded the alarm about breast cancer and its impact on women. But she understood change would not happen without a large enough group of dedicated people coming together to work for that change."

What started with a sacred commitment between sisters (recounted in the introduction to this book) has grown into an international movement. Yet, the first steps were humble: a collection of women gathering early one Sunday morning to run for the cure. "It was a remarkable beginning," recalled Susan Carter Johns, currently vice president of strategic relationships for the organization, who attended that first event in 1982. "In an era of Jane Fonda, leg warmers, and terry cloth headbands, the run was a non-threatening activity where an important message, usually only heard in a doctor's office, could be told."

Susan continued: "Nancy shared the story of her sister and put a face on the disease. It was powerful and personal. She explained the impact of breast cancer on women and connected it to everyone there. She made her story their story. She invited everyone to put a name on her back and run in honor or in memory of someone they knew who had breast cancer, survived it, or passed away from it. The sense of friendship, camaraderie, and determination from everyone coming together that day was palpable."

A Catalyst for the Breast Cancer Community

Women responded to that sense of community, and the organization grew organically. Over the next 25 years, Komen's activities broadened well beyond its signature event as more than 120 domestic and international affiliate groups sprang up to join the cause, and its target audience expanded to reflect a more diverse sisterhood of women—and men (see Figure 6.2).

With such growth, its internal structures, programs, and communications hadn't been able to keep up. The evolving marketplace required

FIGURE 6.2   Start Line, Race for the Cure®

targeted new initiatives and even stronger political advocacy work. Research also showed Komen's original look, name, and messaging were dated and confusing. They did not resonate with key audiences, particularly younger women and certain ethnic groups, among whom breast cancer was increasing at an alarming rate. In this way, the lack of an effective brand message was hampering its mission to reach those most at risk.

"We traditionally had done things very lean and never spent money on advertising," explained Carter Johns. "We relied strictly on free public service advertising, and many of our local affiliates created their own look. So, of course, the brand meaning was getting terribly fragmented. With an explosion in the number of nonprofit organizations and businesses supporting the breast cancer cause, there was increasing confusion in the marketplace about who we were and how we were different. It's hard to build community when your brand meaning isn't clear."

Komen needed to capitalize on its long-standing issue leadership to clarify who it was and what it stood for. The new brand meaning message would need to differentiate it in the marketplace and increase its impact, including outreach to new audiences, with a feeling that was fresh and progressive. The mandate had an accompanying goal of investing an additional $1 billion over the next decade toward finding the cure.

Komen understood that, to reach its audacious goal, the national organization, its affiliates, individual supporters, and corporate partners had to stand together in stronger and more unified ways. External community would be a key part of a five-year journey to revitalize and transform its brand meaning.

An Overview of Principle Five

The long-term success of any nonprofit depends on a critical mass of like-minded people—supporters who feel a sense of connection and are inspired by the organization's mission and values. A breakthrough nonprofit brand understands that it cannot be all things to all people, so it spends time making sure that it is offering the right things to the right people. By prioritizing where it will spend its limited time and resources, a BNB maximizes the return on its investments. Table 6.1 outlines the continuum of this approach.

TABLE 6.1 EXPAND BRAND BY MOBILIZING AN EXTERNAL COMMUNITY FROM BASE TO BREAKTHROUGH

	Base	Build	Breakthrough
How	Cultivate a brand community: Deliver participant benefits as a cornerstone of community building	Foster the brand community: Nurture supporters and develop a robust community by appealing to needs, beliefs, and values	Grow the brand community: Empower brand champions and constantly grow the community by reaching new audiences
Who	One-time or infrequent participants who have a limited or no relationship with the organization	Repeat and increasing supporters who understand the organization and believe in its ability to deliver results	Long-term and lifetime champions who are co-owners of the cause and actively recruit members, regularly advocate, and raise funds for the organization
What	Offer practical value and transactional benefits that align with their needs and/or interests	Provide deeper personalized benefits, rewards, and experiences that more directly connect them to the brand meaning and the services they help provide	Create truest sense of community by introducing them to other cause champions, sharing leadership responsibility, and helping introduce their networks to the organization
Why	Understand who they are and why they are involved. Engage in basic education, linking the cause to the donation, sale, event, etc., in a simple and compelling way	Engage in dialogue; listen and respond while creating a variety of interactive brand or mission-centered experiences	Offer them creative freedom within a structured framework that protects the brand meaning; provide targeted, highly relevant engagement
Where	Create a range of easy ways to get involved through a variety of channels	Add layers, offering a pathway that provides meaningful ways for supporters to continue their engagement with the organization year-round and meets them where they are by offering experiences in a variety of settings	Enable online and off-line action by creating the infrastructure to support the projects they adopt in their personal lives

How-To Success Factors

Building an external community of brand champions requires three key factors to move from base to breakthrough.

1. *Base: Cultivate a brand community*—Deliver participant benefits as a cornerstone of building a community.

2. *Build: Foster the brand community*—Nurture supporters and develop a robust community by appealing to people's needs, beliefs, and values.

3. *Breakthrough: Grow the brand community*—Empower brand champions and constantly grow the community by reaching new audiences.

Base: Cultivate a Brand Community through Participant Benefits

A BNB builds community as an end, not just as a means. It proactively builds a broad community and understands the power of activating it to achieve change. A BNB views community members as vital allies. It carefully identifies and nurtures relationships with individuals whose interests and passions align with its brand meaning. While it takes an inclusive approach, it doesn't dilute its relevance by trying to please everyone. After all, efforts to engage mass audiences too often result in compromises that detract from the level of focus needed for a brand to break through.

Instead, a BNB views itself as a catalyst that enables a well-defined community to advance a common cause. It looks for bonds that unite and works to bring like-minded people together, knowing these connections are critical to its long-term success. Komen isn't just one of countless charities focused on a common disease; it is global movement of people dedicated to finding the cures for breast cancer. Stratford doesn't just sell tickets to plays; it brings people together around important ideas, deep emotions, and pure delight in life, empowering them to rediscover great artistic works. These breakthrough brands view their community members as friends working with them for a common cause.

Starting an Ongoing Journey   BNBs think of building a community as an ongoing journey that begins with individual relationships. They cultivate connections by understanding people and moving them along a continuum of engagement. BNBs start by getting new contacts involved as participants. Only once they have attracted participants do they think about moving them to become supporters by letting them experience the organization's mission and see its positive impact. And once they become true supporters, they are encouraged to serve as champions by fostering a sense of deep belonging and new connections. Remember, it is difficult to garner a champion right off the bat, so attention must be paid to that initial member attraction to and participation with your brand.

BNBs get to know community members and help them to get to know one another through a meaningful dialogue about shared interests, common values, and collective aspirations. There is real value to taking a fresh look at existing and potential supporters. BNBs cultivate curiosity while listening attentively to what supporters say—and what is unsaid. They act as an anthropologist, observing the tribe that gathers around their cause and using those insights to allow supporters to connect on their own terms. The learning is critical in helping to attract new participants who may have similar feelings and desires. No matter the organization's size, it can benefit from segmenting its audiences and providing a variety of products, services, and experiences tailored to the distinctive needs and interests of each group. This is a critical step in developing the relationships that are at the core of vibrant communities.

For many, this is new, even radical thinking. Traditionally, nonprofits built relationships almost entirely based on the organization's needs and wants. Sometimes referred to as "yell and sell," this limited, one-sided model involves the organization explaining what it does and why a supporter should contribute. Yet, return on investment is often much lower than it could be since the message isn't tailored to address the benefits that interest a particular audience. The sooner an organization focuses on building a relationship-driven brand, the sooner it can extend its reach, influence, and impact through a community of supporters and external champions.

A turning point for Stratford was shifting from selling tickets to building relationships by focusing on patrons' benefits that suit their needs. It coordinates a distinctive experience for its patrons. "Our goal is to connect people to the Stratford brand meaning and make the experience a satisfying one," explained Administrative Director Anita Gaffney. "We make suggestions for plays and pretheater chats, provide information about restaurants and hotels, and we follow up to make sure that we have met their needs.

"Moving from transactional sales to building relationships has really been game changing for us. It was a different mind-set, and it took time to adjust from pushing tickets or getting donations to creating experiences and building a sense of belonging. Now the whole organization looks at what our patrons need to make their time with us meaningful and interesting to them. Everyone is involved, not just our marketing, sales, or fund raising team. When the focus is on supporter needs, interests, and aspirations, it is easier to build a long-term meaningful relationship," Anita observed.

Stratford uses a continuum of involvement model of relationship building. The initial connection may be requesting information or attending a play. Yet, the organization seeks to move the relationship further along the continuum by staying in touch to better understand how the relationship can be built over time. "Rather than waiting for attendees to get back in touch one day, we communicate with them," explained Anita. "We thank them, of course, but we also make suggestions based on what we know about them. For example, they might have seen a new Canadian play. We let them know about the work of other Canadian playwrights, or programming that relates to their interests. And it isn't always something they have to pay for or go to Stratford to enjoy. We do online webcasts throughout the year, hosted by our director, Antoni Cimolino (see Figure 6.3). We work to serve their needs and show them we are interested in what interests them."

"Our philosophy is to be the catalyst to connect people to the brand meaning. We want people to feel a sense of community, that there is a place for everyone here," explained Susan G. Komen for the Cure's Susan Carter Johns. "We don't start by asking for anything. We don't lecture. We give people information they want to hear and let them get involved on their terms. The relationship and support builds from there."

Local affiliates customized Komen events, starting with its signature Susan G. Komen Race for the Cure® series, to move people up the spectrum from aware to engaged to enthusiasts. Key to the organization's success was extensive involvement with its corporate partners, which created

FIGURE 6.3   **Antoni Cimolino, Pretheater Presentation at Stratford**

consumer awareness and invited them into Komen as initial participants. "It may sound simple, but you have to make sure people know what you do and have multiple points of entry in order for them to want to be part of your group," said Emily Callahan, senior vice president, Global Marketing and Networks. Komen built a strong organization thanks to a keen understanding of the relationship continuum. It translated those strong relationships into a movement through savvy community building.

Build: Foster the Brand Community by Nurturing Supporters

A breakthrough nonprofit fosters an external community through activities and experiences that engage people on multiple levels. At the base, it rationally attracts participants by communicating in ways that define the benefits of engagement. To build, it appeals to the heart through personal storytelling. The goal here is to begin to build a belief in the organization and a stronger bond with the organization, what it stands for, and the impact it has made. Finally, at the breakthrough level, nonprofits break through by creating a deep sense of belonging, inviting champions to make the organization's approach to the cause a shared responsibility.

Respond to Needs   A BNB views its brand meaning as the way by which supporters can fulfill their own interests or needs. After all, it's not just how people feel about the brand, but how the brand makes them feel about themselves. Make giving reciprocal and understand that, over the long term, many people are increasingly apt to donate, volunteer, or engage with a nonprofit organization because of enlightened self-interest (i.e., what's in it for them as well as the charity) rather than a pure, angelic sense of altruism. For years, research has shown that most significant donors tend to gravitate toward organizations that have some personal relevance, whether that means the organization addresses an issue of special importance to the donor, a loved one has benefited from the organization's work, or someone influential has inspired them to get involved. Individual support could be motivated by a desire to cultivate an area of personal interest, build a skill, or make new friends. A BNB understands those complex motives and delivers practical benefits that are connected to everyday life.

Cultivate Beliefs   While keeping individual preferences top of mind, a breakthrough brand connects individuals to its social mission and the tangible results it is achieving. It provides relevant ways for people to see firsthand the good that they have invested in, which creates a cycle of credibility that is the foundation for long-term trust and support. With this, volunteers spend more time, advocates recruit more supporters, and donors give higher amounts when they experience the impact of their contributions in ways that are personally meaningful to them. Hands-on engagement tends to make people more forgiving of inevitable gaffes and shortcomings, and it inspires them to return year after year.

Connect to Values   As detailed in Principle One, the pinnacle any brand can achieve is to stand for something so well that people adopt it to reflect a part of who they are and as a reflection of their values. This is the ultimate form of loyalty. Of course, to attain such a level takes time, discipline, and investment, but the results make the effort required worthwhile.

Breakthrough: Grow the Brand Community and Empower Champions

Many nonprofits have a tendency to target the obvious suspects. A health group focuses on people who have had the disease. A theater troupe connects only with those people who have an existing passion for theater. It makes perfect sense, but it leaves value on the table.

Reframe the Case to Expand Community   By viewing the world in a slightly different way, a BNB reframes the case for involvement with its organization in ways that appeal to new and larger groups. For example, Stratford appeals to grandparents' interest in sharing cultural experiences with their grandchildren by offering special programs for this group and introducing the next generation of theatergoers to Stratford's world. Komen targets new audiences by going where they are. The organization built relationships with Major League Baseball and NASCAR to reach and engage a broader audience, including males; reached out to African Americans by connecting through churches; and sought to engage Hispanic Americans by going to relevant community centers with language and messages geared specifically to them. The point is to go beyond the usual suspects. Reframing your message and looking in nontraditional places can build a much larger constituency.

Stratford Shakespeare Festival knew it couldn't rely only on people in town or even in surrounding communities. To build a nonprofit brand meaning strong enough to revitalize its town, the organization needed to appeal to diverse communities across Canada and beyond. Its focus on innovative experiences was key.

"Even though we are based in Canada, we have a strong American community who support and attend the theater," stated Anita Gaffney with pride. The brand meaning is powerful enough to have shattered borders in the minds of its constituents. "Our supporters aren't limited by geography. They see Stratford as their theater." Today, an impressive 30 percent of Stratford's attendees regularly make the journey from the United States, drawn by Stratford's ability to offer innovative experiences.

Stratford's mission is to create stimulating, thought-provoking productions of Shakespeare's plays, to examine other plays from the classical repertoire, and to foster and support the development of Canadian theater practitioners. The organization vows that by searching Canada and the world for the finest talent and by providing the training that enables those artists to achieve their most courageous work, Stratford will immerse its audiences in a theatergoing experience that is innovative, entertaining, and unsurpassed anywhere in the world.

"We produce events that get people talking, and make it easy for as many people as possible to be involved. For example, our Play On program is designed to appeal to 18- to 30-year-olds. This group has distinctive needs and interests. It's harder for them to plan ahead, and their budgets are often tight. So, we created lower-priced tickets that they can purchase two weeks prior to a show," Anita explained. "It's tempting to assume that Shakespeare's plays, however well known, are something that only a small and elite group of people would be interested in experiencing. Yet, it could be that nobody has approached them with ways that Shakespeare can fit into their lives. Our goal has been to change attitudes and build a broad community of people who believe in the power of classical theater."

The secret lies in an innovative approach to using Shakespeare as a filter for everything Stratford does. This does not limit the organization to Shakespearean productions; rather, it creates a unifying theme across all of its communications and activities. For example, it may put on a non-Shakespearean performance but include surrounding events that illustrate how Shakespeare and classical theater have influenced the production. Stratford also takes the classics outside the theater walls, offering Shakespeare in the park, broadcast to Cineplexes, and online through streaming media. What's more, it has created an immersive experience at the festival site itself, regularly offering free concerts, preshow talks, and classes to patrons. It delivers the practical value of a great experience for the price of admission and then takes the critical step of ensuring that its offerings are unique compared with whatever else is in the marketplace.

"What we hear from people is they love the quality of Stratford productions and the great variety of performances that we offer, but what differentiates is Shakespeare. They feel it through and through in their every interaction with us. This is what they say they value that they can't get anywhere else. Delivering on our mission and brand promise to our patrons is central to our success," said Anita.

Empower Champions   A BNB innovates in appropriate ways because it has taken the time to understand the true essence of its brand meaning, which makes it easier to find new expressions of that core idea. This approach allows a nonprofit to continue to expand its community and extend its impact. It also frees an organization to empower others to communicate the brand meaning, secure in the knowledge that the brand meaning will be enhanced, not fragmented.

A BNB partners with leaders in target communities and encourages them to bring in new participants. For example, Komen affiliates have point people in each local community who drive the organization's work. These champions advocate on behalf of the cause and bring in new friends. Stratford mobilizes its most passionate supporters to draw others into the experience.

You know branding is at its most effective when others adopt the brand meaning as reflective of their own personal identities and align themselves with the cause. That is a sure sign that the brand stands for something meaningful and has attained the ultimate level of loyalty. Of course, it takes time, discipline, and investment, but the result makes the effort required worthwhile.

Case Study: Stratford Shakespeare Festival Mobilizes an External Community

"Everything we do is designed to build a relationship that connects the organization to current and potential supporters. We don't just sell tickets or ask for donations. We link people to the Stratford brand meaning in a way that is meaningful and relevant to them," explained General Manager Antoni Cimolino. "We get to know them, discover their interests and aspirations. We work hard to create a customized experience that delivers value, links them to our mission, and makes them feel part of Stratford community." That sense that the organization is built around and for its supporters comes from sophisticated target audience segmentation and creative approaches to relationship management.

Listen for Underlying Beliefs and Values   Stratford began its deep segmentation work in the late 1990s. Prior to that, it categorized and cultivated patrons in three groups: customers, members, or nonmembers. As a first step to build on its existing but basic knowledge of its patrons, Stratford looked at the records it had on file and grouped customers based on visit frequency, purchase price, donation amounts, and renewal rates. Then it reached out to people in its database to gather information on their preferences, needs, and values. Questions probed whether discounts influenced their purchase decision, what specific productions they were interested in, which forms of communication work best, and whether they would like to participate in or support workshops, courses, lectures, and a wide range of other potential offerings.

The process helped Stratford identify eight major patron groups. "Five are based on behaviors, how often they attended, what plays and activities were of interest, and what benefits they sought. The other three segments are based on psychographics, meaning their interests, attitudes, values, and lifestyle," explained Anita. "Both approaches have helped us to understand who patrons are, how to talk with them, and how best to meet their needs and connect around what's most important to them. We've shaped marketing programs to build the best possible relationships with supporters. We want to hit the right buttons to get them to come, to get them to return, to get them to increase their purchase, and to have them think about donating to the festival." Based on the insights it has gleaned over time, Stratford has gone as far as doing predictive modeling to determine how particular patron groups might respond to various potential offers.

Stratford has shared its experience and knowledge extensively, with the hope of benefiting other nonprofits. "Some organizations find the idea overwhelming or think they are too small," stated Anita. "We say it doesn't matter what your size or budget, it's important to get started. Look at your current database and start to understand your community's behaviors, interests, and values. Talk to your supporters, survey them, listen, and then respond to what you heard about their needs and values. Even in our first year of segmentation, we saw results."

Create a Sense of Belonging for Champions   Organizational champions are a particularly important group to identify during the segmentation process. "Our goal is to create a highly engaged, flourishing external community," explained General Director Antoni Cimolino (see Figure 6.4). "Stratford is synonymous with the people who support us. So we are forming Stratford champions by infusing them in us and us in them."

Part of the power of Stratford's brand can be found in its distinctive approach to encouraging local government, businesses, and townspeople to

FIGURE 6.4   **Stratford Shakespeare Festival Theatre, Festival Theatre, 2008**

Source: Photograph by Erin Samuell.

champion the cause. The town of Stratford has been given the freedom to innovate around the organization's brand meaning, with a wide range of stakeholders each determining how they will take part. Whether it's bed-and-breakfasts promoting themed Shakespearean getaways or local restaurants creating specialty menus that tie in to the organization's approach to the classics, the town has adopted the festival as its cause. Everyone benefits from this approach, which has created a movement that is larger than life.

What's more, executives from the festival sit on the Stratford Tourism Alliance Board and work with local schools to infuse classical content into classroom lessons and special experiences. These reciprocal relationships, combined with the empowerment of so many passionate third parties, fuel a passion for the festival brand meaning. In an amazing testament to the sense of ownership and engagement Stratford has fostered, the organization's volunteer program has a two-year waiting list.

Evolve to Strengthen and Grow the Community   Through sophisticated donor segmentation, innovative relationship management plans, and rewarding, customized offers for active supporters and loyal champions, Stratford creates mutually satisfying relationships for patrons at all levels. To sustain those relationships, Stratford seeks out new opportunities to listen to its constituents and evolve to meet their needs. "Our supporters are a major source of inspiration and new insight for us," Anita affirmed.

In response, Stratford has evolved its program offerings beyond Shakespeare, even though the bard remains a differentiator and filter for the organization's work. The festival produces other classical theater pieces, stages musicals, and introduces new Canadian plays. "We work to strike a balance between our Shakespearean roots and popular culture. We entice people to come for a musical and then take in a Shakespeare play as part of the same visit," explained Anita. "We make it accessible through preperformance presentations and thorough program information."

Experiment and Meet People   While the festival evolves, Shakespeare remains at the heart of its brand meaning. Since many students study Shakespeare, making it accessible and relevant has been a critical way to extend the community and infuse Stratford into the school system. Live Shakespeare performances literally bring the canon to life for students and help educators teach Shakespeare. "The philosophy of our education department is to give them a deep and rich experience," stated Anita. "We do preclass visits, and we put an emphasis on helping teachers teach the work. We do on-site workshops with our artists and introduce tools and techniques that make teachers more comfortable with the subject." To connect with the American community, the company also completes a 10-day residency at Michigan State University, reaching high schools in the region. This multidimensional approach has resulted in more than 70,000 students connecting with Stratford each year.

Building on its connection with Michigan, Stratford reached out to the African American community in Detroit with a presentation of a performance in Palmer Park. The organization is experimenting with taking a performance to Toronto, the largest city in Canada, about 150 miles west of Stratford. The festival also has created strategic alliances in Chicago, New York, and other cities to help generate widespread buzz.

The organization is not only growing beyond the town of Stratford but also taking Shakespeare off the stage and into countless living rooms and malls. In 2008, its production of *Caesar and Cleopatra,* featuring Christopher Plummer, was shot as an HD film and aired on Cineplex screens in Canada and on the TV arts channel Bravo. Sharing theater with a broader audience—from schoolchildren to moviegoers—is part of the festival's community-building efforts. Growing connections with diverse communities has become a strategic approach to cultivating, nurturing, and growing new community members and advocates.

Cultivate New Audiences   No organization can afford to stay the same. And Stratford knows that its most loyal base represents less than 30 percent of its ongoing ticket purchases. However, ticket sales represent more than 75 percent of its revenue. It must constantly look at innovative ways to engage new audiences. As North America's population has diversified, Stratford has worked to reach out to audiences who might not traditionally have connected with the organization's brand meaning.

To help build links to African American and Caribbean communities, for example, in 2007, the company performed the play *Harlem Duet,* which was written by a black playwright. The organization worked closely with influencers from predominantly black communities in Detroit to determine how to customize ticket offerings and promote the event in nontraditional venues, such as local hairdressers, which are well trafficked by the target audience. The success of the performance has inspired Stratford to engage in additional efforts in Detroit, a promising new market for the organization.

The story of the Stratford Shakespeare Festival is a remarkable one: established by a community of committed local citizens, built through connecting the community to the Stratford brand meaning, and strengthened and grown through innovation and relevance.

Case Study: Susan G. Komen for the Cure Mobilizes an External Community

"Many people look at the breast cancer movement today and assume the profile, exposure, and number of people involved have always been this high," observed Susan Carter Johns. "They don't realize how taboo the subject was in the early days and how much attitudes and behaviors have changed over the past 30 years. We feel proud of the role we have played but know our success was possible because of the critical mass of people who spread the word and positively championed the cause."

Komen became a powerful organizational brand by defining aligned local events, building word-of-mouth, creating and engaging communities of supporters, leveraging corporate partner channels, and, critically, by contributing to tangible outcomes and improvements for women facing breast cancer.

Instinctively following this successful formula, in its first 25 years, Komen built a breakthrough brand and galvanized a powerful social movement. Its success lay in a relatively easy-to-understand brand meaning idea backed by a compelling and authentic story; a focused, integrated approach to its programs, marketing, and development activities; and its ability to inspire internal and external communities to join in the breast cancer crusade.

Over time the organization began to face a range of challenges. Like many nonprofit organizations, Komen was facing internal and external forces that were pushing it to carefully reexamine its organizational and business models. It had grown significantly in its first 20 years. As mentioned in the introductory story, this is when research undertaken by the organization in the early 2000s demonstrated an acceptable level of awareness about the organization but a lack of connection between the organization's key programs and the Susan G. Komen brand. It also indicated that the organization wasn't resonating with certain audiences, particularly young women, where there was an increasing risk of breast cancer. At the same time, there was growing fragmentation, clutter, and confusion in the breast cancer space.[3]

The landscape had changed. A growing number of new and successful nonprofit organizations like the American Breast Cancer Foundation and for-profit companies like Avon[4] were doing great work in and outside of the breast cancer community. Enormous clutter and confusion were becoming hallmarks of the breast cancer movement. Komen was determined to rise above the crowd. Its goal was to stand for something that Komen could uniquely own. It sought a way to differentiate itself in an increasingly crowded space, to reach broader audiences and engage more people—and to invest an additional $1 billion in the next decade. Its approach was as daring as ever. It began a five-year journey to revitalize and transform its brand meaning so it could rally what it hoped would be a revitalized and expanded external community.

Linking Brand and Community   Branding was never top of mind at the organization. "We knew we had to pay attention to what I described internally as our most important asset," recalled Susan Carter Johns, currently vice president, Strategic Relationships, who has been involved with the foundation since its inception. "We needed to take a step back and not just make a cosmetic change. It had to be from the depths of the organization, our DNA. We needed to revisit our core values, which are essential to growth, so that the new brand meaning would connect with existing supporters and attract new constituents." The rebranding process took five years of hard work. "It really was a journey. We looked at our core brand meaning and evolved the way we talked about our role—repositioning ourselves from leaders in the breast cancer fight to leaders in the global breast cancer movement," elucidated Katrina McGhee, senior vice president, Global Business Development and Partnerships.

Six months before a public launch, the new brand meaning was secretly shared with staff, affiliates, and corporate partners—strategically ensuring understanding and buy-in of the elevated brand meaning among core constituents before it was revealed to the broader community. The timing reflected the trust that Komen placed in the champions who were critically important for the cause. They needed to understand and be able to articulate the changes in order to launch the new brand meaning and effectively engage new external audiences (see Figures 6.5A and 6.5B).

The Susan G. Komen
Breast Cancer Foundation

FIGURE 6.5A   **Original Susan G. Komen Breast Cancer Foundation Logo**

FIGURE 6.5B   **New Susan G. Komen for the Cure Logo**

In 2007, on the organization's 25th anniversary, it launched the repositioned brand meaning. Once the Susan G. Komen Breast Cancer Foundation, the organization was renamed Susan G. Komen for the Cure. The new name reflected the organization's heritage and humanity while tapping the existing strong association between Komen and the vision of the cure, which was seen in everything from Race for the Cure® to Bowl for the Cure to Cook for the Cure. Updated graphics presented a consistent face across the organization's far-flung affiliates. Emboldened by the success of its new brand meaning, Komen recently simplified its mission statement to "Save lives and end breast cancer forever."

This evolved brand meaning has built momentum at every level of the organization. By consolidating many brand expressions into one clear, unmistakable voice, the brand meaning has lent greater clarity to the cause and extended the reach of the organization's message. And more importantly, it has boosted Komen's ability to enhance its external community, building on its first 20 years of success.

Inviting Millions to Join as Participants   Although it is pursuing new community outreach initiatives, its approach remains the same. "We don't start by asking for anything. That has been a fundamental part of who we are. First and foremost, we want to build a relationship and get people involved. We encourage them to participate in education activities, share information with others, and even join a local Race for the Cure® event. Our goal is for them to benefit personally, get them to understand and believe in the role Komen is playing in finding the cure. We want to create a sense of community," explained Katrina McGhee, senior vice president, Global Business Development and Partnerships.

"We have a great message of hope, along with viable ways for anyone to become part of making a positive change," noted Susan Carter Johns, when asked to share the secrets of Komen's success. "We have built a community of supporters who believe that fighting breast cancer is their personal crusade. They are our best champions and do so much work on behalf of the movement."

These supporters sponsor friends who walk in the Breast Cancer Three-Day, run in a Susan G. Komen Three-Day for the Cure, run in one of the hundreds of Susan G. Komen Race for the Cure® events, and buy products that benefit Komen through cause-related marketing. In addition to generating revenues, Komen benefits from the marketing might of its corporate partners to disseminate educational messages about the disease on packages, through in-store displays, in brochures, at events, and online. In 2009, the year of the popularly named Great Recession, Komen had more than 250 partners—an organizational record and a testimony to the power of the cause and its influence on consumers. In the fall during National Breast Cancer Awareness Month and again around Mother's Day in May, partner marketing, education, and fundraising messages piggyback on products and services ranging from sports and luxury apparel to household goods, tech products, and automobiles. "Through these partnerships, we have reached millions of people with life-saving messages. We get testimonial after testimonial about what that's done that we could never be able to do alone," Emily Callahan said. "That's a driving force behind our partnerships. We want to be as pervasive as possible to get people to sit up and take notice."

Mobilizing Local Communities—Nationwide   From the start, Komen's focus wasn't just raising money, but empowering women, giving them a voice around the issue of breast cancer, and mobilizing a community to help find the cure. Komen served a catalyst, bringing people together around a vital issue of shared concern.

Over time, more than 120 domestic and international affiliate groups sprang up to mobilize local communities, fueling Komen's success. These independently incorporated 501(c)(3)s are staffed with thousands of volunteers who drive the mission in their neighborhoods, organize the local races, and get the educational messages out. Affiliates are empowered to customize key national programs—the Susan G. Komen Race for the Cure® series, the Susan G. Komen Three-Day for the Cure, and the traveling Komen on the Go program—to reflect the needs of their local communities.

"We've really learned to appreciate the wisdom that comes from people who are actually implementing what we are putting together," said Katrina. "Our number-one strategic imperative is to strengthen them, since they're the heartbeat of the organization, our on-the-ground troops. The majority of our funds are generated from the cumulative impact of donations at all of those local events."

The national organization provides support services to meet each affiliate's needs. For example, it invites affiliates to annual training events, provides proven tools for executing programs, and hosts frequent conference calls to share best practices. "Each affiliate has its own leadership and pays its own expenses," Katrina revealed. "Our goal is to provide a tested framework that lets local groups run themselves. It's amazing how well they do it and how much they extend our reach and impact in the process." The freedom to customize national programs and direct the funds they raise toward local grants creates opportunities for affiliates to connect with individuals who often become avid Komen supporters.

Affiliates are asked for candid feedback and new ideas and encouraged to identify opportunities for continual program refinement. "We treat them the way that we want them to treat the individual supporters in their community. Since they are on the ground, they provide important feedback and critical advice on advancing the cause," Susan explained. "Our local affiliates are like dear friends. Instead of preaching to them, we seek to inspire."

Komen's national office not only provides inspiration, it serves as a platform for the global movement. It coordinates national cause-marketing partnerships, undertakes national lobbying efforts, and builds outreach activities on behalf of the broader community.

Developing Champions for the Mission   Giving affiliates freedom to localize national programs and asking for their feedback fuels their commitment. They embody a deep sense of belonging to Komen, inspiring others to become champions for the cause.

Deeper participation with Komen events is an important way people strengthen their sense of connection, so the organization is strategic in providing a range of ways to engage. These include live fundraising events, such as a 5K walk/run, a marathon, or a three-day event; the educational experience of Komen On the Go, a youth-oriented education and engagement touring vehicle; and online communities, such as its Facebook and other social media outreach. All have been crafted and evolved over the years to be highly relevant to specific targeted groups and to provide multiple levels of engagement within the platform of a single event.

For example, the Race for the Cure® series, which attracted more than 1.6 million in 2009, offers several engagement opportunities, from the race itself, to educational messages, fundraising, and celebrations of survivors. "People have a fun experience at the events. More importantly, I want them to walk away with something that's going to change their behavior and change their lives," said Emily Callahan, senior vice president, Global Marketing and Networks. "Over the long term, I hope they'll become champions and change the lives of others."

Katrina McGhee, senior vice president, Global Business Development and Partnerships, embodies the spirit of a champion. "When I go out and represent Komen, I'm really representing the millions of breast cancer survivors, their families, and those who have lost their battles. I'm representing everybody who believes in the cause, because to me that's who Komen is," she explained with passion. "To mobilize people, to get them to do what you ultimately want, is to first give them what they want. Think back to what our structure does: It allows people to meet a need they have in their own lives to do anything to further the cause, and gives them multiple ways they can do it."

Meet People Where They Are

"When you think of so many nonprofits, you think of a building or a series of statistics," stated Emily Callahan. "When people think of Komen, they think of a group of people—a community of survivors, of activists. We are ordinary people who came together to find the cures. The philosophy at Komen is community building to propel change. We reach as many people as possible and have them take Nancy's promise to her sister and make it their own."

Komen has reached out to different demographic segments, tailoring its message and offerings to their unique needs and values and preferred methods of engagement. "We have expanded our impact by working specifically with multicultural communities and their leaders," explained Emily Callahan. "We welcome everyone and seek to connect with them in a way that is meaningful and relevant. We have targeted diverse communities—African-American, Hispanic American, Native American, Pacific Islanders, and the Lesbian, Gay, Bisexual, Transgender communities—and all have special needs. We are also committed to reaching young women, where there is a growing incidence of breast cancer, and to reaching men.

"We find the passionate people in each of the targeted communities and work with them to harness their energy and get them to be leaders and advocates. We want them to own the cause and provide the tools to take the messages out to their networks," said Emily as she explained the Susan G. Komen for the Cure philosophy of mobilizing an external community of people. "We try to let it be organic and move at the pace that is comfortable for people. It's great if they want to help raise money, but we believe that will come after they feel comfortable and ready."

Komen reached out to leaders in those communities and engaged them through advisory councils that offer feedback on proposed and existing programs and communications plans. Advisors collaborate with Komen to develop special programs and messages designed to effectively reach their communities and build a social network based on the way the community operates. They also help craft dedicated calls to action.

For example, Komen launched the Circle of Promise campaign to increase awareness, support, and action within the African American community, whose women have significantly poorer survival outcomes than white women. Circle of Promise participants become community activists. They are equipped with tailored tools to spread messages within their personal networks, engage in public policy actions such as signing online petitions or sending e-mails to congressional representatives, and ways to donate funds to the cause. A partnership with the powerful African American women's group LINKS is building a community of African American women who are joining with Komen to rewrite their story of breast cancer.

"We have jointly pledged to decrease the mortality of African Americans from breast cancer by increasing awareness of the risks, reducing pervasive myths in the community, encouraging breast self-awareness leading to early detection and treatment, and mobilizing the community to collectively fight for access to quality care for all," added Emily Callahan. The goal is to recruit 100,000 Circle of Promise members. Members sign up through a special Circle of Promise web site and receive welcome kits chock-full of information they can use and share with others (see Figure 6.6).

FIGURE 6.6   Circle of Promise Logo

The organization is building links with other multicultural communities to join together to address their specific needs around breast cancer. Some of the targeted groups don't feel comfortable speaking about breast cancer or don't have reliable information or the tools to get the information out. Komen addresses these communities with culturally appropriate education and awareness tools, some in native languages like Spanish or at events such as the Native American Conference and Powwow to reach Native American populations.

"Our philosophy is based on reaching people where they live, work, and play. Going to people is natural to us," added Susan Carter Johns. "We reach out and connect through their churches, in hair salons, through family education centers. Each group is treated individually. We strive to reach them where they are comfortable—which is where they already are."

Drive Innovation from the Core

"Everything we do is to build a growing network of individuals around a powerful brand idea," explained Emily Callahan, senior vice president, Global Marketing and Networks. "If you're for finding the cure, empowering women with breast health, bringing survivors together, then come join with us. We know this is the message, relevantly presented to specific groups, which will build our community of individual supporters in our next chapter."

The organization has a time-tested way of mobilizing diverse communities. As it prepared for its next chapter, the rebrand work elevated Komen from a national to a global leader in the breast cancer movement. As it looked beyond national borders, the organization hired Boston Consulting Group to document Komen's best practices and five core principles. The model has been turned into an education and training program called Course for the Cure.

"As we move out and help other communities around the world, we need to replicate a core framework that maintains the Komen standards and approach while meeting local needs. For example, in the Middle East, they are particularly interested in our education model because there is so much secrecy and shame around the disease. Another area of interest is cause marketing, because they are positioned to work well with companies for revenue and awareness benefits. In Latin America, it's more about education and engaging a community in the cause," explained Emily, who has been actively involved in the global push. "We are proud of what we have achieved in the United States and the impact it has had here. And we're excited about taking our model and adapting it to countries where this issue is just starting to get traction."

"Overall our focus is Komen as a catalyst. We want people to think of Komen as a global leader in making a difference in saving lives and ending breast cancer forever," explained Susan Carter Johns. "There is a place for everyone in the movement to participate, to help, to engage, so we can advance the cause together."

The Komen story is a remarkable one—built by millions of ordinary people. Thanks to the power of its brand meaning to rally a remarkable external community, Komen has become a powerful movement for global change.

PRINCIPLE FIVE: SUMMARY

Any organization that thinks their cause is too narrow, obscure, or unknown only has to look at the inspirations of Stratford and Komen: a loyal community mobilized around Shakespeare and classic theater and a movement launched at a time when breast cancer was unknown and unspeakable. Any organization of any size or scope can break through by rallying an external community using the innovative principles and techniques drawn from our BNBs.

- *Base: Form a brand community*—Deliver participant benefits and cultivate individual relationships as a cornerstone of building a community.
  - Know a critical mass of people is vital to propel social impact.
  - Build a community as an end, not just a means.
  - Focus on building a relationship first; donations will follow.
  - Understand who your patrons are and why they are involved.
  - Act as a community connector, bringing people together around common interests.
  - Nurture and grow community by engaging in dialogue, listening, and responding.
  - Be inclusive, but don't try to please everyone.
  - Understand that direct experiences with the brand meaning trump communications.
  - Create a variety of interactive brand meaning or mission-centered experiences.
- *Build: Foster the brand community*—Nurture supporters and develop a robust community by appealing to their needs, beliefs, and values.
  - Create a vibrant and engaged community of participants, supporters, and champions.
  - Offer participants practical value and transactional benefits that align with their needs and/or interests.
  - Provide supporters deeper personalized benefits, rewards, and experiences that more directly connect individuals to the brand meaning.
  - Build credibility and loyalty by doing what you say you will do.
- *Breakthrough: Grow the brand community*—Empower brand champions and constantly grow the community by reaching new audiences.
  - Connect with your most passionate champions and work with and through them to mobilize their networks.
  - Create truest sense of community and create champions who say, "This is my kind of organization!"
  - Grow supporters through innovation.
  - Continuously and creatively look for more friends.

- Reframe your case to engage new and untraditional supporters with the right messaging, relevant experiences, and thoughtful connections.
- Regularly share results with your community in a way that is authentic and transparent.

CHAPTER 7

Principle Six: Cultivate Partners to Extend Your Brand Reach and Influence

"Partnerships build and strengthen our brand, its reach and credibility. We ensure careful alignment of passions, goals, values, and target audiences. So, at the core of each partnership is a win-win relationship."[1]

—ELLEN RÉTHORÉ, VICE PRESIDENT, MARKETING AND
COMMUNICATIONS, KIDS HELP PHONE

"NatureBridge and the National Park Service have a symbiotic partnership as our brands are integrally linked. The more we work together, the stronger we both become."[2]

—STEPHEN LOCKHART, MD, PhD, CHAIRMAN,
BOARD OF DIRECTORS, NATUREBRIDGE

KIDS HELP PHONE'S BRAND JOURNEY

The story has become a legend. It was August 1989, and a young nonprofit was at a turning point. Kids Help Phone (KHP)—a toll-free, 24-hour, bilingual, and anonymous counseling, referral, and information service for children and youth in Canada—had launched three months earlier. That night began quietly for the counselors at the organization's phone center. As they pondered what it might take to get kids to call, the phone lines suddenly lit up. The number of calls went through the roof—and they have not stopped since.

In a groundbreaking partnership, MuchMusic, Canada's popular national music television station, had just broadcast Kids Help Phone's toll-free number on the screen. Thanks to its reputation among its youthful audience, MuchMusic made it acceptable, almost cool, for kids to ask for help. "Call and talk with a professional counselor in confidence about whatever issue is on your mind," intoned the hip station's VJs.

There is no denying that kids have a powerful and emotional connection to popular music. Yet, at the time, many nonprofits viewed corporations—and particularly corporate-owned media—as potentially detrimental to their brands. That concern meant that few charities were willing to try the experiment represented by the new partnership. Kids Help Phone was willing to take the risk, but it wasn't just a lucky gamble. The move was grounded in a joint commitment to the well-being of the young people in Canada and similar brand values, including being nonjudgmental, open, innovative, and entrepreneurial. Driven by an emphasis on mutual benefit, the unlikely partnership has not only survived but has continued to grow in depth and influence.

At the heart of Kids Help Phone (KHP) is the compelling brand idea of providing help and hope to young people across Canada. During a history that now spans more than 20 years, KHP has recognized the power of partnerships to build its brand reach and influence well beyond anything KHP could achieve alone. Driven by a desire for impact and a willingness to take risks, KHP has built a broad spectrum of connections, from simple, short-term relationships to truly transformative multilevel and multiyear partnerships that became integrated into the DNA of each organization's brand.

Extending the Brand through Long-Lasting Partnerships

"Our brand meaning and beneficiary audience is the filter we use when considering a partnership. The well-being of children in Canada is at the core of Kids Help Phone. Potential partners must share this passion," explained Ellen Réthoré, vice president, Marketing and Communications, at KHP. "But it can't just be about our mission. We know that isn't enough to sustain enduring relationships. We have a strong belief in directly benefiting our partners as well as our beneficiary audience."

FIGURE 7.1   Coffee Crisp Chocolate Bar Promotes Kids Help Phone

From the beginning, the organization built deep relationships that were innovative; the approach was unheard-of at the time. Its four founding corporate partners—BMO Financial Group, Bell Canada, Nestlé Canada, and Parmalat—communicated KHP's mission with vigor. They put the nonprofit's logo and background information on product packaging, from milk cartons to children's cereal boxes to Smarties, all great places to reach kids and those who care about them. They also included KHP in their own corporate advertising and in-store displays. By leveraging corporate distribution channels, Kids Help Phone enhanced its credibility, extended its reach, and connected with key audiences in unexpected places and in surprising ways, all at no cost to the organization. Perhaps just as remarkably, all four original corporate partners remain active and critical members of the KHP team 20 years later! (see Figure 7.1).

What is the secret of this success? Relationships based on shared values, aligned audiences, and agreements that meet the goals of both partners while protecting and enhancing each brand.

NATUREBRIDGE'S BRAND JOURNEY

"We learn our values early. Much of what we care about growing up turns out to play a large role in what we care about as adults. This is why the work of NatureBridge and its partnership with the U.S. National Park Service is so critical," NatureBridge Board Chair Stephen Lockhart stated with passion.

Since 1971, NatureBridge, originally named Yosemite National Institute, has introduced almost a million students to U.S. national parks through residential field science education and leadership programs. Currently, it annually serves more than 40,000 participants from diverse backgrounds. NatureBridge is the National Park Service's premier residential environmental education partner.

The partnership concept is simple. NatureBridge provides environmental content and programming for children, and the National Park Service provides the context that inspires curiosity and brings the curricula to life. After 39 years, the relationship continues to grow in scope, impact, and mutual benefit, making it clear that the approach just plain works.

As a pioneering government–nonprofit collaboration, the benefits of the alliance may not have been obvious to everyone, particularly in the early days. However, the two organizations are linked by a powerful shared purpose: connecting youth to the natural world and inspiring them with concern for the planet through intensive experience in our national parks. NatureBridge students stay on site at a designated national park for three to five days, long enough to have a profound impact on their attitudes and behaviors toward the environment and nature.

"We don't just educate young people, we transform them, their views of themselves and the world around them," explained Board Chair Stephen Lockhart. "NatureBridge is creating the next generation of environmental stewards, park visitors, park staff, and even park philanthropists. I've met park employees and supporters who went through the program and are involved with the park today as a direct result of those early experiences."

NatureBridge was designed to meet the needs of local science teachers who were looking for hands-on educational opportunities, as well as the National Park Service, which wanted to connect with a greater number of children and use its in-park residential facilities year-round as opposed to solely during warm-weather periods.

Early successes and interest from other parks close to Yosemite led to the program's expansion. The debut of Headlands Institute at Golden Gate National Recreation Area was in 1977, and Olympic Park Institute at Olympic National Park launched in 1987. Each institute has its own board of volunteers but was part of the same overarching organization, Yosemite National Institute (see Figure 7.2).

FIGURE 7.2   NatureBridge Students

A Shared Commitment Leads to a Cocreated Vision

Over its 39-year history, the partnership between the two organizations has evolved and grown. From the early days of a simple win-win agreement, it has deepened into a transformational partnership where each feels a sense of shared value and commitment.

In 2006, NatureBridge, through a National Park Service Centennial Challenge grant, began to realize its revised vision: to replicate its model nationally. "We had a time-tested model, and we knew we could impact a broader constituency by expanding our work in other national parks across the United States," explained Jason Morris, vice president, External Affairs and Programs, NatureBridge. This goal is being realized. In spring 2010, NatureBridge added its fourth campus. Based at Santa Monica Mountains National Recreation Area, close to Los Angeles, when scaled up, this site will have the potential to affect thousands of additional kids annually.

"That's the power of partnership," explained Stephen. "Our partnership with the National Park Service has clear alignment, a symbiotic relationship, mutual benefit, good communications, respect, and trust. And we have learned from this success. As we move forward, we're expanding our partnership to include corporations, media, and other nonprofit organizations for greater reach and impact."

A CASE STUDY: AN ICONIC NAME UNIQUELY TRANSFORMED

The challenge: Yosemite National Institute (YNI) was the founding name for an environmental education program initially set in three different national parks. While part of YNI, each program had its own name that evoked its local park resources. For example, the program based near San Francisco was named Headlands Institute at Golden Gate National Recreation Area. Most users experienced only one of the institutes and viewed it as a great local program, without realizing it was part of a more robust organization. This overly narrow view hampered overall organizational development efforts. As the group planned to expand from a regional nonprofit to a national one, it realized a name change was essential to effectively repositioning the brand meaning.

The solution: Lexicon, a branding firm, shaped a simple, elegant solution (see Figure 7.3). They proposed creating a name that would link all the institutes together, showcase the social mission, and also allow the iconic, beloved individual national park identities to shine through. The name and accompanying tagline, NatureBridge: Connecting Youth to the Natural World, clearly communicates what the organization stands for and acts as the overarching name of the organization. But each institute maintained its distinct name and is linked as a campus of NatureBridge. When speaking about the overarching program, Nature-Bridge is the *hero,* or lead brand name; regarding individual institutes, the local names acts as the hero brand and receives top billing.

FIGURE 7.3   NatureBridge Logo

AN OVERVIEW OF PRINCIPLE SIX

A critical piece of the breakthrough nonprofit brand journey is the evolution from an entirely independent entity to one with strategic partnerships. To become a BNB, you must define and live your relationships as mutually beneficial, respectful alliances that meet the goals and objectives of both partners, while protecting and enhancing both brands. When approached this way, alliances can offer access to new expertise, relationships, and assets that increase your brand credibility, capacity, and capital.

In developing a partnership strategy, a BNB stands for something special, based on deep values, and so has nothing to fear from connecting to other brands. A BNB builds partnerships on a foundation of authenticity, credibility, and clear and honest communications.

It does not confine its partnerships to one type or group. Instead, a BNB forges strategic relationships with a variety of organizations across sectors, including media, corporations, government, educational institutions, other nonprofit organizations, and volunteer groups. It recognizes that each type of collaborative partnership can play a role in helping the nonprofit achieve greater brand influence and reach.

Not all partnerships are the same. Many nonprofits cultivate a mix of several types, each with a distinct purpose and benefits. Breakthrough brands emphasize partnerships that show the potential to become transformative—for both organizations—over time (see Table 7.1).

How-To Success Factors

Base: Establish transactional relationships—Prepare internally to ensure win-win relationships that are culturally and systematically incorporated into the organization's DNA.

Build: Align transitional relationships—Proactively seek strategic alignment and build across both parties' objectives for higher levels of engagement and therefore benefit to both.

Breakthrough: Nurture transformational relationships—Create true partnerships and move along the continuum to transformational where they become integrated across the organization and establish co-ownership.

Base: Prepare Internal Framework for Transactional Relationships

At its base, a BNB establishes the necessary internal support to develop mutually beneficial alliances. It starts with building a culture that

TABLE 7.1   BNB PARTNERSHIP CONTINUUM, FROM BASE
TO BREAKTHROUGH

	Base	Build	Breakthrough
How	Establish transactional relationships: Prepare internally to ensure win-win relationships that are culturally and systematically incorporated into the organization's DNA. Start with simple transactional agreements	Align transitional relationships: Proactively seek strategic alignment and build across both parties' objectives for higher levels of engagement and, therefore, benefit for both; cultivate relationships to build trust and respect	Nurture transformational relationships: Develop true partnerships and move along the continuum to transformational, where they become integrated across the organization and establish co-ownership
What	Transactional: Tangible benefit(s) with goal of creating a win-win relationship that can grow over time; straightforward engagement by single function/department on both sides	Transitional: Relationship deepens as partners deliver community and business results together; added levels of engagement and assets brought to bear with greater cross-organizational involvement	Transformational: Deep cultural engagement where partners feel a sense of belonging and co-ownership due to shared value created; organization-wide engagement or integrated into DNA; integrated across organization, that they are part of the organization and have a sense of ownership
Why	Singular or focused objective per partner	Greater commitment with multiple objectives	Shared values for greater influence and reach
Where	Often one-off or short-term	Extended to multiple pushes or years	Builds over time and becomes long-term
Who	Singular communication to limited audience	Multiple messaging opportunities to increase reach to targets	Multiple pulsed and dynamic messages to reach targets where they are in the course of their daily lives
When	Few to several relationships, with limited management and complexity; most common form of partnership	Fewer aligned relationships due to increased time and commitment	Fewest due to depth of time and resource commitment on both sides

encourages a partnership mind-set and the systems and structure to facilitate their development.

Leadership Drives Commitment   To prepare for a new approach to partnerships, start at the top. An organization's board and senior staff need to lead by example, modeling a collaborative approach to relationships by asking what you can give before asking what you can get. They should make partnership development a personal priority, actively participating in meetings and investing in the stewardship of key relationships. Your executive director shouldn't show up only if there is a problem to solve but also when there is a milestone to celebrate or a new opportunity to share. Integrate a partnership approach into your culture through performance goals and by inviting members of multiple departments to the table when new partnerships are being considered or existing partnerships evaluated.

"Partnerships have always been a priority for our senior leadership and, as a result, our organization. They model strong relationship behavior and encourage relationships. There is an expectation that partnerships will be developed right across the organization, in an integrated and cross-functional way," explained Ellen Réthoré of Kids Help Phone. "For example, our counselors are involved in reviewing marketing partners. Our marketing and fund development teams are involved with partnerships built by our programming team. This core tenet ensures organization-wide buy-in and involvement, and it helps us avoid problems down the road."

"When we started, we were far more inward-facing," recalled Jason Morris, of NatureBridge. "Yet, our board and senior leadership realized that for us to have a bigger impact, we would need to actively think about the National Park Service as a true partner. Our leadership began asking about what they needed, which helped develop a strong and open relationship. That learning has been applied as we've connected with corporations and other partners."

Identify Internal Goals for Partnership Program   A breakthrough nonprofit organization has clear goals and objectives for any partnership they want to build. This can include everything from raising awareness to generating revenue to executing programs. "Our initial partnership with MuchMusic was very much based on our need to reach young people to help them understand our service and what we could do for them," explained Ellen Réthoré. "They also provided credibility and a much needed endorsement of our organization. While any partnership must meet the goals of both, it's important to be clear what you want to achieve within the relationship."

Catalogue Value-Add Assets   No matter how simple or complex, win-win relationships require each organization to add value. This means understanding what you can contribute to prospective partners. By cataloguing assets in advance, your entire organization will be on the same page about what is and isn't negotiable—even before initial discussions with outside organizations. By understanding the full value you bring to the table, you are more likely to garner interest from organizations you approach and to build more rewarding, multifaceted relationships. This approach also assists with prospect brainstorming, as your team can use its asset list to identify the type of organizations that would benefit from your distinctive offerings.

Asset Checklist

- ☐ Brand reputation and recognition
- ☐ Who you serve (audience alignment)
- ☐ What you do (mission and goal alignment)
- ☐ Where you do it (geography alignment)
- ☐ Impact of work (reach and influence)
- ☐ In-house expertise
- ☐ Program, event, and campaign collaboration possibilities
- ☐ Connections in community
- ☐ Volunteer opportunities (for employees and other stakeholders)
- ☐ Media and marketing relationships
- ☐ Communication tools
- ☐ Chapters, branches, or affiliates
- ☐ Grassroots networks
- ☐ Volunteer base
- ☐ Celebrities
- ☐ Issue expertise
- ☐ Spokesperson(s)
- ☐ Social media network presence (Facebook, Twitter, etc.)

Dedicate Staff and Resources   Nonprofits serious about building partnerships must have a structure to facilitate collaboration. A nonprofit is most likely to develop a breakthrough approach to partnerships and ultimately a breakthrough brand when it dedicates appropriate staff time and resources to that goal. It is important to invest in building a relationship action plan, seeking and securing partnerships, and managing them for success.

Depending on the complexity and sophistication of the partnerships, you may need to appoint a dedicated manager to oversee the relationship from the front end, when seeking and selling the prospective joint venture, through to the back end of evaluating results and recalibrating for the future.

Create an Approval Process and Risk Assessment Framework   Partnering for the sake of partnering is not as effective as strategically seeking relationships that offer a strong brand meaning fit. A decision-making framework can help your team analyze the benefits and identify potential risks involved with potential alliances. Organizational buy-in is strengthened by a consistent approach and proper due diligence.

Kids Help Phone and NatureBridge both have a staff and board review and approval process for potential partnerships of a certain size and scope. When considering a potential collaboration, each uses a framework like the one shown in Table 7.2.

A simple decision-making framework is critical to being agile and ready to partner. Determine the structure that works best for the organization. "We've turned down more partnership opportunities than we have agreed to," admitted Jason of NatureBridge. "That's because we want to have engaged partners who become part of our team. We've come to expect aligned values, shared interests, and common goals. We have a thorough system of checks and balances. Every significant relationship goes through the board for final sign-off. That helps ensure fit and congruence," he concluded.

"We're careful about who we partner with," offered Ellen of Kids Help Phone. "First, they have to be completely supportive of our mission and aligned around protecting children. They can't be thought of as doing anything that would harm children in any way. We talk with our professional counselors and explain what the potential partner does and solicit their feedback on how the brand meaning could be perceived and whether it is a good fit. We do research to ensure there is no negative news, no part of the operations that could be controversial or contrary to our mission. We

TABLE 7.2   PARTNERSHIP ANALYSIS FRAMEWORK

	Yes	No	Comments (e.g., are NOs fixable?)
Strategic alignment			
1. Is there brand meaning alignment?			
2. Is there mission and goals alignment?			
3. Is there program and activity alignment?			
4. Is there audience/consumer alignment?			
5. Is there geographic alignment (local, regional, national)?			
Organizational capacity			
6. Do you have the capacity to meet the expectations of the partnership?			
7. Human resources?			
8. Necessary assets to contribute to success? (See list of possible assets.)			
Financial implications			
9. Does it meet the minimum dollar amount for contribution (if marketing partner)?[3]			
10. Is the revenue greater than the costs that will be involved?			
11. Is it neutral?			
12. Does it generate additional revenue?			
Marketing and reach potential			
13. Does it build membership, donors, and volunteers?			
14. Will it market messages to target audiences?			
15. Will it heighten awareness of the nonprofit organization?			
16. Will it target new markets—get the message out to new audiences relevant to the nonprofit organization?			
17. What is the scope of their employee base? Their potential to engage? At what level—executive, staff?			
Reputational and compatibility fit			
18. Does it compete with existing corporate partners?			
19. Is the company, product, or service noncontroversial?			
20. Does the potential partner have a good reputation?			

TABLE 7.2   (*CONTINUED*)

	Yes	No	Comments (e.g., are NOs fixable?)
21. Is there partner compatibility—open communications, mutual respect, and trust?			
22. Does the partner demonstrate a commitment to social responsibility?			
Length and depth of partnership			
23. Is the program one-off/short-term or a longer-term, deeper relationship? (Score according to need.)			
Risk assessment			
24. What are the risks? (Risk assessment undertaken will vary according to each sector. For example, in youth arena, like Kids Help Phone, this could mean review by counseling professionals; in the environmental field, review by scientists or, in the case of NatureBridge, field staff.)			
25. List other considerations particular to your sector or community.			
NUMBER OF YES/NO			

also gauge their partnership know-how, whether they are action-oriented, and how they can add value—and how we can add value to them. It takes time. We have turned down potential partners—but our brand meaning is too valuable to risk on a connection that might not work. If we move forward after our evaluation, we strongly commit to our joint success."

Engage with Aligned Transactional Partners   Having the culture, processes, and procedures in place enables an organization to be open to possible partnership opportunities. At the base, organizations are open and ready to partner, if the right one comes along.

Alignment and fit are central to the success of any partnership. "All of our partnerships have shared values and a shared commitment to the well-being of children in Canada," explained Elle Réthoré of Kids Help Phone. "Whatever the type of partnership—with other nonprofits, education institutions, government, or corporations—we look for common values, shared passion, shared audience, and an opportunity for mutual benefit.

We are committed to the idea that any relationship must be win-win, and we always look at ways it can help make a relationship work for both organizations."

While many of the initial Kids Help Phone partners are now deep long-term relationships, many were started as a short one-off agreement. The organization continues to build partnerships—most often started as trans-actional one-off relationships. "We have a number of partnership agreements with law enforcement agencies all across Canada," shared Ellen. "For example, the Royal Canadian Mounted Police has a program called Race against Drugs. We have a partnership where they share information about Kids Help Phone in their presentations. In return, we are available to respond to any calls that come in as a result of the program. It's a powerful but simple partnership arrangement."

"Our initial relationship with the National Park Service was very much a transactional agreement," explained Jason Morris of NatureBridge. "There was a great fit, shared values, shared goals, and a natural align-ment—essential to any partnership. But we basically ran the environmental institutes, and they provided the national park facilities. We had an agree-ment, and it was definitely of mutual benefit, but it wasn't much beyond the focus of the programs."

Short-term transactional agreements can yield important insights, re-quire the least amount of investment, and hold the promise of growing to the next level. Many are organic or come about because of an existing relationship.

Put It in Writing   Once initial negotiations are complete, work with your partner to finalize agreements and build the foundation for a sustain-able structure that can be executed immediately but can also grow with time. It is vital to put all discussions and decisions in black and white. Writ-ten agreements minimize risk and maximize understanding. They allow you to identify and reconcile potential misunderstandings, minimize risk, and outline clear processes and program structures.

Depending on the complexity of the partnership, the written agreement can be as simple as a letter or memorandum of understanding or as formal as a detailed project plan signed by both parties. Regardless of the depth or approach, always consider getting the agreement reviewed by a lawyer. Many attorneys provide pro bono support to charitable organizations.

Regardless of whether you are considering an alliance between two small, local charities or a national corporate arrangement, an agreement should cover the following key elements:

- Description of goal(s), objectives, purpose: rationale for partnership
- Responsibilities: expectations of each partner
- Terms of the agreement: length of agreement, including start and stop dates
- Milestones: what happens and when
- Payment and/or financial resources: how much, when, and any minimum guarantees
- Decision-making and approval process: outline how decisions will be made, by whom, and when, including how review and approval of all materials or related decisions will take place
- Use of logo: how trademarks can and cannot be used and the approval process
- Recognition: can include, for example, logo on the organization letterhead, priority placement on the organization site, recognition posters and banners used at all events
- Communications: how partnership details and successes will be communicated, to whom, by whom, how often
- Disagreements: explain any steps that will be taken in case of a disagreement or unforeseen programmatic results
- Termination: how and why the agreement may be terminated and by whom
- Notice: who the key contacts will be at each organization
- General: anything that has not been covered, including confidential and proprietary information of both the organization and the company and hold harmless clauses

Build: Align Transitional Relationships

Breakthrough nonprofit brands build up their partnership programs by proactively seeking strategically aligned partners where they can combine assets to create value for both. Transitional partnerships offer greater value

to both parties, although they usually require more sophisticated management and messaging.

Prospect Intelligently   Finding the right partners is part science and part
art, combined with hard work. While there is no magic bullet, there are
steps that can help you work smarter, not harder, when identifying potential targets and preparing for initial meetings.

Consider Those Closest to the Organization   Prospecting intelligently
starts with identifying those closest to your organization. That offers the
greatest chance of forming a meaningful partnership. Consider the 60-30-
10 rule. It suggests that approximately 60 percent of all resources be dedicated to current relationships, 30 percent to a targeted group of prospects,
and 10 percent to the universe of all potential partners, no matter how im-
probable. It is more efficient to extend an existing relationship than to secure a new one. Current supporters who already are excited about your
organization are often the most effective partners. Existing relationships
also start off with a comparatively high level of mutual respect and trust.

Yet, new relationships must be developed on a regular basis to promote
ongoing vitality. Many will start small and build as trust is established and a
nonprofit proves it can be an effective cause partner. Prospecting can include outreach to:

- Contacts of the board of directors (as your board evolves, consider
  populating it with an eye to potential partners)
- Contacts of staff and volunteers
- Employers of your midrange or major donors
- Past partners or lapsed connections
- Partners working with similar types of organizations
- Potential sector partners, such as banks, retail
- Those with an expressed interest in your mission, target audience, or
  geography
- Advertising and marketing associations and/or agencies, which
  sometimes help broker corporate cause partnerships

**Focus on Organizations with Similar Target or Employee Audien-
ces**   Partners with similar target or employee audiences provide strong

partnership opportunities. NatureBridge's relationship with Kleen Kanteen, a manufacturer of eco-sensitive water bottles, aligns an environmental education organization with a company whose core customers care about the environment. Kids Help Phone has reciprocal, deep relationships with education partners.

"Shared goals unite our partner community," observed Ellen Réthoré of Kids Help Phone. "Commonality is at the core of our partnerships. We have common cultures, passions, and values. We also serve similar audiences. So the partnerships just make sense. For example, we work closely with educators and have developed critical relationships with teachers, schools, and academics focused on children's needs. We put a lot of time and effort into each and every one, but they are natural and not forced."

Get to Know Partners Every endeavor succeeds or fails because of the people involved. Take the time to get to know the people on the other end of the phone or across the table. Cultivate a culture of curiosity about potential partners and what makes those outside organizations tick. Effective partnerships take a willingness to think beyond short-term self-interest and the confidence to share your organization's brand meaning in new and more calculated ways.

Do Your Homework Before approaching any prospect, whether an old friend or a new contact, it pays to do as much research as possible. Conduct deep media and blogger audits; review your target's web site, annual reports, and, if relevant, foundation and/or corporate citizenship reports. This will give you a head start on the initial conversation.

- Analyze the potential partner and create a profile—answer questions about the organization's what, who, when, where, why, and how. For example, what is its business, and what is its competitive position in the marketplace? How many employees does it have? Where is it located? What is the employee demographic? Who are its constituents/customers? Who are its future constituents? How does it communicate with its consumers? Who are its suppliers? What is its current community involvement? What media coverage has it received? Who are its supporters? Detractors?
- Research organizational reputation.

- Revisit and prepare to discuss any personal connections you have with the organization—or that it has with you.

- Assess its business goals, needs, and challenges.

- Review your asset checklist, and look for a match between its needs and your assets, programs, and resources.

- Determine the most appropriate contact at the organization and whether the timing is right.

- Outline how a partnership could help you achieve your mission goals and how it could help your prospect achieve theirs.

Once your research is in hand, plan an in-person meeting to begin the partnership exploration. In preparation:

- Determine the best members of a customized relationship development team. This could include your staff, volunteers, and/or board members. Always invite those who bring knowledge of the prospect's business goals and activities.

- Meet with everyone from your organization who will attend the prospect meeting; advance planning will ensure you have a shared agenda and will allow you to discuss expectations and goals and provide background information.

- Hold an initial phone conversation with the identified contact at the prospect organization (or their assistant or relevant team member) to confirm the meeting and to collect additional preliminary information on business and social goals, target audiences, and existing non-profit partnerships.

- Include high-level decision makers as soon as possible.

Make the Approach   That first meeting is about listening. Use it to ask questions and gain critical information rather than to put forward a formal proposal. Make sure your questions are not ones that could be answered with more thorough background research. Instead, show up prepared and knowledgeable, and use your time together to build rapport and gather key information that rounds out what is publicly available. This approach ensures you can make a detailed, targeted proposal that reflects what you learn.

Understanding your target's objectives, audiences, partnership criteria, and what success looks like for them is essential to forming a match. Your prospect's objective(s) could include awareness, program development, employee recruitment and/or retention, reputation lift, and/or increased sales. Other objectives could be access to new markets, new geographic areas, or a new stimulus for innovation. With this information in hand, you can summarize what your brand meaning stands for and how it can best address your prospect's needs.

Questions to ask your prospect include:

- What are your organizational goals for the next year? five years?
- Who are your core or most important audiences? Are you trying to reach or strengthen your relationship with any new audiences?
- What are your most important goals or priorities for community engagement?
- How would you describe your current and past nonprofit partnerships? What worked and didn't work? How did you leverage those relationships? What assets do you put toward their partnerships?
- What would you want to get out of a partnership formed with my organization? (Prompt your prospect to consider audience alignment, employee engagement opportunities, or reputation linkages.)

Building a mutually beneficial alliance requires looking at how your goals and needs can align with your potential partner's. Building transitional relationships means focusing on combining assets and creating value for both organizations. The following process can ensure the highest level of success.

Customize to Make It Real   Whether you are in talks with a prospect or trying to enhance an existing relationship, it is important to proactively offer custom options for activities and benefits that respond to the other organization's needs. Tailor proposals to suit the individual circumstances, assets, and interests of each partner, providing tangible examples of activation and outlining the assets available for the partner's benefit (see Table 7.3).

Many relationships start with one activity and expand as increased exposure and trust lead to new ideas for enhanced engagement. Nonprofits earn

TABLE 7.3   **MAKING THE MATCH**

Partner Objectives	Match
Awareness	Contribute promotional support, such as advertising, collateral materials, PR/media relations, events
License to operate	Focus giving to areas where the prospect operates or is strategically focused
Acquisition/loyalty	Outline how your supporters align with your prospect's target audience
Recruit and motivate	Offer turnkey employee engagement opportunities
Perception and reputation	Demonstrate how a connection to your cause could improve perception of your prospect's organization
Social return	Show how the new relationship will deliver measurable social impact
Business returns	Establish and jointly track clear ROI and performance metrics

respect by delivering on or exceeding expectations, which bring opportunities to continue or even expand collaborations. NatureBridge's partnership with the National Park Service grew as the nonprofit delivered value. Kids Help Phone's multiple 20-year partnerships are a true indicator of its ability to deliver benefits other organizations appreciate.

The best partnerships are distinguished by reciprocity and mutual benefit. Sometimes, both sides come together to brainstorm the best possible program. When you consistently focus on your partner's needs, they are more likely to advocate for, recommend, remember, and support your organization.

Conduct Joint Planning and Create Joint Strategy   Once a deal is successfully locked, revisit the objectives of each organization, as well as the shared objectives at the heart of the relationship. Create a goal map, clearly outlining what each partner needs and expects, with mutual goals in the center. See Table 7.4, for example.

Together, the partners determine realistic expectations for what the alliance will achieve, who is responsible for what, tangible benefits for each partner, and how the program will be evaluated. Joint planning should take place before the program launches and should outline the specific value that will be created for each partner. Predetermined check-in points

TABLE 7.4	SAMPLE GOAL MAP	

Nonprofit Goals	Shared Goals	Partner Goals
• Generating revenue • Extending reach to new audiences • Building on relationship with existing audiences • Creating awareness • Achieving specific mission-oriented goals	• Reaching similar audiences • Building reputation • Achieving social goals • Innovation	• Awareness • Program development and implementation • License to operate • Employee recruitment/retention • Reputation lift • Increased sales • Access to new market, new geographic areas • New stimulus for innovation

serve as a focus for program implementation and provide opportunities to adapt the strategy as needed.

"We actively cultivate alignment through intense conversations. We build a personal relationship and discuss the strategies and tactics of working together for mutual benefit and impact," NatureBridge's Jason Morris shared.

Seek Cash Plus   While every organization needs dollars in hand, savvy nonprofits recognize the value to be found in more creative tender. These currencies allow organizations to expand the scope of relationships, driving greater value for both partners. For example, in-kind support can include employee volunteers and skill-based expertise, such as accounting and marketing. In-kind support in the form of goods and services can save nonprofits precious dollars and add value to their work; these contributions can include computers, office space, travel, vehicles, food for events, or advertising. As financial resources become more restricted and demand for nonprofit services continues to increase, these alternative forms of support are increasingly important.

Actively Manage Partnerships   Often, nonprofits divide relationship development (sales) and execution (delivery) into two functions and have different staff members manage each. One person who is skilled in building relationships handles the initial organizational introduction. This includes structuring the grounds for collaboration, program details, and finalizing the agreement. Depending on the size and scope of the proposed alliance, this may be done at a relatively junior staff level or at the most senior level within the organization. Transitional relationships almost always engage at least one senior nonprofit manager from the start. If a deeper, longer-term partnership or transformational relationship is being built, it is ideal to engage in senior leader–to–senior leader relationship building.

Program execution comes next, and it requires dedicated staff. This typically needs to be managed on two levels. The first is tactical: ensuring agreed-upon commitments are met by people in various relevant area(s) of the organization. Usually, a day-to-day contact person facilitates seamless communications between the partners, particularly when multiple departments are involved. The second level of program execution is strategic: maintaining the relationship and looking around corners for new opportunities to meet or exceed stated objectives.

Kids Help Phone, for example, has a formalized stewardship program for each of its corporate, community, and media partnerships, with dedicated resources and staff to ensure execution. Each partnership plan outlines core activities, key communication points, and engagement opportunities, such as events for partner employees. An internal steward is designated as the contact responsible for coordinating across Kids Help Phone's various organizational functions. "Everyone plays a role in connecting with our partners, but we have leads who coordinate each program," explained Ellen.

At NatureBridge, the organization uses an account management system. A partnership framework designs a relationship that seeks to ensure mutual benefit in an atmosphere of open communications and trust. The communications team works on messaging and joint communications. A different set of people manages the relationship on a day-to-day basis. "That's one of the great things we learned from our partnerships with the National Park Service and schools. When the fit is strong, the desire to work together to connect children to the natural world is overwhelming," Jason stated.

Expand Partners Creatively but Seek Strategic Alignment   Initially, prospecting is usually focused on the most naturally aligned potential partners. As an organization grows in partnership sophistication, to avoid leaving money on the table they can move beyond the most intuitive partner prospects. A creative technique nonprofits can employ is to seek a combination of low and high mission alignment. A simple but effective process developed by Cone involves brainstorming potential partners and analyzing alignment at three levels: high, medium, and low.

- *High alignment:* Nonprofits are likely to find a relatively small group of organizations that offer an obvious and clear fit. Kids Help Phone's long-term partnership with Bell Canada is an example of high alignment. The Kids Help Phone mission depends on connecting with young people through technology, and Bell Canada is a leading communications technology company in Canada. NatureBridge and the National Park Service enjoy clear mission alignment.

- *Medium alignment:* In the middle zone are a greater number of companies that are moderately aligned with a nonprofit's brand meaning. These are companies where a useful connection could be made. Kids Help Phone and MuchMusic is an example. The station appeals to young people who enjoy music and might also need the services provided by KHP.

- *Low alignment:* These are potential partnerships where the fit is not initially obvious. Only deep investigation brings the brand meaning alignment to light. Intel's partnership with NatureBridge is an example. While the connection may not be apparent at first glance, Intel has provided handheld devices that students use to collect science data in the field. In return, the NatureBridge provides employee engagement opportunities and undertakes cobranded marketing with Intel.

Measure, Measure, and Measure   Ultimately, a partnership must create value for both parties if it is to endure. Measuring results on a predetermined basis provides the opportunity for learning and lays the groundwork for growth. Partnerships need to be evaluated based on initially laid-out outputs (tangible numbers and results) and outcomes (intended program benefits and impact). Approaching this assessment jointly enables both organizations to learn from both successes and challenges.

Clearly stating what you want the partnership to achieve up-front helps in back-end analysis. At a tactical level, what does success look like for each program element? For each partner? Elements to evaluate include:

Outputs: What tangible, measurable results is the partnership designed to achieve? This can include:

- Dollars raised through a program, event, or promotion
- Media impressions garnered
- Number of people reached through the program and/or number of employees engaged
- Social impact, such as an increase in the number of low-income students exposed to national parks

Outcomes: What are the intangible program benefits, outcomes, or impacts? While these can be hard to measure, they can include such things as enhanced capacity of the nonprofit organization, reciprocal access to new and broader publics, new relationships built, broader awareness of each organization and its mission, increased credibility of the nonprofit because of the relationship, leveraged dollars, attitudinal and/or behavior change among target audiences, and lives transformed.

Breakthrough: Nurture Transformational Relationships

Building a successful partner community doesn't stop with the signing of the agreement. It involves ongoing management and a continual investment of time and energy. How the execution and delivery of a partnership agreement is handled will determine its effectiveness, how satisfied you and your partners are, and whether the relationship can be sustained and grown.

Establish and Practice Mutual Respect Kids Help Phone's student ambassador program demonstrates the organization's commitment to reciprocal relationships and mutual respect. "We currently are in 30 communities with 2,000 student ambassadors in 450 schools," explained Alyson Waite, manager, Student Ambassador Program. "The goal is twofold: to help promote awareness of KHP and create a connection to the service in local communities. But equally important for us is to provide the student ambassadors with life-changing personal growth opportunities. We help them cultivate leadership skills that enhance the quality of their lives and advance them as they move into adulthood. We tailor their experiences because we know each ambassador has different strengths and interests, and we want it to work for them as well as us."

Whether with high school students or multinational corporations, the keys to building a successful relationship can be strikingly similar: Open communications, authenticity, and respect are all critical. It's important to remember each partner's cultures and constraints. Remember:

- *Equal, but different:* Cross-sector partners must respect each other and view each other as equal partners. At the same time, partners—particularly when they work in different fields or are from different sectors such as business or government—live in different worlds. They have a different language and culture. Commit to being equal and to understanding the differences.

- *Language:* Each sector and even each organization has its own language. Learning their language is as important as helping your partners learn yours. How do you do that? "Immersion is the best way," explained Jason Morris of NatureBridge. "You go sit in meeting after meeting, and you listen. Take notes and ask questions later. We have learned the vocabulary of our National Park Service partners, and we translate our work into their language. It's far easier than getting them to understand your vocabulary, and it demonstrates your deep connection to the relationship."

- *Culture:* Business is in the business of selling products and making money; government in developing and implementing policy; and nonprofits in delivering services and providing community support. By this very nature, the cultures of organizations in each sector will be different. Business needs to demonstrate results. Traditionally, many nonprofits have been slower and take a more consensus-oriented approach. Respect and a willingness to understand and meet each other's needs are critical to success.

Actively Manage Relationships, Not Just Programs   For deep, long-term, sustainable partnerships, there cannot just be one owner on the partner side. Successful nonprofits become embedded in the partner organization, creating relationships with key players at various levels and in several departments. Ideally, they demonstrate benefits for more than one department or help satisfy more than one organizational goal.

This is critical for many reasons. It helps your partners when they sell new contracts internally. It allows you to bring new and exciting assets to the partnership. And it helps ensure a successful transition when you are faced with turnover or reassignments at the partner organization.

For example, key to Kids Help Phone's success has been its ability to connect with multiple levels and multiple parts of its constituents. "We look well beyond our original contact in a company. We connect with their employees, consumers, suppliers, and other important groups. Our aim is to embed ourselves in the company culture and build a multilevel relationship," reported Meghan Reddick, director, Marketing, at KHP. "Our relationships are all about the people. Yet, people come and go all the time. If one person leaves and his or her replacement has an affinity for supporting another children's cause, we can withstand it. Our relationships are so deep and broad we aren't dropped for other organizations. Recently, for example, Empire Theatre purchased our long-term partner Famous Players movie theater. When the new owners did a survey about which organizations to support in the community, the deep and broad relationships we developed put us at the top of the list."

Carefully planned relationship management is a priority at KHP. "We make an extra effort to engage our premier partners' executive teams in leadership roles in our organization," Ellen Réthoré confided. "One of Bell's most senior Montreal-based executives is on our volunteer chapter council in that city. Several other founding corporate partners are members of our board and executive committee. This allows them to really understand our work and the outcomes we deliver. There is a sense of involvement and ownership that has strengthened their connection and commitment to our organization."

Communicate Continuously   Communication—both internally and externally—is a key to building any partnership. Internally, as brand ambassadors, staff needs to understand the parameters of a partnership, including activities agreed upon, benefits promised, and the partner's core goals. This is particularly important for a national organization with local offices. Employee communications, such as a partnership sheet that outlines the program, can be an effective way to create the understanding that leads to the delivery of consistent messages. Externally, active communication keeps the organizations connected and up-to-date on activities that the partnership is making possible. Communication also helps to generate ideas and to surface issues or challenges with the partnership arrangement.

Communications should be a two-way flow of information that fully engages both partners. It should be frequent, open, and honest.

"Large organizations can seem abstract. But it's real people sitting at desks. Get to know them. The more actively you communicate, the better. The more passive you are, the quicker and more systemically it breaks down," suggested Jason Morris of NatureBridge. "For example, we wanted to keep our students and staff safe and informed by using the radio frequencies that the National Park Service operates within its parks, and our positive, active relationship facilitated the permission. But if they only hear from us when we need something, the partnership looks self-serving."

"We meet regularly and often with our partners," explained Meghan Reddick. "Some of the best ideas have come from casual conversations. When new opportunities arise, we're top of mind."

Provide Expected and Unexpected Benefits and Opportunities While it is critical to deliver on what is expected, truly transformative partnerships often hinge on going above and beyond. Seek to offer unexpected opportunities for the partner to engage with your mission, and evolve the partnership dynamically, based on what gains the most interest. One way to do this is to stay on top of news relating to your partner and proactively offer new ideas and opportunities as the external environment shifts. Regular meetings that bring your staffs and volunteers together also can improve execution and generate new ideas and excitement. Engaging in mission-related activities together can help build ownership, strengthen relationships, and pump up the fun. As a little extra surprise, consider inviting key players to planned events or activities that are outside the partnership agreement. Such thank-yous or unspecified benefits can move relationships from "getting from" to "giving back" or even "growing together."

Involving partners' employees in nonprofit events builds an internal sense of community for them, and it strengthens the pride their employees feel from working for a company that's engaged in great work. For example, Bell Canada has supported KHP's annual walk for the past nine years. The company puts its marketing, brand, and people behind the event, engaging its staff as organizers, participants, and champions. Explained Meghan, "In our walk, we get senior leaders involved as volunteers and administrative staff as team captains. The walk enables employees of our

FIGURE 7.4   Bell Walk for Kids Help Phone

corporate partners to connect outside of the office and see each other in new ways. Our corporate partners also enable their employees to walk with family and friends and raise money for KHP. They essentially stop the presses at their own workplaces in order to support us. It's amazing for us and them" (see Figure 7.4).

Celebrate, Then Innovate   Success should be celebrated. Milestone dates and accomplishments can be used to bring partners together to recognize the great work that has taken place, to communicate to internal and external audiences, and to learn and plan for the future. Outputs and outcomes should be shared in all relevant communications and collateral, wrap-up reports, speeches at key events, newsletter thank-yous, and case studies. This helps both parties feel good about the value brought to the relationship and generates excitement to build on in future years.

While celebration is important, partnerships constantly need to evolve. Measuring results can help here as well. Where certain areas may have seen strong results, perhaps some did not. Consider phasing out or tweaking activities that saw less success and increasing focus on activities that gained more traction. Wrap-up meetings, brainstorming sessions, and annual retreats also provide authentic opportunities to share experiences—good and bad—and to grow and innovate—together. Following is a checklist to help you forge longer, stronger partnerships.

Breakthrough Partnership Checklist

As a nonprofit, ask your partners to:

- ☐ Value you as a partner in achieving your shared mission
- ☐ Work together to maximize positive social and business impacts
- ☐ Strive to build a relationship that exceeds expectations
- ☐ Respect and protect the integrity of your brand meaning
- ☐ Engage you in ongoing, meaningful, and honest dialogue
- ☐ Share responsibility for the long-term success of the relationship
- ☐ Provide you with a talented, creative, and experienced team
- ☐ Do what it takes to meet your key objectives
- ☐ Set realistic expectations and deadlines
- ☐ Publicly recognize your relationship and the results it delivers

As a partner to a nonprofit, ask them to:

- ☐ Value you as a partner in achieving your shared mission
- ☐ Work together to maximize positive social and business impacts
- ☐ Build a relationship with you as a key member of your team
- ☐ Respect and protect the integrity of your brand meaning
- ☐ Recognize your capabilities and capitalize on them whenever possible
- ☐ Remain open to creating new solutions to shared challenges
- ☐ Cultivate direct and constructive communication
- ☐ Provide you with access to a talented, creative, and experienced team
- ☐ Publicly recognize your commitment and societal impact
- ☐ Establish realistic expectations and deadlines
- ☐ Provide the tools and information you need to be successful
- ☐ Starting with short-term transactional agreements can yield important insights, require the least amount of investment, and hold the promise of growing to the next level.[4]

KIDS HELP PHONE NURTURES A PARTNER COMMUNITY

By adapting as technology has evolved, staying on top of the issues that are important to kids, and literally spending day and night connecting with kids directly, KHP has earned the respect and trust of educators, academics, social service providers, corporate partners, and, most important Canada's young people. What organization wouldn't love the kind of partnerships that Kids Help Phone has built? The organization's partnerships have been central in building KHP's brand meaning, vibrantly growing and transforming it from a little-known organization to one of Canada's most treasured and prominent children's charities.

With four founding 20-year corporate partners, one 20-year media partner, and multiple other corporate, media, community, and education partnerships, KHP is breaking through. Today, KHP serves more than 2 million children annually and operates from coast to coast in Canada in both English and French. The organization has a 90 percent awareness level among youth, a presence in more than 55 communities, and a strong reputation for professional work.

"Kids Help Phone was built through mutually beneficial partnerships that are mission, values, and audience aligned. Our joint commitment to the well-being of kids in Canada is palpable," Ellen Réthoré noted. "We wouldn't be the organization we are today without all of our different partners. They are truly part of our brand DNA, and we are equally part of theirs."

Keeping It Fresh—The Next 20 Years

"We keep relationships fresh by evolving ourselves," Ellen pointed out. "We've recently undertaken research on public perception and understanding of our organization. It's been very enlightening and is helping to frame new messages and develop new programs. Lots of people think we only serve troubled children. Our new messages will focus on our broad work with young people and the ways we have adapted to changing community needs—addressing issues like gangs and emerging mental health challenges. We'll be launching a fully transformed kids' web site with new and enhanced online counseling services and, in support, a national advertising campaign and youth awareness materials. That provides new opportunities for partners to benefit from their relationship with us, and for us to rethink how we work with them." This partnership mind-set will help set the stage for success in the organization's next 20 years.

NatureBridge Nurtures a Partner Community

As NatureBridge looks to grow its presence nationally, it is taking its relationship with the National Park Service (NPS) to a new level.

Move from Transactional to Transformational Partnership

NatureBridge's experience illustrates the way an organization can move away from a highly transactional model toward a philosophy that became the cornerstone of a truly transformational partnership. The organization was initially built on a fee-for-service revenue model. As a result, it attracted the relatively narrow section of the local population that could afford to attend. This largely upper- and middle-class group benefited from the experience but could choose from a range of similar program options. Yet, less affluent young people had few, if any, opportunities to connect with nature. Additionally, at that time, the student body did not reflect the state's diversity, and the organization risked losing relevance. Recognizing these challenges, in 1997 the board launched a diversity commitment.

"It was a watershed moment for us and our NPS relationship," recalled Jason Morris. "Our initial connection was much more transactional. We grew out of the environmental movement of the 1970s and had the relatively focused mandate to provide nature-based education in select parks. We delivered programming for students, but only those who could afford our fees. Eventually, we got to the point where that wasn't enough to differentiate us—to our audience or our partners." The board asked itself how it could strengthen relationships with core constituents: students, educators, school boards, and, most importantly, the National Park Service.

In response, NatureBridge launched a plan to diversify the student body, staff, volunteers, and board of each of its participating institutes. At the transitional stage, it raised funds for scholarships that would enhance participant diversity and broaden its work. Initial support of $150,000 has grown to more than $2 million annually. Board members were recruited from more diverse populations, and a new human resources program emphasized hiring to better reflect the diversity of each region.

"We truly began to represent the Park Service's vision of accessibility and broad engagement. That solidified our relationship and took it to a higher level. We weren't just educating students, we were reaching out to new audiences that were important to our partner," Jason observed. NatureBridge became more relevant to a larger number of students, increasing its impact. That made it a more attractive and important partner, strengthening its connection with schools and the NPS. In turn, those partnerships made NatureBridge a more dynamic organization. It was a virtuous cycle. "Over time, we proved our ability to fund-raise and brought even more value through the addition of funding partners, so the cycle continued," Jason concluded.

NatureBridge's relationship with the NPS grew to become truly transformational. "Our board and staff started connecting beyond the local park staff to the regional and then to the national office of the Park Service in Washington," continued Jason. "We met with them, engaged in a dialogue about our roles and the future vision for our respective work. People at all levels within the Park Service began to understand the congruence between our organizations and become excited about our ability to help it achieve its goals. With our new strategic direction to expand into other national parks across America, we are truly transforming the way we work together."

"We've taken a very professional approach to our new strategic direction. We brought in branding expert Lexicon to help us create a new brand identity [see the box earlier in this chapter]. We moved our offices to downtown San Francisco so we could have a more public presence," explained Stephen Lockhart. "All of this is strengthening our position with the Park Service and with other partners."

Growing Range of Partners for the New Future

As NatureBridge grows in size and scope, it has attracted corporate attention. "Our experience with the National Park Service has taught us a lot about partnerships, their value, and what's needed to make them work," Jason Morris noted.

The organization has built aligned relationships with Intel, Oracle, and the National Geographic Society, to name a few. These partnerships have enhanced the work of NatureBridge field educators. Intel, for example, has provided handheld devices that students use to collect biomonitoring science data. In return, NatureBridge supports the company's needs, from employee engagement opportunities to promotional marketing.

PRINCIPLE SIX: SUMMARY

Breakthrough Nonprofit Brands:

- Proactively build partner communities to extend their brands; mobilize additional capital, capacity, and credibility; and leverage ideas, insight, and influence.

- Use their brands as the filter and focus for building partnership, knowing there is much to be gained by working with others.

- Live their partnerships; these mutually beneficial, respectful relationships meet the goals and objectives of both parties, while protecting and enhancing each partner's brand meaning.

- Share values, passion, and audience alignment with their partners. Relationships are tailored for mutual benefit, create a sense of ownership, and are built to empower both partners to deliver on mutual goals.

- *Base: Establish transactional relationships*—Prepare internally to ensure win-win partnerships are culturally and systemically incorporated into the organization's DNA.
  - Establish culture and partnership mind-set through leadership, establishing goals, and dedicating staff.
  - Put structure and process in place for success.
  - Undertake initial relationships; put in writing through agreement.

- *Build: Align transitional relationships*—Proactively seek strategic alignment and build across both parties objectives for higher levels of engagement and, therefore, benefit for both.
  - Proactively seek aligned partners and understand their needs.
  - Establish reciprocal relationships and joint strategy to achieve mutual goals and benefits.
  - Look for multiple ways to work together including new currencies.

- *Breakthrough: Nurture transformational relationships*—Develop true partnerships and move along the continuum to transformational where they become integrated across the organization and establish co-ownership.

- Actively manage partnerships.
- Provide engagement opportunities.
- Overcommunicate, underpromise, and over-deliver.
- Empower within a framework.
- Create a sense of ownership.
- Celebrate and continually evolve.

CHAPTER 8

Principle Seven: Leverage Your Brand for Alternative Revenue and Value

"Goodwill's entrepreneurial spirit is core to our brand. Around North America and the world, community Goodwills strive to improve opportunities to grow business so they can help more people who need assistance every day."[1]

—JIM GIBBONS, PRESIDENT AND CEO, GOODWILL INDUSTRIES INTERNATIONAL

"During this tough economy, people who have never been in our stores are recognizing the caring and good value Goodwill provides. When people shop at our stores or utilize our many other social services, they directly experience the Goodwill brand and the good we do."

—KIM ZIMMER, SENIOR VICE PRESIDENT, COMMUNICATIONS AND PUBLIC AFFAIRS, GOODWILL INDUSTRIES INTERNATIONAL

GOODWILL INDUSTRIES, BRAND JOURNEY

Being in the business of doing good is the mandate of every nonprofit organization. But running businesses and earning income to achieve community good is core to Goodwill's brand DNA. The roots of today's Goodwill Industries International began as a simple idea. In 1902, the Rev. Edgar Helms, a young Methodist missionary, arrived at Morgan Chapel in the poor community of Boston's South End. There he found struggling immigrants from Germany, Poland, Italy, and other countries who had little money, no jobs, did not know the language, and were losing hope. To help meet their immediate needs, Helms took burlap bags to the northern part of Boston and went door to door asking wealthier Bostonians for whatever clothing and household items they could spare. His original intent was to give the materials away, but to his surprise, the immigrants were too proud to simply accept a handout. Never one to give up, he took his idea a step further. Helms enlisted members of his church to repair and clean the clothing and fix any damaged items. Then he set up a small operation to sell the donated clothing and goods at reasonable prices. Helms used the income to provide wages to the workers—and the first Goodwill store was born. Ultimately, the funds generated helped give immigrants basic education and language training. Workers earned a paycheck and learned valuable skills, giving them a hand up, not just a handout.

A Powerful Idea Evolves

Some 100 years later, Helms's idea has grown into something even more powerful. Today, Goodwill Industries operates a network of 183 independent, community-based organizations in the United States, Canada, and 14 other countries. As one of the first community enterprises, Goodwill's basic goals have not changed significantly over the years; however, the types of people Goodwill serves and its programs have evolved. Goodwill today provides job training, employment placement services, and other community-based programs for people who are disabled, lack education or job experience, or face employment challenges. The organization's mission is to enhance the dignity and quality of life of individuals, families, and communities by eliminating barriers to opportunity and helping people in need reach their fullest potential through the power of work.

To achieve its mission, the tradition of community enterprise remains at the core of Goodwill. True to its roots, the organization continues to sell donated clothes and other household items in more than 2,300 retail stores and, since 1999, online at www.shopgoodwill.com. But as it has evolved and grown, Goodwill has moved beyond product and retail sales, taking its brand meaning to a higher level of breakthrough community enterprises that more deeply engages beneficiary and supporter stakeholders (see Figure 8.1).

FIGURE 8.1   Goodwill Logo

Local Goodwill agencies generate revenue, create jobs, and teach employable skills by contracting with businesses and government agencies to provide a wide range of commercial services. These services include packaging and assembly, computer recycling, manufacturing, call centers, food service preparation, and document imaging and shredding. Goodwill produces income by helping businesses fill gaps caused by labor shortages, time constraints, and limited space or equipment. It is a $3.3 billion organization, and more than 1.5 million people in North America benefit from Goodwill's services. That's approximately one person placed in a job every 42 seconds of every business day. Eighty-four percent of its revenues are channeled directly back into Goodwill's programs and services. It's a unique operating model that relies on revenue generating ventures and community enterprises. Business ventures generate revenue sources, but the revenue is directed to social benefits rather than shareholder value.

United as a Caring Community Enterprise

Each Goodwill organization is an independently registered charity and operates autonomously in a Goodwill-designated territory. "We live in two worlds—our own local one and a wonderful network of Goodwill organizations across the country. We have strong name recognition, but people don't necessarily understand the qualities for which we want to be known," explained Gidget Hopf, CEO of ABVI[2]-Goodwill, Rochester, New York, and chair of the national branding committee. The organization was founded in 1911 as the Association for the Blind and Visually Impaired (ABVI). In 1994, ABVI became a member of Goodwill Industries International, an affiliation that has enhanced the organization's ability to offer employment opportunities.

David Hadani, former board chair, added, "When I first got involved in Goodwill, I thought it was a thrift store operation. I had no understanding of the depth and breadth of the Goodwill brand meaning. Like many non-profits, Goodwill's brand stood for the organization's programs and earned revenue model. We needed to intentionally build a brand meaning to more accurately represent the scope of our mission and values."

Building a breakthrough nonprofit brand (BNB) requires a fine balance between leadership commitment and grassroots engagement. In early 2002, the board made a commitment to focus on the brand and its development. It took a number of years. The board formed a national brand committee to show the commitment and investment needed to discover the brand meaning and define the compelling, unifying brand position and promise.

The committee undertook an extensive discovery research process that involved thousands of people. "We wanted to develop a brand meaning that would represent the organization as a whole but also work with and augment local Goodwill brand messages. We got great feedback," stated Gidget Hopf. "We got buy-in as we surveyed our constituents, employees, customers, consumers, board, donors, and a broad conglomerate of people to find the authentic core of our brand meaning."

Caring Community Enterprise was adopted as the universal brand con-nector. "Being a community enterprise makes us unique and is at the heart of what we do," said Gidget. "The link between our brand meaning and commerce to achieve community good is core to what we stand for. We defined Goodwill's brand promise to unite caring and enterprise to empower people and build communities that work."

More than any of our breakthrough nonprofit brands, Goodwill is driven by an earned income and social enterprise model. They use a con-tinuum of enterprise ventures to derive revenue from sources other than purely altruistic donations and bring substantial value to the organization. As we will see in this chapter, nonprofits of all sizes and scope are leverag-ing their brand meaning to take advantage of market forces that have rewarded those in the private sector.

An Overview of Principle Seven

Developing revenue-generating products and services and running com-munity enterprises is an untraditional means of enabling people to experience a brand in action. At the same time, it can generate alternative revenue and create additional value. Unlike for-profit enterprises, non-profit organizations return profits to the social purpose rather than maximizing returns to shareholders.

Nonprofit enterprises are not new. Nonprofit organizations have a long history of earning income. Today, earned income accounts for a growing source of revenue for most nonprofit organizations, where, depending on the type of organization, anywhere from 25 to 50 percent is earned income.[3]

Breakthrough nonprofit brands use their brand meaning to extend reach, generate untraditional revenue, and build brand equity through their entrepreneurial endeavors. In so doing, they can achieve the following benefits:

- *Earn undesignated revenue:* Earned income is most often undesignated revenue that can be used by organizations to cover operational and mission-related expenses. "The thrift shops generate the lion's share of Goodwill's revenue, strengthen our financial independence, and allow us to achieve so much more," explained David Hadani. "At Goodwill, we say no money, no mission" (see Figure 8.2).

- *Extend brand awareness:* "When people donate or come into a Goodwill store, we view it as an opportunity to explain our mission and

FIGURE 8.2   **Goodwill Store**

communicate key messages," explained Kim Zimmer, senior vice president, Communications and Public Affairs. "We make sure our mission is front and center." The organization's cause-marketing initiatives also involve opportunities to communicate what the organization stands for. "We use our cause-marketing partnership with Mrs. Goodbee Talking Dollhouse, for example, to encourage children to donate clothing and toys to Goodwill. It is an opportunity to teach about personal and community responsibility and connect that message with us," continued Kim. "Promoting the organization and having a call to action is incorporated into community enterprise ventures wherever possible."

- *Experience the brand:* Community enterprises give stakeholders and others a chance to experience the brand meaning in action. "When people come to our Goodwill stores, they understand what we stand for and how we bring our mission and values to life," added Kim Zimmer.

- *Strengthen reputation:* "Running thoughtful and well-managed community enterprises strengthens an organization's reputation," stated former Goodwill Board Chair David Hadani. "We've built a reputation that has enabled us to work with companies and government. Our Dell Reconnect Program is a great example of the trust and respect for our brand meaning." Dell supports the return of electronic goods to Goodwill, which in turn recycles almost 90 percent of the material. The program started in Austin, Texas; its success has led it to be rolled out in 30 states.

- *Reach new audiences:* A number of Goodwills have established boutiques near colleges to introduce the organization to new stakeholders. "College students are an audience we have focused on over the past five years," explained Kim Zimmer. "A group of Goodwills experimented with boutique and vintage-type stores. Their success has resulted in others establishing them. By introducing young adults to Goodwill, we begin to build a relationship that hopefully will last well beyond their college years." As a continued way to attract younger shoppers, Goodwill Industries launched its e-commerce web site in 1999: www.shopgoodwill.com. Millennials as a generation are highly values driven in where they shop, eat, and work, as well as where they donate. "Our recent expanded branding will help position us to connect with them," shared David Hadani. "Millennials have a very strong relationship and connectedness to entrepreneurship and community enterprise. This generation is very hands-on and is interested in immediacy. They want to have a direct impact. Creating a bond with the next generation is critical for sustainability of any organization."

- *Achieve social benefits:* At the breakthrough level, community enterprises' objectives are not just about making money but also about delivering social benefits to the community at the same time. Many community enterprises are committed to improving the lives of local people. Goodwill provides jobs and skills training for those they serve.

Building earned income ventures requires taking calculated risks, balancing them with good business practices and governance. BNBs that undertake earned income strategies are continuous learners, adapting and shifting practices to maximize impact and revenue.

In developing community enterprise ventures, a continuum exists that ranges from sales of products and services that earn revenue and extend reach to higher-level mission-based community businesses that generate both money and strong mission-based objectives. Each type shares common success factors—a culture of entrepreneurship and innovation, combined with brand relevance that converges with market opportunities and organizational capability.

While there are shared success factors, the different types of enterprise require scaled levels of strategies, structures, and processes to be successful. This principle will explore the overarching success factors. It will look at the continuum of enterprise activities and offer insights and tangible examples of the different types of community venture that can help an organization use its brand to leverage additional revenue and value. See Table 8.1 for the continuum.

How-To Success Factors

The purpose of this chapter is to give organizations an understanding of the value of their brand meaning to leverage alternative revenue and

TABLE 8.1   LEVERAGING BRAND FOR ALTERNATIVE REVENUE: CONTINUUM FROM BASE TO BREAKTHROUGH

	Base	Build	Breakthrough
How	Prepare for transactional point of sale opportunities: Establish an internal culture of enterprise; look for market opportunities that converge with brand relevance and establish organizational capabilities	Build on structure and experience: Move up the continuum to undertake more sophisticated earned income ventures and aligned community enterprises	Enter into integrated mission-based community enterprise business ventures to drive double bottom line: Achieves financial and mission-based goals to parallel others
What	Makes use of organizational visual brand identity Point of product purchase sales Earned income from product sales Transactional Short term; a moment Simple, easy, and/or quick decision Unengaged Subject potentially to unrelated business income tax Lowest risk	Aligned with brand meaning Personal experiences and personalized sales tied to higher purpose of organization that give direct experience of brand Greater connection that generates revenue and reach Higher risk	Driven by brand meaning Businesses with integrated mission-based goals and financial goals Highest level of engagement and connection to supporter and beneficiary stakeholders Deep engagement with brand meaning More sustainable revenue and value Turn expertise into business Longer-term operations Can have higher risk but greatest value over time
What: Types of Ventures	Product sales on site, at events, or online Licensing (images or logos) on products, properties Online store Product-driven cause marketing	Stores Restaurants Personal sales Cause marketing in-store promotions Aligned fee for service events or programs	Publishing Fee-for-service Consulting: ideas, expertise Licensing of ideas Joint venture businesses Community enterprises that achieve

	partnerships (e.g., portion of the proceeds, donate at register) Parking lots; coat checks	Concessionaires: businesses run by others where a portion of the proceeds returns to the organization	mission goals, such as employing and/or training beneficiaries
Why	Typically lower revenue per transaction; high potential for brand extension and/or awareness among the masses	Typically low to medium revenue per transaction; high potential for brand extension, as well as increased loyalty among targets	May range from low to high revenue; potential for brand extension among most lucrative targets; high potential for driving social impact and/or mission
When	Often one-off or short term	Longer than one moment in time	Sustained period of time or renewable operation
Who	Establish internal working group to put structure in place and experiment Often led by marketing and development team	Build on knowledge and establish a stand-alone group or area to drive community enterprise activities	Stand-alone business enterprise department Business ventures with partners (corporate, government, or other nonprofits) to share the risk and benefit from each other's strengths

benefit through earned income and community enterprise ventures. It will provide basic information to ensure organizational readiness.[4] The spectrum of community enterprises is showcased to demonstrate the impact each can have on an organization's brand reach, influence, and ability to generate alternative revenue.

1. *Base:* Prepare internally for transactional point of sale opportunities—Establish an internal culture of enterprise. Look for market opportunities that converge with brand relevance and establish organizational capabilities.

2. *Build:* Use structure and experience—Move up the continuum of earned income ventures and aligned community enterprises.

3. *Breakthrough:* Deepen community enterprise ventures—Enter into integrated mission-based community enterprise business ventures to drive the double bottom line of financial and mission-based goals that break through.

Base: Prepare Internally for Transactional Points of Sale

At the foundational level, a BNB establishes the internal supports essential for undertaking basic transactional point of sale activities. Transactional points of sale are basic earned income activities such as product sales, licensed products, and/or basic cause-related marketing ventures, most often tied to visual brand identity such as the logo or other organizational assets. Starting with simple transactional point of sale activities can yield important insights, require the least amount of investment, and hold the promise of growing to the next level.

Preparing to enter into point of sale activities requires organizational readiness and often a shift in culture. An organization must develop an enterprising mind-set and be willing to take carefully considered risks to develop simple transactional earned income activities.

Culture of Enterprise and Innovation A culture of enterprise doesn't just happen. It becomes part of the way an organization thinks and operates. At the base, an organization has to be prepared to be entrepreneurial, experiment, take risks, and not be paralyzed by analysis. This has to be integrated throughout the organization. "Goodwill is the entrepreneurial spirit that started with Edgar Helms and runs central and core to our organization," stated David Hadani.

Added Wendi Copeland, "There is an expectation of entrepreneurship, experimentation, and risk taking. We look for opportunities, listen to the community, and we're not afraid to proceed. We have values that explicitly talk about innovation, and we use the phrase 'we embrace continuous improvement, bold creativity, and change.' At Goodwill, we talk about being at the cutting edge but not the bleeding edge."

Seek Convergence to Realize the Enterprise Sweet Spot   Wendi works with individual Goodwill organizations to help build their enterprise capabilities. "I recommend three core factors that must converge before an organization enters into a community enterprise," she stated. "Look for the community enterprise sweet spot—where brand relevance converges with market opportunity and organizational capability. Each potential venture must be dealt with on a case-by-case basis; the key thing is to review each area and address any issues thoughtfully and honestly, not just by default."

Brand Relevance   "When thinking about entering into the nonprofit business world, I first recommend that they stake out a vision for the organization's earned income and enterprise activities," explained Wendi. "It has to make sense for the brand and help to achieve the organization's goals for it to become a reality."

"Even if it's just a simple line of branded products, which is the base level of enterprise," explained Wendi "you have to analyze if it makes sense for the brand. You can get caught up in the excitement of creating a new enterprise or commercial activity, so this is a very important first step." Wendi asked local Goodwill enterprises to challenge themselves by answering a few basic but important questions: Does the revenue opportunity align and add value to the brand meaning? Does it enhance its mission-based work? David Hadani concurred, noting it's important to stay focused and find a niche that affords an organization the opportunity to be successful.

At the base level, earned income ventures use the organization's visual and verbal brand identity to generate revenue and create basic awareness of the organization. The most prevalent types of point of purchase sales are:

Products: Most often they feature the organization's logo. Susan G. Komen Run for the Cure, for example, sells products such as T-shirts, coffee mugs, and lapel pins featuring the colorful and well-recognized organizational logo. The products extend awareness of the organization but don't achieve a specific mission-related goal. Another example of a product that is not mission related is UNICEF's Christmas card program. The card makes use of children's art, but the benefits are tied to raising awareness while generating additional revenue.

Licensed products: Licensing is a business that grants the right to use a legally protected trademark, name, graphic, logo, slogan, likeness, or other similar intellectual property in conjunction with a product or service for a royalty or fee. A formal licensing agreement outlines the prescribed amount of time the license is granted, the specific geographic area, tracking of sales, marketing and distribution vehicles, and dates royalty payments will be made. In exchange the nonprofit receives payment in the form of a royalty, usually a percentage on the product sales.

Product driven cause-related marketing relationships: Donations are made to a nonprofit cause based on transactional sales and are usually meant to drive sales and build customer loyalty for the company. In a product purchase, a percentage of the revenue is donated to a cause based on product sales. Other donation triggers could be the use of a coupon, adding a widget to a Facebook page, visiting a web site or opening a new account. Product sales programs encourage passive consumer participation and most often are offered for a defined period of time and tied to a specific product/service.

These earned income ventures often don't directly advance the mission but add value through added awareness and income. Regardless, like any enterprise venture, they must be appropriate and make sense for the brand. Because nonprofit brands are values driven, any enterprise activity must be consistent with organizational values. No organization can afford to compromise the brand or erode staff morale for the sake of potential revenue.

Market Opportunities The second consideration is analyzing the marketplace and determining if there are unaddressed opportunities to seize. "Our founding story is a great example of an unmet community need and market opportunity," said Goodwill's Wendi Copeland. "Goodwill Enterprises saw an opportunity for people to donate slightly used clothes that could be resold in a store, run largely by beneficiaries of the Goodwill program."

A nonprofit group that hopes to earn revenue in the marketplace must provide a product or service that brings customers value at a fair price. "We have standards as to the quality of the donated goods for our thrift stores," added Kim Zimmer. "People who shop at our stores want to know that they're getting good quality at a low price. It's rare to find people that are willing to buy a product just to serve the organization's mission—if they were, they would more likely be donors."

At the base level, market opportunities include products that could be sold directly by the organization from their or partner locations, on the web, at events, or during special seasons such as Christmas. It could also include licensed opportunities if an organization has a potential opportunity to license its brand identity. Cause-related marketing (CRM) product sales can be developed with local, regional, national, and global businesses. Research is required to determine if there is a sufficient market opportunity to form a CRM relationship.

Organizational Capabilities Where brand relevance, market opening, and organizational capabilities meet is where there is opportunity. For an organization to be successful, it must have or be able to get the capabilities to undertake the commercial activity or run a community venture.

"Organizations have to make sure they have the capabilities or can buy the talent to successfully undertake any venture," stated Wendi Copeland, outlining the third requirement for enterprises. "Hiring new employees or consultants to help with implementation is perfectly acceptable, but you've got to make sure you've thought through what it takes to implement a community enterprise. Don't go by intuition or emotion. Do research and analyze every prospect. Recognizing and assessing opportunities is a skill, not intuition. Ask questions, probe potential issues, and challenge assumptions—all are important to success."

UNRELATED BUSINESS INCOME TAX (UBIT) GENERAL RULES

Even though a nonprofit organization is tax exempt, it still may be liable for tax on its unrelated business income (UBIT). This is income from a trade or business, regularly carried on, that is not substantially related to the performance by the organization of its exempt purpose or function except that the organization needs the profits derived from this activity. An exempt organization that has $1,000 or more gross income from an unrelated business must file Form 990-T, Exempt Organization Business Income Tax Return. For additional information, see the Form 990-T instructions.[5]

The UBIT applies to all organizations exempt from tax under section 501(a) except certain U.S. instrumentalities. State and municipal colleges and universities are also subject to the UBIT, even if they are not exempt under section 501(a).

All organizations subject to UBIT, except trusts, are taxable at corporate rates on that income. All exempt trusts that are subject to these provisions and non-exempt would be taxable at trust rates on UBIT. However, an exempt trust may not claim the deduction for a personal exemption that is normally allowed to a trust.[6]

Explained Kim Zimmer, "We are very careful to make sure that our businesses all relate to achieving our mission. To my knowledge, we've not had any issues that have threatened our charitable tax status or required us to pay income tax."

Strategies, Structure, and Systems   Breakthrough nonprofit brands put strategies, structures, and systems in place to enable enterprise and maximize success. "Once the business opportunity analysis is complete, we work with Goodwills to help develop their business plans," explained Wendi Copeland. "Whether the business opportunity is basic such as product sales or an aligned business venture, it pays to have a strategy, structure, and systems in place to ensure success."

"Any type of enterprise activity requires careful thought and planning. Even when we did something as simple as being a third-party bookseller on Amazon.com, we developed a strategy that outlined goals and execution.

We determined the structures and systems needed to ensure success," shared Gidget Hopf.

Carefully Crafted Strategies Even for the base level earned income activities, business plans are essential to outline goals and mobilize resources. The business plan should provide details of how you are going to develop the earned income activity, when you are going to do it, who is going to play a part, and how you will manage the finances. Clarity on these issues is particularly important if you're looking to finance the investment. As with any business activity, one of the main issues is finding funding to help convert an idea into a viable business activity. Having a business plan is essential to present to the board, or senior leadership. The process of building the plan will also provide focus on how earned income activities will need to operate to succeed.

Any earned income or community enterprise plan should include:

- An executive summary: This is an overview of the business you want to start, and it is vital. Board or senior leadership judgments about the earned income opportunity are often based on this section alone.

- A short description of the business opportunity: who you are, what you plan to sell or offer, why, and to whom.

- A description of your target audience: Knowing your audience, their interests, buying patterns, and how to reach them is vital to success.

- An outline of your marketing and sales strategy: why you think people will buy what you want to sell and how you plan to sell to them.

- A presentation of your management team and personnel: your credentials and the people you plan to recruit to work with you.

- Details of your operations: your premises, production facilities, management information systems, and information technology.

- Consideration of third-party sales: In the case of a licensed product program or cause-marketing product sale, it is highly recommended that a formal agreement be drawn up to outline the terms of the program, tracking of sales, the financial contribution, use of the nonprofit's logo, name and brand identity and sign-off, and promotional and advertising support. The agreement will ensure clarity around roles, responsibilities, expectations, and execution.

- Financial forecasts: This section translates everything you have said in the previous section into numbers.[7]

"I would advocate for organizations to think big, but start small," advised David Hadani. "The issue that many organizations face when trying earned income activities or starting a business is they have grand plans, a mission and strategy so big it is almost unexecutable. Try something and scale it as you learn has been a key factor in many of Goodwill's successful enterprises."

Get the Right People in Place   "Over the past eight years I've been involved with Goodwill, I've seen some of the best entrepreneurial businesspeople that I've ever worked with. They are responsible and accountable to the community and each other. That is very important for success in business," stated David Hadani with conviction and pride. "Leaders here are very focused on organizational success. There is no fear about who is going to get the credit."

Earned income points of sale rarely requires full time staff to manage activities. At the base level, BNBs traditionally establish an internal working group to put the strategy and structure in place to experiment with earned income ventures. Staff who have had experience in this area are invaluable in aiding the organization's effort to leverage the brand for alternative revenue and value.

Establish Systems for Ongoing Evaluation and Risk Management
Systems need to be put in place for regular check-ins to ensure financial accountability and risk management. "We have sophisticated staff to run these enterprises for us," explained Wendi Copeland. "They are experienced social entrepreneurs who are constantly evaluating each and every business and any potential risks."

Even the most basic activities require regular checking in, evaluating successes and challenges to tweak or evolve plans. Mitigating any risk early can provide critical learning and a higher opportunity for success.

These guidelines provide a framework for staff, volunteers, partners, media, and others to consistently use the brand identity.

Experiment and Learn   Edgar Helms started with simple earned income community enterprises—selling used clothes. At the base, community enterprises involve low risk with revenue and awareness benefits. Many are product sales, often featuring an organization's visual and/or verbal identity. Parking lots and coat checks are enterprise activities that also add revenue.

UNDERSTAND AND PROTECT BRAND VALUE IN THE MARKETPLACE

Brands are valuable assets that in the nonprofit sector are often the most valuable single asset. Practically speaking, the value of the brand translates into everyday economic benefits including:

- Premium pricing for memberships, programs, and services
- Lower cost of promotion and marketing through higher recognition by consumers, media, and community influencers
- Reduced threat of competition

UNDERSTAND BRAND VALUE

Breakthrough nonprofit brands understand the role their brands can play in earned income ventures and community enterprises. For example, ABVI-Goodwill decided to sell books as a third-party seller on Amazon. To their surprise, the first night they sold more than 100 titles; the second night, 130. "We really believe it was because of the Goodwill brand," explained Gidget Hopf, executive director. "There is a lot of positive feeling and trust in who we are."

Evaluating the value of a nonprofit brand is often as much an art as a science. A nonprofit valuing its brand is an idea that doesn't come easily to the charitable world. It can be hard to translate a charitable cause or humanitarian effort into dollars and cents.

Knowing the value of the brand can help an organization understand what it is contributing to its community and shape its future. Genuinely and honestly answering these questions will help you determine the value of your brand.

- *Financial performance:* Total revenue less indirect expenses = social contribution
- *Differentiation of brand:* How the brand is differentiated and preferred in the marketplace
- *Reputation strength:* Size of market, leadership, stability, relevance, level of support, community reach, and protection of brand[8]

Large nonprofits are hiring brand evaluation firms to help determine the exact dollar value of their brand. One of the most famous is Habitat for Humanity, which first undertook a brand valuation in 2001. Valued
(continued)

(continued)

at $1.8 billion, equivalent to Starbucks at the time, the organization used the information to strengthen its corporate partnership pricing.[9]

PROTECT BRAND VALUE

Breakthrough nonprofit brands protect their brands from infringement or misuse by obtaining and by defining their trademarks and writing visual brand guidelines that outline acceptable usage.

Trademark process: Your distinctive identity is worth protecting. Registering it provides the broadest scope of protection. A brand can be registered at the state and federal levels. The federal level secures the most benefits in trademark infringement.

Brand identity usage guidelines: BNBs establish and adhere to clear brand usage guidelines that outline acceptable use of the visual and verbal identity of logo, color, typography, and name. The guideline, usually developed by a communications or advertising agency or an internal graphic designer, provides a framework for elements such as:
- Logo with or without tagline
- Logo version in color and in black-and-white
- Logo sizes
- Logo spacing
- Logo when shown with partner (corporation, foundation, government, other nonprofit organization)
- Logo exceptions
- Typography
- Color—primary, secondary
- Samples of logo usage

Examples of Base-Level Earned Income Activities from Our Case Studies

Goodwill Industries International

- *Product sales:* Shopgoodwill.com (see Figure 8.3) enables virtual purchase of Goodwill-donated products. "We are always on the lookout

FIGURE 8.3   Shopgoodwill.com

for new ideas," explained Gidget Hopf. "It's part of our entrepreneurial spirit. Goodwills experiment and try new things all the time. Shopgoodwill.com is a great example of an idea that has become a national endeavor. It was the brain trust of the CEO in Orange County and was started in 1999, well before online shopping was as acceptable as it is today."

Product sales: ABVI-Goodwill sells donated books as a third-party Amazon seller. "We had thousands of books in our inventory," explained Gidget. "It's a great way to sell at limited expense with significant exposure."

American Heart Association

- *Product sales:* The American Heart Association actively embraces entrepreneurship and product sales as an innovative way to extend reach and earn income. Supporters can demonstrate their commitment by shopping at shopheart.org.—the online cause site where proceeds from a wide range of merchandise, from T-shirts to jewelry to mugs, contribute to the fight against heart disease and stroke.

Food Bank For New York City

- *Cause-marketing donation at the till:* Food Bank For New York City works with more than 300 businesses during their autumn Go Orange campaign. This cause-marketing initiative sees businesses accepting cash donations to the Food Bank and providing Go Orange buttons in return that a donor can wear to support the organization. Cause-marketing ventures are mutually beneficial relationships between companies and nonprofit community organizations. A company uses the power of its marketing, brand, and people to help promote and raise money for the cause while enhancing its own brand meaning.

Susan G. Komen for the Cure

Product sales: Through its online Promise Shop, an extensive range of merchandise is offered. Products include T-shirts, promise rings, mugs, ties, pajama sets, and jewelry, all featuring the colorful and highly recognizable organizational logo, at www.shopkomen.com.

U.S. Fund for UNICEF

- *Product sales:* Famous for its Christmas cards and calendars featuring the art of children around the world, UNICEF was also an early community enterprise organization. It sells the products in its own sales offices and works with other retailers that sell on behalf of the organization. UNICEF also has a web site called inspiredgifts.org, selling gifts that engage purchasers to deliver its brand meaning: Believe in Zero. Items from midwifery kits and nutrition and vaccine products, to bicycles/motorcycles for aid workers can be purchased.

Build: Capitalize on Brand and Experience to Build the Next Level of Community Enterprise Ventures

Community enterprises that make a more personal connection through direct experiences and personal sales elevate an organization's brand meaning. This second level of community enterprise provides more engagement opportunities and experiences with the brand but requires a stronger culture of enterprise, a more sophisticated understanding of the marketplace, and a deeper level of management and organizational capabilities.

Strengthen Culture of Enterprise and Innovation   As a caring community enterprise, Goodwill empowers and enriches lives by using an entrepreneurial spirit. "The Goodwill founder, Edgar Helms, was a man who tried different community enterprises when he first started the organization," explained Wendi. "If it didn't work, he went back and tried something else."

This approach continues to describe the Goodwill ethos and is embedded in the organization's culture. Goodwill has a strong enterprising spirit and a culture of risk. They grow by approximation. An enterprise is tried; practices are adapted to make it a success through continuous learning. The drive and commitment to Goodwill is palpable. Leaders are encouraged and empowered to take a risk. It's an expectation. There will be some failures. Doing everything 100 percent is probably being way too safe.

As an organization moves up the continuum of enterprise activities, the level of internal enterprise required rises accordingly. At the build level, enterprise activities move beyond basic earned income ventures to include mission-aligned businesses such as stores or restaurants.

Brand Relevance: Align to Brand Meaning   At the build level, brand relevance is strengthened. The goal becomes making a direct connection to the brand meaning in action. At this level, earned income ventures and aligned business activities are tied to the higher organization's purpose. Higher engagement and greater connection to the brand meaning deliver greater brand value. Opportunities include retail operations, aligned fee-for-service programs, or deeper cause-marketing promotion:

Market Opportunities   Understanding possible market opportunities or niches requires research as more risk is involved in higher level enterprise ventures. Building on experience and learning, BNBs ensure market opportunities exist before launching into deeper business ventures. And the more complex internal support structures they require are in place.

Organizational Capabilities   As earned income and aligned business move up the continuum, the level of business planning, staff capabilities, and support structures must grow with it. Often a stand-alone group is formed to drive community enterprise activities. Business plans require more depth. Staff, volunteers, or board members with business expertise become valuable allies in strengthening an organization's enterprise capabilities.

As Goodwill moves into higher level businesses, it realizes the need for experienced individuals to power success. "Our goal is to hire people you have to run to keep up with," explained Wendi Copeland. "We have a rigorous process that involves multiple interviews and behavioral questions. I want to hear what they've done and how they did it. I like to talk with people who have worked with them. Skills are important, but I also want to hear passion in their voices. We need true believers working at Goodwill."

Business plans and risk management structures also have to continue to grow in depth and rigor. The business plan framework outlined remains relevant but should include more analysis and information as to the what, how, who, why, where, and when.

Examples of Build-Level Community Enterprises   Goodwill Industries operates community enterprises at the local, regional, and national level. "Our entrepreneurial spirit has led us to try some very interesting businesses—some that succeed and some that don't, but we try nevertheless," enthused David Hadani.

Goodwill Industries International

- *Thrift stores:* Virtually every Goodwill runs a thrift store supported by donations of new or gently used items like clothing, appliances, electronics, and furniture. There are more than 2,300 Goodwill retail stores in the United States and Canada.

- *Selling expertise:* Over the last 25 years, ABVI (see Figure 8.4) Goodwill has become an expert in adapting technology for people who are blind. "Everything today is online so we're looking into

FIGURE 8.4   **Goodwill ABVI Call Center**

opportunities to turn our expertise and knowledge into a business venture," explained Gidget Hopf.

- *Food services operation:* ABVI-Goodwill delivers meals and serves them to all the senior centers in Rochester, New York. This allows users to directly experience Goodwill's brand in action. The organization recently leveraged its infrastructure to serve children's day care centers and has established an on-site restaurant at their main office.

- *Cause-marketing promotion:* Goodwill launched a new cause-marketing promotion initiative in spring 2010 called Do Good. Donate. The promotion is designed to engage corporate partners to promote the good of donating items to Goodwill. Goodwill designed a new logo for its corporate partners to include in cause promotions, and in some cases on products themselves, to remind consumers to responsibly donate their items and help strengthen local communities. Levi's was one of the first partners to support the program by launching Care Tag for Our Planet. Levi's® included the Do Good. Donate logo on the care tag in jeans, with a reminder to owners to donate them to Goodwill when they are no longer needed. The logo offers a unique vehicle to educate consumers about how to recycle their products responsibly. Donating to Goodwill not only diverts unwanted items from landfills but also helps people who need it most in local communities.

- *Aligned community venture:* "We incubate ideas by trying," continued Gidget Hopf. "For example, we have lots of fabric from the clothing in our stores. We sent up a sewing team and let them experiment, making unique products. Our goal is to try and create mass market products at an affordable price." The organization also seizes opportunities and is nimble and experienced enough to know what works and what is needed for success. "Because our population at ABVI-Goodwill is blind, we were able to be a recipient of a Welfare-to-Work grant and move quickly on implementation," she added.

American Heart Association

- *Cause-marketing promotions:* Cause-marketing partnerships extend revenue and reach through proceeds from product sales and promotions. For example, in 2010, together with fashion expert Tim Gunn, the

Campbell Soup Company asked customers to design an original Campbell red dress. Three finalists were chosen, and a $1 donation was made for every vote for a favorite entry.[10]

Susan G. Komen for the Cure

• *Cause-marketing promotions:* Multiple and deep cause-marketing partnerships such as Yoplait's Save Lids to Save Lives helps the organization annually reach millions of people with a message of hope while raising money for breast cancer research, education, screening, and treatment.

U.S. Fund for UNICEF

• *Person-to-person sales:* An early pioneer of door-to-door fund raising, UNICEF's Trick or Treat boxes are now synonymous with Halloween.

• *Cause-marketing promotion:* Most recently, UNICEF has partnered with Pampers® with a donation to purchase one immunization for every package of diapers sold. Through its extensive advertising and in-store promotional campaign, Pampers has helped UNICEF extend its reach while generating additional revenue for the cause of childhood survival.

Breakthrough: Deepen Community Enterprises to Achieve Mission and Financial Goals

The double bottom line—the simultaneous pursuit of financial and social returns on investment—is the ultimate benchmark for a community enterprise. Leveraging an organization's brand to successfully pursue this type of community enterprise is a breakthrough for nonprofits. These types of community enterprises provide the highest level of engagement and connection to supporter and beneficiary stakeholders. Building this level of community enterprise poses the greatest risks also can provide the greatest rewards. The rewards that come from this type of deep alignment can be more than worth it with careful consideration and diligent execution.

Entrepreneurial Mind-Set Integrated into Organization   "Entrepreneurial thinking isn't just about creating a business idea or a product," shared Gidget Hopf. "It's how you approach your work; it's a way of thinking, whether you're a social worker in the rehabilitation department, in the HR department, or you're in bookkeeping or finance. Driven to innovate and try new enterprises is embedded in the culture."

According to David Hadani, an important part of the Goodwill brand is to believe in the people they serve and do whatever they can to provide meaningful work and opportunities to learn new skills. "We're driven to continue to try new community enterprises, learn, innovate, and evolve. We know that the need is great and the courage that is required to make the ultimate choice to walk through the doors and ask for help—nothing is harder than that," he continued. Hadani added that it's not good enough to communicate your brand; trust and sustainability are an essential part of it. The trust element is so important because it's a relationship between you and your stakeholders.

While each Goodwill organization operates independently, the commitment to share learning, experiences, and ideas to advance the cause is real. "When I joined Goodwill 15 years ago, it was to do a turnaround," shared Wendi Copeland. "My CEO told me to call other organizations to find out what was working for their organization. My experience told me that would not work. I was wrong. Everyone I spoke to shared important learning and insights that were critical in reviving the organization."

Failure is viewed as an opportunity to learn and evolve. "Many organizations see the statistics that 85 percent of earned income and community enterprise activities fail within the first three years of operation, and that becomes a reason not to try," reflected Wendi. "There is no question that it is hard work, and while culture encourages it, an organization has to be realistic about community enterprise opportunities."

Brand Relevance: Organizational Integration   Gidget Hopf, executive director, ABVI-Goodwill, said, "Our drivers are people, profits, and the planet. Creating jobs is the bottom line for us. Our local Goodwill brand promise is 'socially entrepreneurial spirit uniquely qualifies us to prepare and empower people affected by vision loss to realize their goals and dreams.' Any revenue opportunity has to create jobs for our beneficiaries. We also need to make profits. We repeat the no margins means no mission mantra."

Breakthrough community enterprises are driven by an organization's brand meaning and are aligned with and driven by mission goals. Ventures can include turning expertise into businesses or running businesses that benefit the organization's beneficiary audience, thereby helping achieve mission.

Market Opportunity   As the highest level of risk, careful consideration must be given to market opportunities and research undertaken to maximize success. Partnerships with other nonprofit organizations, businesses, or contracts from government help to spread risk while ensuring a market for the enterprise. See Chapter 7, Cultivate Partnerships, to review the principles and practices for effective partnering to build and strengthen the brand.

Organizational Capability   Stand-alone business enterprise departments are a must for this level of nonprofit enterprise venture. Expertise, training, and support are vital. "We invest in our people and have leadership development programs from the executive level to managers," continued Wendi. "The program is geared to building the leadership we need for the future. We spend a lot of time training and supporting staff in enterprise development. That is something that is very unique to Goodwill."

"We're continuously evolving, sharing, and are very much a learning organization. We believe in standing on each other's shoulders. This is very motivating," added Wendi. "If we hire really intelligent people and then tell them to keep the status quo, we will not keep them. We must be on a trajectory of innovation leap, catch your breath, innovate again, then catch your breath. We have to be adaptive because the environment is ever-changing, and if you're standing still, then you're falling behind."

JOINT VENTURES

Community enterprises can be undertaken through a collaborative or partnership model. Product licensing or traditional product-based cause-marketing activities are implemented through a corporate partnership model. Joint ventures can involve a single or multiple partners from government, business, or even other nonprofit organizations.

"We encourage our member associations to look for ways to collaborate on ventures," said Goodwill's Wendi Copeland. "Joint ventures or partnerships with government, corporations, or other not-for-profits are a great way to bring additional venture and human capital to the table, extend impact, and help minimize individual organizational risk."

"One of the key points we make with our Goodwills," explained Wendi, "is not to think that an organization has to undertake a community enterprise on its own. None of us has enough resources to achieve what needs to be done in our communities. We encourage collaboration. We must find ways to extend our arms without having all the money."

"Strategic partnerships are becoming more important," stated David Hadani. "Ones that allow you to make it easier to accomplish your mission or make an ecosystem that makes it easier for everyone to combine to achieve. It's the move from community enterprise 1.0 to 2.0. Work with others to drive a business model that will be more successful together. Our partnerships with Dell Reconnect and Levis Strauss are examples of this."

Examples of Breakthrough-Level Community Enterprises

Goodwill Industries International

- *Government-contracted services:* "We are a trusted business partner with government," explained David Hadani. "The Goodwill brand meaning is so strong that we undertake many government contracts to provide services and products for them."

- *Manufacturing operations:* At ABVI-Goodwill, manufacturing plays a major role in its operation.
  - *Self-stick notepads:* 3M provides the raw materials for self-stick notepads and ABVI-Goodwill converts the raw materials into finished pads in multiple colors and sells them to the U.S. government.
  - *CD-ROMs:* The organization had an idea to manufacture CD-ROMs, which they now sell to the U.S. government for data storage.
  - *Training uniforms:* The organization's manufacturing operations sew physical training uniforms for the U.S. Air Force so even those who can't serve in the military feel like they're doing their part.

- *Cleaning products:* ABVI-Goodwill has a green initiative that produces a cleaning product line sold to the federal government, including all branches of the military and civilian departments.

- *Telephone call centers:* ABVI-Goodwill is certified to run the 211 call center, the national Lead Poisoning and Toxic Substance Hotline for the Environmental Protection Agency, and the 24/7 Lifeline (a suicide hotline). The program has created important jobs for the many blind people who answer the calls.

- *Recycling operations* (Dell Reconnect): In partnership with Dell, Goodwills recycle computers, printers, and computer peripherals. The aim is to salvage 90 percent of a computer to keep it out of landfills by ensuring most of the computer parts are treated and safely removed. The program generates revenue, provides important jobs, and has earned a lot of goodwill for Goodwill Industries (see Figure 8.5).

- *Good Guys:* A youth mentoring initiative in schools and the community has worked well in seven Goodwills. As a result, 57 Goodwills in 38 states presented a joint proposal to the Office of Juvenile Justice to replicate the Good Guys initiative across the country.

Inspiration Corporation: Aligned training business

- *Mission-based community enterprise:* Cafe Too is a restaurant open to the public that is used as a hands-on learning experience for students involved in Inspiration Corporation's food service training program. The program is designed to build skills and provide employment opportunities in an atmosphere of dignity and respect to people facing barriers to self-sufficiency. Inspiration Corporation is also developing a new community enterprise restaurant and food service training center in East Garfield Park, Chicago, which is set to open in late 2010.

FIGURE 8.5   Dell and Goodwill Reconnect Logo

Memorial Healthworks! Kids' Museum license program and consulting services

- *License program and consulting services:* Healthworks! has extended its brand reach in an innovative way by licensing the Healthworks! concept to other community medical centers. Consulting services are available to support the implementation. This program spreads the Healthworks! epidemic from the full-scale HealthWorks! model to licensing HealthWorks! exhibits to delivering HealthWorks! original field trips, camps, and events.

NatureBridge: Fee for service

- *Program fees:* The initial business model was as a dedicated self-sustaining organization raising revenue from program beneficiaries. Today, more than 80 percent of NatureBridge's funds come from income earned from program fees related to science education, youth leadership, and teacher-training programs.

Stratford Shakespeare Festival: Full spectrum from products to retail to ticket sales

- *The whole gamut of community enterprise activities:* The Stratford Shakespeare Festival in Ontario, Canada, runs retail outlets and produces and sells multiple logo products and Shakespeare-related items. As a breakthrough community enterprise, the organization generates 60 percent of total revenue from ticket sales.

GOODWILL AND THE ENVIRONMENT

"The environment is becoming a significant driver for our organization, as it is for Goodwill Industries across North America. We believe our green business emphasis and approach is a positioning that could be a strategic competitive advantage for the organization," explained Senior Vice President of Communications and Public Affairs Kim Zimmer.

(continued)

(*continued*)

As a result, green businesses and training have become a focus for Goodwill. "We are embracing environmental responsibility as a growing element for our brand. There are real market opportunities, and we have the organizational capabilities to be part of the green movement. Goodwill is providing green construction training and services. There are unique manufacturing requirements and guidelines associated with green building. We've moved into green custodial services that use cleaning material and distinctive methods that require a different type of training," explained Kim. "We're always looking for new enterprise ideas, and in particular parts of the country, there are real opportunities for green jobs. California and parts of Texas, for example, have state policies that are advancing the need for trained and qualified people in these areas."

Making It Real

Goodwill launched its **Donate Movement** in the summer of 2010 to help users better understand the positive effects of their good deeds by calculating the real-world impact donations have on people within local communities, and how it helps make a healthier planet. For more information see: http://donate.goodwill.org/

Embrace Community Social Responsibility: People, Profits, and Planet

Although a nonprofit organization is a charitable organization when it undertakes a community enterprise venture, the rules are changing. While the lens of corporate social responsibility is clearly focused on the actions of the private sector, organizations in all sectors are being held to a higher standard. Many businesses have endorsed the principles of corporate social responsibility and have put checks and balances in place to ensure their marketplace operations are as responsible as possible. Almost all businesses understand the growing expectation for socially and environmentally responsible outcomes as a result of their actions.

Goodwill Industries is adopting the People, Profits, and Planet approach to their businesses. "Job creation is number one for us, and we are looking for meaningful work and to pay our people a living wage," explained Gidget Hopf. "We also talk about things like responsible recycling, waste and salvage, after market, and how not to fill the land-fill but be responsible with clothing and goods."

EXPERIENCING THE GOODWILL BURN

"The Goodwill burn" is a phrase frequently used by staff, volunteers, and board members involved in the movement. David Hadani, the past national board chair, explained, "Goodwill burn is the passion for the organization, the commitment to it. It's the thing if I took one of you to one of our businesses, I would bet all the money in my pocket that you would walk out of that operation with the burn. It's an understanding of what we do and a desire to be a part of it."

Added Wendi Copeland, "The Goodwill burn is something that true believers have. They believe that people need an opportunity, and though they have a God-given right to fail, people get up in the morning and want to succeed. Goodwill is about making sure people have that opportunity. They invest in the lives of people around the country, to give them a chance to be successful through the power of work."

Goodwill thrives and is dedicated to fulfilling the goals of its vision, which states: "We at Goodwill Industries will be satisfied only when every person in the global community has the opportunity to achieve his/her fullest potential as an individual and to participate and contrib-ute fully in all aspects of a productive life."

PRINCIPLE SEVEN: SUMMARY

Breakthrough Nonprofit Brands:

- Understand the role community enterprise can have to advance an organization's brand relevance and reputation, extend brand reach, strengthen existing relationships and build new ones, generate untra-ditional revenue, and enhance brand equity in the marketplace.

- Embrace community enterprises as a way to experience the brand and build and strengthen relationships in the community.

- Build a culture of entrepreneurship, innovation, and learning.

- Consider community enterprise opportunities based on the conver-gence of brand relevance, market opportunity, and organizational capabilities.

- Develop strategies to enable successful implementation, put the right people in place, establish systems, facilitate community enterprises, and enable risk assessment, continuous learning, and innovation.
- Protect brand value through the trademark process and development of brand usage guidelines.
- *Base: Establish*—an internal culture and systems to undertake transactional points of sale. Put the processes, people, and procedures in place to leverage the brand to generate income and create additional value.
  - Experiment and learn with simple transactional community earned income activities.
- *Build: Capitalize*—on brand and experiences to build personal sales and experiences. Move to the next level of community enterprise that involves more personal experience and sales.
  - Greater opportunity to experience and understand the brand and align with brand meaning.
- *Breakthrough: Deepen activities*—by entering into community enterprise ventures that achieve the double bottom-line benefits of mission and money. These community enterprises engage their beneficiary and supporter stakeholders.
  - Establish double bottom-line community enterprises that achieve mission-based and money goals.
  - Bring the brand meaning to life and show the mission in action. Integrates brand meaning into commercial enterprise ventures.
  - Work with others to maximize resources and success and spread the risk.
  - Embrace the growing importance of being a socially responsible community enterprise: people, profits, and the planet to strengthen brand value and equity.

Conclusion: The Breakthrough Nonprofit Brand Journey

> *"Any job is never done. You wake up every morning and there's something new. I think with our respective brand it's that commitment to continue to work with it that makes it powerful. We've learned that you can't outsource that to an advertising agency or a branding firm. We live the core values everyday."*[1]

> —David Hadani, Volunteer Board Member, Past Chair,
> Goodwill Industries International

The opportunity and need for nonprofits to build breakthrough brands (BNBs) has never been stronger. An explosion in the number of nonprofits, the growing need for their important community contributions, and the complicated environment in which they operate means these organizations have only one real choice. They must strategically build and manage their brands to stand out and strengthen purpose, build passionate connections, and create trusting relationships or face ever-dwindling support and organizational decline. This book's mission is to demonstrate that breakthrough branding, regardless of an organization's size, is vital for its future. Indeed, it is the new nonprofit imperative.

BREAKTHROUGH NONPROFIT BRANDS ARE A VALUABLE ASSET

Breakthrough nonprofits understand that branding is more than a cosmetic makeover or communications tool. Finding and defining an organization's brand meaning is critical to an organization—the living, breathing DNA that brings its mission and values to life.

Breakthrough organizations view brand as a collection of perceptions people form from its every communication, action, and interaction. It is what people collectively say, feel, and think about an organization. It is its reputation, identity, and goodwill in the community. Brand is the nonprofit's most important asset. Those organizations that manage and build the perceptions they want and work to bring them to life maximize their brand's strategic value.

As Food Bank For New York City's President and CEO Lucy Cabrera stated, "The focus on our brand meaning rallied and inspired staff. It is such an important asset that has helped us engage hundreds of new partners and friends who have united with us over the past seven years. It has been our rallying flag for staff, volunteers, and board members. The results have been remarkable—doubling fund-raising revenue, raising significant awareness of the cause, and reinforcing the Food Bank as the go-to hunger relief organization in New York City."[2]

A steadily growing number of visionary nonprofits are breaking through by intentionally building and carefully managing this vital asset. Breakthrough nonprofit brands use it to create a strategic sustainable advantage to maximize the trust and loyalty required for the continuous flow of resources necessary to fulfill their mission. They understand the future lies in building a brand that lasts long beyond any single management team. They build their brands to last.

BREAKTHROUGH NONPROFIT BRANDS DIFFERENTIATE TO STAND OUT

Nonprofit brands break through by defining their brand meaning—what the organization stands for, the powerful idea that sets it apart, and its relevant to core stakeholders. They understand that focus is intrinsic to keep their brand meaning from becoming emotionally shallow and weak. They understand their core constituents and the values that drive them. This creates emotional and personal bonds with the organization that drive enthusiastic support and encourage like-minded people to get involved.

BREAKTHROUGH NONPROFIT BRANDS ARE BIGGER THAN THEMSELVES

Breakthrough nonprofit brands go beyond the organization. They represent a cause that is bigger than the nonprofit—a cause that key constituents believe in and care about. This higher purpose and the outcomes they seek are based on deep values. And it is these values that drive people's passion, becoming a force and magnet for those who care about the cause at the core of a nonprofit's brand meaning.

BREAKTHROUGH NONPROFIT BRANDS RALLY COMMUNITIES

A nonprofit breaks through by taking its brand meaning a step further. It leverages this to build long-term trusting relationships. It focuses strategically on cultivating long-term communities within and outside the organization—while working to engage new audiences in its cause. Breakthrough nonprofit brands use stories and personal supporter experiences to communicate and engage with their audiences to satisfy and exceed expectations. As a result, initial supporters become a vibrant community of brand champions who unite behind the cause and adopt and promote it as if it were their own.

BREAKTHROUGH NONPROFIT BRANDS HAVE COURAGEOUS LEADERSHIP

Leading a nonprofit organization can feel like mission impossible: so many social and community needs, so many conflicting interests, so many different directions to pursue. Being a leader is about focusing organizational energies and channeling them effectively. BNB leaders understand the power of a focused, compelling brand meaning to unite employees and rally stakeholders inside and outside of an organization.

Building a BNB takes courageous leadership to drive its conscious development, ensure disciplined focus, and promise consistent delivery. A breakthrough organization's brand meaning is a central management preoccupation for the chief executive officer, board, and executive team driving governance, operations, and mission achievement. All-out efforts are made to ensure decisions inside the organization align and represent the clear brand meaning to current and prospective supporter communities. Courageous leaders break down internal silos and create a cohesive team that brings the whole organization together around the brand meaning for maximum impact.

BREAKTHROUGH NONPROFITS USE THEIR BRAND TO DRIVE STRATEGY

Breakthrough nonprofit brands have an unmistakable sense of direction. They understand that a focused, distinct brand meaning makes the organizational strategy clearer, more motivating, and attractive to all stakeholders. With discipline and consistency, a breakthrough nonprofit brand becomes the organization's central operating principle. It determines the focus and outcomes an organization seeks and filters what an organization will and will not do. It provides a framework to align mission-based programs, communication outreach and engagement, and development activities. Consistency and focused, disciplined delivery are hallmarks of BNBs.

BREAKTHROUGH NONPROFIT BRANDS EMBRACE INNOVATION

Breakthrough nonprofit brands project a sense of infectious momentum that comes from continuous improvement and innovation. Such innovation comes as a result of understanding stakeholders and what the brand means to them. They constantly search for ways to deliver better results in areas that mean the most to stakeholders. They look at their brand meaning in a different way to engage new supporters, seek untraditional revenue sources, or deliver new innovative programs. Breakthrough nonprofit brands are consistent but understand the value their brand meaning framework provides to drive great creativity and innovation. The organization dares to live its brand meaning in ways that are brave and different, creating a new definition of leadership in its field. They make sure goals are achievable and don't compromise their brand integrity. They look at their actions through the lens of "what does this do for our brand?" and ensure harmony.

BREAKTHROUGH NONPROFIT BRANDS CREATE OWNERS, INSIDE AND OUTSIDE

A BNB is a catalyst and connector between the value it provides and the values it stands for. Breakthrough nonprofit brands view themselves as catalysts, bringing people to the brand and helping them understand what it means. They look for bonds that unite, knowing these connections are critical to their success. The BNBs exist not to serve their own needs but rather to find common links between themselves and their supporter community. They focus on pursuing solutions that advance the cause and act as a convener, inviting others to join the movement. By having their brand meaning as a rallying flag, internal and external stakeholders champion the cause as their own (see Figure C.1).

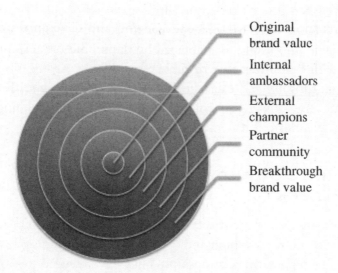

Original brand value

Internal ambassadors

External champions

Partner community

Breakthrough brand value

FIGURE C.1   Value of Brand Grows with Community

Breakthrough Nonprofit Brands Enjoy Alliances to Extend Reach and Impact

Breakthrough nonprofit brands stand for something distinctive based on deep values. They have nothing to fear from connecting with other brands, if there is alignment. That's because they know it is almost impossible for one organization to fight for a cause single-handedly and win. They define a space within a cause movement in which they can best deliver, and they build partnerships to extend brand reach, influence, and impact knowing that sharing common ground can make everyone a winner.

Breakthrough Nonprofit Brands Build Sustainable Organizations

The organizational values and mission of BNBs rarely change. But their operating practices and business strategies are constantly evolving to meet and/or define needs in the marketplace. They define what they uniquely stand for, and they are consistently focused and relentlessly disciplined. They use their brands to determine outcomes relevant to their core stake-holders. A BNB doesn't try to be all things to all people. Breakthrough nonprofit brands have the courage *not* to do things. They ensure this brand-centric philosophy is embraced by the whole organization. They leverage their brand meaning to build a sustainable organization that has strong donor loyalty and can recruit top executives, rally staff members, provide meaningfully engage volunteers, drive diversified funding streams, and ultimately make a greater social impact.

Ongoing Journey and Long-Term Commitment

The 11 best-in-class nonprofits featured in this book are recognized leaders in their field. They have built and lived their brand meaning in ways that have enabled long-term relationships. They have secured passionate, on-going commitments from people who have adopted the cause as their own and recruited others to join in. And they have achieved significant social impact and are constantly propelling their organizations forward. These organizations are truly remarkable, and their contributions to this book demonstrate their commitment to elevate the work of all nonprofits.

While they are leaders, not one of these organizations has achieved breakthrough in every principle. All view their brands as works in progress and ongoing journeys of self-assessment and innovation. They believe in the value and importance of branding for stability and future growth, and they encourage all nonprofits to move forward with the long-term commitment needed to build a BNB.

Your Brand Future

What is the future of your brand? How does your nonprofit brand currently stack up against the leading principles and practices of BNBs? Where does it need to go in the future?

The brand continuum assessment tool shown in Table C.1 can assist your organization in analyzing each of the Principles to determine where you fit on the brand continuum from base to breakthrough. Through the use of the journey chart in Appendix A, you can plot your current position and work to elevate your brand meaning in the head, heart, and hands of stakeholders to build sustainable competitive advantage and transform your organization into a powerful force for community good.

The Breakthrough Nonprofit Brand Journey

As nonprofit organizations continue to evolve and grow in importance, so, too, will the public's expectations of how they will address social issues and achieve mission results. Branding has become a must-do organizational strategy for the twenty-first century, the new nonprofit imperative.

Building a brand that breaks through is a means, not an end. We look forward to our own journeys as we continue to help nonprofit organizations build their brands to advance their missions, live their values, and power their contributions to community. As Winston Churchill said, *"Every day you may make progress. Every step may be fruitful. Yet there will stretch out before you an ever-lengthening, ever-ascending, ever-improving path. You know you will never get to the end of the journey. But this, so far from discouraging, only adds to the joy and glory of the climb."*[3]

We agree. May your journey begin.

TABLE C.1 BRAND CONTINUUM ASSESSMENT TOOL

	Base	Build	Breakthrough
P1 Discover your authentic brand meaning	Conduct basic research to discover the rational portion of brand meaning and convince supporters' "heads"	Conduct additional research to discover emotional portion of brand meaning to touch supporters' "hearts"	Engage with "hands" of supporter and seek their participation to refine brand meaning
P2 Embed your brand meaning across the organization	Align and focus mission-based programs, communication outreach, and development activities to drive brand meaning	Integrate and leverage your brand meaning in your organization structure and HR systems	Institutionalize and embed processes in systems to facilitate effective organizational implementation of the brand meaning
P3 Rally internal brand champions	Explain and educate to communicate brand meaning and key messages to internal stakeholders	Engage and empower to give staff and volunteers the power to "live" the brand via daily actions and interactions	Energize and motivate to instill a sense of pride and build an internal community to further drive the brand meaning externally
P4 Develop 360° brand communications	Create unique and strong verbal and visual identity that reflects the brand meaning	Integrate online and off-line communications and create compelling communications that brings the brand meaning to life and is customized for target audiences	Act as a catalyst and empower supporters to cocreate brand communications and drive actions.

P5	Expand your brand by mobilizing an external community	Cultivate a brand community by delivering participant benefits as a cornerstone of community building	Foster the brand community by nurturing supporters and develop a robust community by appealing to needs, beliefs, and values	Grow the brand community by empowering brand champions and constantly grow the community by engaging new audiences
P6	Cultivate partners to extend your brand reach and influence	Prepare systems to support transactional win-win relationships	Strengthen alignment to transition relationships that strengthen objectives for both partners	Nurture true transformative partnerships that are integrated across both organizations and create co-ownership of them
P7	Leverage your brand for untraditional revenue and value	Establish internal culture and systems to undertake transactional point of sale efforts to connect to brand meaning	Capitalize on brand and experience to build personal sales and experiences that align with brand meaning	Deepen to create mission-aligned business ventures driven by brand meaning and achieve financial return and mission goals

Base = At the base, a nonprofit brand presents the organization's focused and differentiated brand meaning that is relevant to its core stakeholders. It helps the *organization stand out*. The base level articulates a brand people can rationally understand and count on.

Build = To elevate the brand to the next level, a higher-order need is satisfied that connects to stakeholders on an emotional level. The organization makes a passionate commitment to *stand up* for a *cause* and the solutions it seeks — something that is bigger than the organization. The build level connects to the heart of their constituents and what they care about and believe in.

Breakthrough = The breakthrough level builds a *community* of owners. This powerful, differentiated brand meaning becomes the rallying flag, engaging diverse stakeholders who champion the cause as their own. Supporters inside and outside the organization *stand together*. Building the brand to this level results in the greatest return on investment by engaging the hands and inspiring action.

Brand Journey Assessment Tool

Building a breakthrough nonprofit brand is a journey, not a destination. Where is your organization on the brand spectrum? Answer the following questions to assess where your brand stands in the brand building continuum. Reflect on the results, and use them to make decisions about what to prioritize based on your organization needs.

Seven Principles and the Questions to Ask	Rank 1–5 (5 = highest)
Discover the Authentic Meaning of Your Brand	
Head: Can you rationally explain the unique, meaningful, and relevant idea that your brand stands for?	
Heart: Have you layered on a cause and outcomes the organization wants to achieve?	
Hands: Do you inspire others to join in? Have you explained what people can expect when they interact with your organization?	
Embed Brand Meaning across Organization	
Have you aligned mission-based programs, communication outreach, and development strategies to drive brand meaning?	
Is brand meaning integrated into the organization through appropriate HR structure to bring it to life?	
Have you embedded processes in organizational systems to facilitate effective organizational implementation of the brand meaning?	
Rally Internal Brand Ambassadors	
Have you educated and explained the brand to internal staff and volunteers and provided them with simple-to-use tools to ensure everyone is an owner?	

Rally Internal Brand Ambassadors	Rank 1–5 (5 = highest)
Do you engage and empower your internal team? Do hires appropriately reflect the brand and are they empowered to live the brand meaning?	
Are staff and volunteers regularly energized and feel motivated by a brand that is fresh and exciting? Do they feel a sense of pride and part of an internal community that helps to further drive the brand externally?	
Develop 360° Brand Communications	
Have you created a unique verbal and visual identity to reflect the organization's brand meaning?	
Have you built an integrated online and off-line communications strategy that brings the brand meaning to life? Do you connect the right message using the right channel to the right stakeholder?	
Do you act as a catalyst and empower supporters and champions to build and share your brand story? Does your communications drive actions?	
Expand Your Brand by Mobilizing an External Community	
Do you deliver benefits for participants and build relationships as a cornerstone of community?	
Do you nurturey our supporters to develop a robust community that appeals to their needs, interests, and values?	
Do you empower brand champions and constantly growth the community by engaging new audiences?	
Cultivate Partners to Extend Your Brand Reach and Influence	
Have you prepared systems internally to support transactional win-win relationships?	
Do you seek more aligned transitional relationships that strengthen the objectives of both partners?	
Do you nurture true partnerships that are transformational, that integrated across both organizations, and that create co-ownership?	
Leverage Your Brand for Alternative Revenue and Value	
Have you established an internal culture and systems to undertake simple point of sale efforts to connect people to the brand meaning and generate additional revenue?	
Can you capitalize on your brand meaning to build personal sales and experience to move up earned income opportunities and business ventures?	
Have you created mission-aligned business ventures driven by brand meaning to achieve financial return and mission goals?	

Snapshot of Nonprofit Case Studies

KIDS HELP PHONE

Kids Help Phone

Mission

Kids Help Phone's mission is to improve the well-being of children and youth in Canada by providing anonymous and confidential professional counseling, referrals, and information through technologically based communications media.

Vision

"To continue to improve and grow Kids Help Phone to ensure we deliver the most effective, timely and valuable counseling, referrals and information to every child or youth in Canada, from five to 20, who could benefit from our support."

Key Services

- By phone and by web, counselors respond to kids' needs, explore options, and equip them with skills to meet life's challenges in a climate of hope and respect for individual differences. Kids Help

Phone helps kids make healthy decisions based on their needs, personal values and beliefs, and well-being.

- Counselors are paid professionals who meet the highest possible academic and professional standards.

- Uses the ever-evolving changes in communications technology to reach out to children and youth.

- Contributes to the awareness and public dialogue on children's issues and to the development of policies and practices that improve the well-being of kids in Canada.

Values
- Maintains the innovative, entrepreneurial, and exploratory spirit the founders had when they started the organization in 1989.

- Practices and programs must reflect the highest standards of ethics, openness, and honesty. All funds raised must be used responsibly in the furtherance of Kids Help Phone's mission and vision.

- The passion and commitment of the organization's volunteers is fundamental to the success of fund raising and awareness programs, and each volunteer has the right to choose how to use her or his time and expertise to support activities.

- Young people have the right to contribute to the well-being of their own generation by volunteering their time and energy to the organization's awareness and fund raising activities.

- The staff has the right to the opportunity to develop their skills, to be treated fairly, to be recognized for their accomplishments, and to be stimulated to approach their work with passion and commitment.

- The organization's staff is responsible for the successful operation of the organization, and the board is responsible for long-term direction and the achievement of the mission.

Year Founded: 1989

Revenue in 2008: $12.2 million

Number of Volunteers in 2008: 10,000+

AMERICAN HEART ASSOCIATION

Mission

American Heart Association (AHA) is a national voluntary health agency whose mission is to reduce disability and death from cardiovascular disease and stroke.

Vision

By 2020, to improve the cardiovascular health of all Americans by 20 percent while reducing deaths from cardiovascular diseases and stroke by 20 percent. For this impact goal, the AHA categorizes cardiovascular health as poor, intermediate or ideal, depending on where people are in each of seven areas. Metrics for children vary based on pediatric recommendations and guidelines; ideal cardiovascular health for adults is defined by the presence of seven health measures, known as Life's Simple 7:

- Never smoked or quit more than one year ago
- Body mass index less than 25 kg/m^2
- Physical activity of 150 minutes+ (moderate intensity) or 75 minutes+ (vigorous) per week
- Four to five key components of a healthy diet consistent with current AHA guidelines
- Total cholesterol of less than 200 mg/dL
- Blood pressure below 120/80 mm Hg
- Fasting blood glucose less than 100 mg/dL

Key Services

- Discover and process science.
- Develop and communicate consumer health information.
- Advocate the American Heart Association's positions to key audiences.
- Generate resources.

Values

Integrity: We pursue our mission with honor, fairness and respect for the individual, mindful that there's no "right way" to do the "wrong thing." We uphold values of the AHA in every action and decision and are committed to act in good faith, comply with the rule of law and with AHA policies.

Excellence: We believe that striving to be the best in our work, our relationships, our ideas, and our services is the greatest demonstration of our pledge to customer satisfaction. We are determined to do the best at what matters most. Our success depends on our employees' and volunteers' ability to deliver the level of consistent excellence expected by all who rely on us.

Vision: In an effort to support our mission, we are willing to take prudent risks. We strive to be proactive, innovative and creative in all we do.

Dedication: We remain dedicated to our customers and our cause. We hold ourselves to the same standards of excellence that make the AHA a premier organization. We are committed to discovery and continuous improvement in developing and implementing our programs, products and services.

Inclusiveness: We're dedicated to a single purpose, fueled by diversity of thought and action. We serve responsibly as members of communities in which we live and work. Our intent is for employees and volunteers to be diverse, to maximize the relationship between our customers and the AHA.

Sensitivity: We value our employees, volunteers and customers and treat them with respect as individuals. We operate with openness and trust, fully granting others respect and cooperation.

Year Founded: 1924

Revenue in 2008: $641,646

Number of employees in 2008: 2,906

Number of Volunteers (donors, event participants, volunteers) in 2008
20 million

THE U.S. FUND FOR UNICEF

unicef ✪
united states fund

Mission

The U.S. Fund for UNICEF saves and protects the lives of children by supporting UNICEF's work through fund raising, advocacy, and education in the United States. Our mission is to work toward the day when zero children die from preventable causes by doing whatever it takes to give them the basics for a healthy childhood.

Vision

No child should die from a preventable cause, but 24,000 do every day. We believe that number should be zero.

Key Services

- **Medicine and Immunization:** UNICEF is the global leader in vaccine supply and has saved an estimated 20 million young lives through immunization. UNICEF does whatever it takes to distribute medicines, malaria nets, and other lifesaving assistance to children in need in more than 150 countries around the world.

- **Nutrition:** UNICEF provides high-protein therapeutic foods and vitamins to combat malnutrition.

- **Water and Sanitation:** From building pipelines to installing water pumps to trucking in supplies in humanitarian emergencies, UNICEF provides clean, safe water to children and their families. UNICEF also supplies latrines and educates communities about life-saving hygiene practices.

- **HIV/AIDS:** UNICEF provides food, medicine, and education to children orphaned by AIDS and works with HIV-positive mothers to prevent the transmission of the virus to their newborns.

- **Emergency Relief:** UNICEF provides lifesaving assistance—including tents, blankets, medicine, food, and water—to children and their families caught in war or natural disasters.

APPENDIX B SNAPSHOT OF NONPROFIT CASE STUDIES

- **Education:** UNICEF provides children the opportunity for a better life through education by delivering school supplies to millions of children each year, training teachers, and rebuilding schools destroyed during emergencies.

Values

UNICEF's ability to save lives is unparalleled because of its unique combination of:

- **Expertise:** Renowned for an extraordinary level of technical expertise exemplified by a network of highly skilled field staff and teams of professionals in public health, disease prevention, logistics, political systems, human rights, education, and emergency response.

- **Efficiency:** UNICEF employs low-cost but highly effective, sustainable solutions that save millions of lives.

- **Reach:** Operating in more than 150 countries, UNICEF has far-reaching programs that help children survive and thrive. UNICEF provides assistance in even the most remote, hard-to-reach areas of the world.

- **Access and Influence:** UNICEF has strong working relationships at the family, community, regional, and country level—with direct access to policy makers and local organizations in every country where it works.

- **Innovation:** UNICEF has helped develop simple, affordable, and innovative solutions to complicated problems. A few examples: birthing kits, oral rehydration salts, portable School-in-a-Box kits, and solar-powered cold storage units to transport vaccines.

- **Resolve:** UNICEF is not daunted by war, disaster, or disease or by geographic, political, or logistical complexity. UNICEF's mission of saving children's lives will continue until no more lives are lost to preventable causes.

Year Founded: 1947

Revenue in 2008: $229 million

Number of Employees in 2008: 200

Number of Volunteers in 2008: 20,000+

SUSAN G. KOMEN FOR THE CURE

Mission

Our Promise: To save lives and end breast cancer forever by empowering people, ensuring quality of care for all, and energizing science to find the cures.

Vision

Our Vision: A World without Breast Cancer "We aim to invest more than $2 billion over the next decade in breast health care and treatment for the underserved and in research to discover the causes of breast cancer and, ultimately, its cures."

Key Services

- Research
- Public health education
- Health screening services
- Health treatment services

Values—Is Hope

Inclusion to embrace the uniqueness of every individual
Stewardship to be accountable for our performance, individually and collectively
Honesty to foster a community of trust and integrity
Openness to seek out new ideas and new ways of thinking
Passion to demonstrate personal commitment to our promise
Empowerment to entrust others and hold yourself accountable

- **More early detection**—Nearly 75 percent of women over 40 years old now receive regular mammograms, the single most effective tool for detecting breast cancer early (in 1982, less than 30 percent received a clinical exam).

- **More hope**—The five-year survival rate for breast cancer, when caught early before it spreads beyond the breast, is now 98 percent (compared to 74 percent in 1982).

- **More research**—The federal government now devotes more than $900 million each year to breast cancer research, treatment, and prevention (compared with $30 million in 1982).

- **More survivors**—America's 2.5 million breast cancer survivors, the largest group of cancer survivors in the United States, are a living testament to the power of society and science to save lives.

Year Founded: 1982

Revenue in 2008: $350 million see below revenue box

Number of Employees in 2008: 160

Number of Volunteers in 2008: 100,000 +

$350 million in net revenues in FY08 from:
- Susan G. Komen Race for the Cure® Series (43% of total revenue, $159 million)
- Donors (21% of total revenue, $77 million)
- Cause marketing (14% of total revenue, $51 million)
- Breast Cancer Three-Day (11% of total revenue, $42 million in FY08)
- Direct mail: 8% of total revenue, $28 million, average gift of $32.95
- Other (3% of total revenue, $12 million). Examples include interest, dividends, investment gains, and merchandise sales

INSPIRATION CORPORATION

inspiration corporation | CATALYST FOR SELF-RELIANCE

Mission

In an atmosphere of dignity and respect, Inspiration Corporation helps people who are affected by homelessness and poverty to improve their lives and increase self-sufficiency through the provision of social services, employment training and placement, and housing.

Vision

Inspiration Corporation serves as a catalyst for self-reliance in its vision to end homelessness and poverty in Chicago.

Key Services

- The Employment Project: Offers career services, employment prepa ration training, tuition subsidies, employer outreach, and job placement and retention services throughout Chicago.
- Cafe Too: A food service job-training program and social enterprise restaurant.
- Inspiration Cafe and The Living Room Cafe: Serve meals in restaurant-style settings and provide supportive services, including case management, in a therapeutic community.
- Housing services: Offers rent subsidies and supportive services to help individuals and families find and maintain permanent housing.
- Open case management: offers case management, information and referral services, and direct financial support to any community members, typically to address a temporary crisis or transition.
- Community voice mail: Offers free voice mail to people who are homeless or phoneless.
- The Engagement Center: Provides daytime social services, laundry, showers, and bag lunches.

Values

- Inspiration Corporation is committed to providing outstanding services in an atmosphere of dignity and respect, while working to achieve its mission of ending homelessness and poverty in Chicago.

Year Founded: 1989

Revenue in 2009: $7,819,132

Number of Employees in 2009: 70

Number of Volunteers in 2009: 1,500

People Served: 3,000 Chicagoans affected by homelessness and poverty

Results

In the fiscal year 2009

- Placed 107 long-time homeless individuals and families into subsidized apartments
- Placed 126 men and women into jobs and 58 people into further education and training opportunities
- Provided community voice mail to 1,523 homeless and phoneless individuals
- Served 35,575 nutritious meals
- Provided open case management to 665 people
- Provided direct support grants of $184,540 emergency and transitional needs

NatureBridge

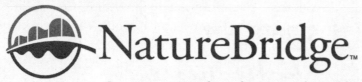

Connecting Youth to the Natural World ™

Mission

NatureBridge is dedicated to teaching science and environmental education in nature's classroom to inspire a personal connection to the natural world and responsible actions to sustain it.

Vision

We believe that we can change the world and inspire generations of environmental stewards, one child at a time.

Key Services

- Field science education for students grades K–12
- Teacher training programs
- Summer camps
- Summer wilderness field research for high school students

Values

NatureBridge believes that environmental education is essential to every child's development and should be a fundamental part of the American education system. We foster personal growth, interpersonal skills, scientific knowledge of the natural world, and responsible actions to sustain it, in order to inspire our students to adopt a stewardship ethic in their homes, schools, and local and global communities.

Year Founded: 1971

Revenue in 2007: $12 million

Net Revenue: $1.2 million

Number of Employees in 2008: 101

Stratford Shakespeare Festival

Mission

The Stratford Shakespeare Festival is a repertory theater company, permanently located in Stratford, Ontario. Our mission is to produce, to the highest standards possible, the best works of theater in the classical and contemporary repertoire. We pursue this mission through a special emphasis on the works of William Shakespeare; the development and celebration of work by classic, contemporary, and emerging Canadian playwrights; and an extensive range of training and enrichment opportunities for both our artists and our audiences. The ultimate goal of our mission is to provide ongoing and evolving opportunities for artistic growth for Canadian theater artists, artisans, and audiences.

Vision

A national institution of international renown, the festival is committed to maintaining and promoting the highest level of artistic excellence, to cultivating the widest possible audience, and to providing theater-related education and training for Canadian artists.

Key Services

- Stratford Shakespeare Festival welcomes all visitors to enjoy a show at any one of the four theaters. Families and groups are welcomed, and all theaters are handicap accessible.

- Special programs and prices are offered for families and groups.

- Stratford Shakespeare Festival relies on visitors from all over and is easily accessible with online purchasing.

- Stratford Shakespeare Festival makes information and donating accessible on their web site for individual and corporate support to sustain activities.

- Stratford Shakespeare Festival offers teachers and students opportunities to teach and learn while engaging them in scavenger hunts, courses, online activities, publications, teaching materials, and teacher conferences.

Values

In our creative exploration of the great works of the dramatic imagination, we aim to rediscover and reinvent those works for each new age, in order that they may continue to entertain, enlighten, and inspire audiences of all ages and origins.

Year Founded: 1953

Revenue in 2008: $57 million (Canadian)

Number of Employees in 2008: 650

Number of Volunteers in 2008: 200+

MEMORIAL HEALTHWORKS! KIDS' MUSEUM

Mission

Memorial HealthWorks! purpose is to "Infectiously contaminating kids of all ages, everywhere to learn, have fun, and make great life choices . . . let the epidemic begin!"

Vision

"Our community is the healthiest in the nation, and Memorial is a national model of excellence."

Key Services

- Dynamic and interactive health education through field trips, camps, parties, hands-on exhibits, and community outreach
- Replication opportunities:
  - Full-scale HealthWorks! facility
  - HealthWorks! area in an existing facility
  - Field trip and camp program licensing and delivery

Values

HealthWorks! supports Memorial Health System's mission by seeking innovative partnerships and creating new resources, with special emphasis on today's children . . . tomorrow's healthy, fulfilled citizens.

Year Founded: 2000

Revenue in 2008: $623,183

Number of Employees in 2009: 15

Number of Volunteers in 2008: 40

College Forward

college forward

Mission

College Forward provides college access and college persistence services to motivated, economically disadvantaged students in order to facilitate their transition to college and make the process exciting and rewarding.

Vision

"We believe that access to higher education is the right of every young Texan."

Key Services

- Orientation to the college experience

- Preparation for college entrance examinations

- Assistance with college applications

- Assistance in securing financial aid

Values

- College Forward believes education changes lives and that a college degree is the best way to break the cycle of generational poverty.

- Students always come first.

- Fun and excitement are critical elements for successful programming.

- The higher the standards, the more students will achieve!

Year Founded: 2003

Number of Volunteers in 2008: 79

Food Bank For New York City

Mission

The mission of the Food Bank For New York City is to end hunger by organizing food, information, and support for community survival and dignity.

Vision

Food Bank For New York City works to end hunger and increase access to affordable, nutritious food for low-income New Yorkers through a comprehensive group of programs that combat hunger and its causes.

Key Services

- Food sourcing and distribution
- Community Kitchen & Food Pantry of West Harlem
- Nutrition education for children and adults
- Children's programs
- Network services for food-assistance programs, including workshops, intranet, and annual conference
- Financial empowerment, including food stamp prescreening and outreach and free tax assistance for the working poor
- Community supported agriculture (CSA)
- Disaster relief

Year founded: 1983

Revenue in FY 2007–2008: $52.1 million

Net Assets in FY 2007–08: $7.6 million

Number of employees in 2008: 173

Number of volunteers in 2008: 5,000

GOODWILL INDUSTRIES INTERNATIONAL

Mission

Goodwill Industries International enhances the dignity and quality of life of individuals, families, and communities by eliminating barriers to opportunity and helping people in need reach their fullest potential through the power of work.

Vision

Every person has the opportunity to achieve his or her fullest potential and participate in and contribute to all aspects of life.

Key Services

- The clothing and household goods donated are sold in more than 2,200 Goodwill retail stores and on our Internet auction site, www.shopgoodwill.com.
- The revenues fund job training and other services to prepare people for job success.
- Goodwill also generates income helping businesses fill gaps caused by labor shortages, time constraints, and limited space or equipment.
- The organization trains and employs contract workers to fill outsourced needs for document management, assembly, mailing, custodial work, grounds keeping, and more.
- More than 84 percent of Goodwill's total revenues are used to fund education and career services, and other critical community programs.

Values

- **Respect**—Treats all people with dignity and respect.
- **Stewardship**—Honors heritage by being socially, financially, and environmentally responsible.
- **Ethics**—Strives to meet the highest ethical standards.
- **Learning**—Challenges each other to strive for excellence and to continually learn.
- **Innovation**—Embraces continuous improvement, bold creativity, and change.

Year Founded: 1902

Number of Employees in 2008: 86,000

Glossary

advocacy: When a company or nonprofit promotes a cause or issue through attempts to influence legislation and funding, often as part of a public affairs campaign.

beneficiary constituency: Stakeholders who are intended to receive and benefit from the services and programs of a nonprofit organization.

brand: A collection of perceptions about an organization, formed by its every communication, action, and interaction.

brand adoption: Recognition and favorable attitudes toward a brand that increase brand loyalty.

brand architecture: How an organization structures the various named brand entities within its portfolio and the nature of the relationships among them. Organizations can have a master brand, sub-brand(s), or separate or independent brands.

brand equity: The value of a brand. From a consumer perspective, brand equity is based on consumer attitudes about positive brand attributes and favorable consequences of brand use.

brand expressions: Conveys the character of the brand through visual and verbal components and differentiates it from competitors.

brand extension: Widening of the range of products sold using a particular brand.

brand fragmentation: A lack of brand consistency that results from transmitting mixed messages (or separately branded messages) or using various communication channels that operates independently.

brand meaning: The singular overriding idea that conveys what the organization stands for. It defines the leadership position that sets it apart and is meaningful to supporters.

brand personality: The words you would use to describe the character of your organization if it were a person.

brand platform: Defines how the organization will focus on building value-added customer relationships.

brand position statement: Succinctly communicates the brand meaning and provides direction for where the brand is going. Repeated consistently across your organization's communications.

brand promise: Answers the question of what one can expect when one interacts with the organizations.

comarketing: A partnership between two or more companies or organizations to jointly promote each other's products, services, or ideas.

core constituents: The most important group or groups supporting an organization, whose continuing support is crucial for survival and success.

customer acquisition cost: The cost associated with acquiring a new customer or donor. It includes research, marketing, and advertising costs.

demographics: Analyzes an audience based on factors such as age, geographic location, marital status, ethnicity, education, and socioeconomic status.

Maslow's hierarchy of needs: A psychology theory proposed by Abraham Maslow that states there are five layers of needs beyond the physical for all humans: psychological, safety, love/belonging, esteem, and self-actualization.

mission drift: When a nonprofit finds that it has moved away from the organization's mission.

nongovernmental organization (NGO):   A nonprofit organization that is not affiliated with the government or a corporation.

public service advertising (PSA):   Advertising with a central focus on public welfare that is generally sponsored by a nonprofit institution, civic group, religious organization, trade association, or political group.

psychographics: Analyzes an audience based on their lifestyles, behavior, and attitudes.

same-service organizations: Organizations that provide the same services as other organizations.

social capital: The value of relationships among individuals founded on trust, mutual understanding, and shared values.

sponsor: An individual, organization, or institution that supports an event, activity, person, or organization financially or through the provision of products or services.

supporter constituency: Individuals, groups, foundations, corporations, and/or government entities that support the work of an organization through financial or other types of support, such as advocacy, human resources, or marketing.

three-dimensional BNB value proposition: Breakthrough nonprofit brands use a three-dimensional model to define its brand meaning. They are rational, emotional, and engagement dimensions. By differentiating itself in each of these dimensions, a nonprofit builds a breakthrough brand meaning.

Notes

■ **INTRODUCTION**

1. The American Breast Cancer Foundation was established in 1997, and Avon launched its now-famous focus on breast cancer in 1994.
2. Examples of October's Pink Promotions: UPS: Passionately Pink for the Cure, Yoplait: Save Lids to Save Lives, Energizer: Power to Keep Going, Ford: Warriors in Pink, American Airlines, BMW North America, Boston Market, The Carlisle, Collection, Coldwater Creek, Hallmark Gold Crown, Kitchen Aid, Lean Cuisine, M&Ms Brand Chocolate Candies, Mohawk Industries, New Balance, Payless Shoe-Source, Pier 1 Imports, Quilted Northern Ultra, Rally for the Cure, Re/Max, United States Bowling Congress, The Val Skinner Foundation, Wacoal America.
3. Presentation, Katrina McGhee, July 2007.
4. Interview, Susan Carter Johns, March 30, 2009.
5. Survey of Association of Fundraising Professional members; American Marketing Association, Nonprofit Special Interest Group; and Imagine Canada members, undertaken Spring and Summer 2008.
6. Ibid.
7. Collins, J. *Good to Great and the Social Sectors: A Monograph to Accompany Good to Great*. Jim Collins, 2005, p. 23–25.
8. http://www.fastcompany.com/ magazine/84/love.html
9. See http://nonprofit.about.com/od/trendsissuesstatistics/a/giving2008.htm.
10. National Survey of Volunteer Organizations, Imagine Canada, 2004.
11. From Peter Drucker Foundation, 1999 found at http://www.fia.org.au/Content/NavigationMenu/Fundraising_Resources/NonprofitSector/default.htm
12. Similarly in Canada, trust and respect for the charitable sector has been consistently strong. The Muttart Foundation, an Edmonton, Alberta-based private funding organization, released in late 2008 results of their fourth public opinion survey of Canadians on their views about charities and issues affecting charities:

"Talking about Charities," found at www.muttart.org/download/TAC2008/TAC2008-03-CompleteReport.pdf. Proof positive of the growing significance can be seen with the latest valuations of leading nonprofit brands: The Habitat for Humanity brand was valued at $3.1 billion in 2006, up from their $1.8 billion valuation in 2001—at the time on par with the Starbucks brand. The American United Way brand, a leading charitable fund raising organization, was valued at $34.7 billion in the early 2000s. The World Wildlife Fund is the eighth most-trusted brand in the United States and the second most-trusted brand in Europe, according to the Edelman Trust Survey.

13. The 2010 Edelman Trust Barometer reports a modest global rise in trust in business—especially the United States, where trust in business jumped 18 points to 54 percent. In the United States, trust in government climbed 16 points in one year. Throughout most of the Western world, NGOs remain the most trusted institution. Across all regions, trust in this institution has increased over time.

14. Edelman Trust Barometer 2009 Report, p. 8.

15. Ibid.

16. Survey of members of the Association of Fundraising Professionals; American Marketing Association, Nonprofit Special Interest Group; and Imagine Canada members, Spring 2008.

17. Interview, Susan Carter Johns, March 30, 2009.

18. From http://www.leadershipnow.com/druckerremembered.html

■ CHAPTER 1

1. Interview with David Placek, November 2008.
2. Interview with Emily Callahan, March 2009.
3. This statistic was presented in a number of resources used in the development of this book. See Bibliography for resource list.
4. *Brand* and the *organization* are used to mean the same thing. We do this as a deliberate choice.
5. Interview with Kim Pucci, December 2009.

■ CHAPTER 2

1. Interview with Caryl Stern, December 3, 2008.
2. Interview with Lisa Fielder, November 3, 2008.
3. All facts and quotes presented in this case were taken from interviews with staff of the U.S. Fund for UNICEF or publicly available information.
4. All facts and quotes presented in this case were taken from interviews with the staff of College Forward or publicly available information.
5. Change in organizational leadership is not on the list because brands should outlast any single management team. A new CEO or CMO is not a sufficient reason to reevaluate a brand.

6. From research undertaken by the U.S. Fund for UNICEF.
7. An Economic Policy Institute report concluded: "The worst scoring students from high SES [socioeconomic status] families complete college as frequently as the best students from low SES families." See http://www.epi.org/economic_snapshots/entry/webfeatures_snapshots_20051012/.
8. See http://www.thecb.state.tx.us/Reports/PDF/1481.PDF.
9. See www.tgslc.org/pdf/educ_attain.pdf.
10. This is significant, because only 9 percent of Hispanic adults in Texas have earned a bachelor's degree—almost 4 times lower than non-Hispanic whites (33 percent). A report by Texas Guaranteed noted: "Among the six largest states, Texas ranks third in the percent of Whites with a degree, ties for second (with New York) for African Americans, and ranks last for Hispanics."
11. "The Price of Persistence: Barriers to Post Secondary Success for Low Income and First-Generation Students." Report produced by College Forward.

■ CHAPTER 3

1. All facts and quotes presented in this case were taken from interviews with staff of Food Bank For New York City or publicly available information.
2. All facts and quotes presented in this case were taken from interviews with staff of the American Heart Association or publicly available information.
3. Stats provided by the American Heart Association, February 2010.

■ CHAPTER 4

1. All facts and quotes presented in this case were taken from interviews with staff and the founder of Inspiration Corporation or publicly available information.
2. All facts and quotes presented in this case were taken from interviews with staff of Memorial HealthWorks! or publicly available information.
3. Inspired by Patrick Hanlon, *Primal Branding* (New York: Free Press, 2006).
4. The turnover rate at Inspiration Corporation in 2009 was 10 percent, including their restaurants, which traditionally have more turnover of staff.

■ CHAPTER 5

1. All facts and quotes presented in this case were taken from interviews with staff and volunteers of the U.S. Fund for UNICEF or publicly available information.
2. All facts and quotes presented in this case were taken from interviews with staff of the American Heart Association or publicly available information.
3. All facts and quotes presented in this case were taken from interviews with staff of Kids Help Phone or publicly available information.

4. All facts and quotes presented in this case were taken from interviews with staff of College Forward or publicly available information. See http://collegeforward. org/aboutus_history.html.
5. All facts and quotes presented in this case were taken from interviews with staff of Inspiration Corporation or publicly available information.
6. See http://www.goredforwomen.org/inspiring_stories.aspx#wilson.

■ CHAPTER 6

1. All facts and quotes presented in this case were taken from interviews with staff of Stratford Shakespeare Festival.
2. All facts and quotes presented in this case were taken from interviews with staff of Susan G. Komen for the Cure.
3. See Introduction notes for list of breast cancer activities.
4. The American Breast Cancer Foundation was established in 1997, and Avon launched its now-famous focus on breast cancer in 1994.

■ CHAPTER 7

1. All facts and quotes presented in this case were taken from interviews with staff and volunteers of Kids Help Phone.
2. All facts and quotes presented in this case were taken from interviews with staff and volunteers of NatureBridge.
3. Many nonprofits put a minimum dollar amount in place to be cause-marketing partners to ensure value for the association with their brand.
4. Thanks to Cone Inc. staff for this checklist. See http://www.coneinc.com/ whatdoyoustandfor.

■ CHAPTER 8

1. All facts and quotes presented in this case were taken from interviews with staff and volunteers of Goodwill Industries International or publicly available information.
2. ABVI stands for Association for the Blind and Visually Impaired.
3. See http://papers.ssrn.com/sol3/papers.cfm?abstract_id=1024484, and in Canada, see http://www.statcan.gc.ca/pub/61-533-s/61-533-s2005001-eng.htm.
4. See http://www.irs.gov/publications/p598/ch01.html.
5. There are numerous books, articles, and training programs that inform nonprofits of the detailed steps necessary to develop community enterprises.
6. See http://www.nonprofitexpert.com/income.htm.
7. See http://www.businesslink.gov.uk/bdotg/action/detail?r.s=sl&r.lc=en&type= RESOURCES&itemId=1073791229.

8. From Interbrand—http://www.interbrand.com/paper.aspx?paperid=77&langid = 1000.
9. John Quelch and James Austin, "Mining Gold in Not-for-Profit Brands," *Harvard Business Review* (June 2004): 24.
10. See http://www.goredforwomen.org/sponsor_programs.aspx.

■ CONCLUSION

1. Interview with David Hadani, July 21, 2009.
2. Interview with Lucy Cabrera, February 2009.
3. See www.quotationspage.com/quotes/Sir_Winston_Churchill.

Bibliography

▒ BOOKS

Aaker, D. *Managing Brand Equity: Capitalizing on the Value of a Brand Name*. New York: Free Press, 1991.

Adamson, A. *BrandDigital, Simple Ways Top Brands Succeed in the Digital World*. New York: Palgrave MacMillan. 2008.

Adamson, A. *BrandSimple, How the Best Brands Keep It Simple and Succeed*. New York: Palgrave MacMillan. 2006.

Andresen, K. *Robin Hood Marketing*. San Francisco: John Wiley & Sons, 2006.

Atkin, D. *The Culting of Brands: Turn Your Customers into True Believers*. London: Penguin, 2004.

Bacon, J. *The Art of Community: Building the New Age of Participation*. Sebastopol, CA: O'Reilly Media, 2009.

Barraket, J. *Strategic Issues for the Not for Profit Sector*. Sydney, Australia: University of South Wales Press, 2008.

Bately, M. *Brand Meaning*. New York: Routledge, 2008.

Bornstein, D. *How to Change the World*. New York: Oxford University Press, 2007.

Bornstein, D. *How to Change the World: Social Entrepreneurs and the Power of New Ideas*. New York: Oxford University Press, 2004.

Checco, L. *Branding for Success*. Silver Spring, MD: Trafford, 2005.

Chiaravalle, B., and B. Findlay Schenck. *Branding for Dummies*. Hoboken, NJ: John Wiley & Sons, 2007.

Clifton, R., and J. Simmons. *The Economist: Brands and Branding*. New York: Bloomberg, 2003.

Collins, J. *Good to Great and the Social Sectors: A Monograph to Accompany Good to Great*. Jim Collins, 2005.

Collins, J. *Good to Great: Why Some Companies Make the Leap and Others Don't.* New York: HarperCollins, 2001.

Collins, J., and J. Porras. *Built to Last: Successful Habits of Visionary Companies.* New York: HarperCollins, 2002.

Cooke, P. *Branding Faith: Why Some Churches and Nonprofits Impact Culture and Others Don't.* Ventura, CA: Regal from Gospel Light, 2008.

Crutchfield, L., and H. McLeod Grant. *Forces for Good: The Six Practices of High-Impact Nonprofits.* San Francisco: Jossey-Bass, 2008.

Daw, J. *Cause Marketing for Nonprofits: Partner for Purpose, Passion, and Profits.* Hoboken, NJ: John Wiley & Sons, 2006.

Drucker, P. *Classic Drucker.* Boston: 2008 Harvard Business School Publishing, 2006.

Drucker, P. *The Essential Drucker.* New York: Collins Business Essentials, 2001.

Drucker, P., with J. Collins. *The Five Most Important Questions You Will Ever Ask about Your Organization.* San Francisco: Jossey-Bass, 2008.

Fisher, R., and W. Ury, with B. Patton, Eds. *Getting to Yes: Negotiating Agreement without Giving In.* New York: Penguin, 1991.

Gad, T. *4-D Branding: Cracking the Corporate Code of the Network Economy.* Sweden: Bookhouse, 2001.

Gilmore, J., and B. Pine. *Authenticity: What Consumers Really Want.* Boston: Harvard Business School Press, 2007.

Gobe, M. *Citizen Brand: 10 Commandments for Transforming Brands in a Consumer Democracy.* New York: Allworth, 2002.

Gobe, M. *Emotional Branding: The New Paradigm for Connecting Brands to People.* New York: Allworth, 2001.

Googins, B., P. Mirvis, and S. Rochlin. *Beyond Good Company: Next Generation Corporate Citizenship.* New York: Palgrave MacMillan, 2007.

Hall, P. *Inventing the Nonprofit Sector.* Baltimore: Johns Hopkins University Press, 1992.

Hanlon, P. *Primal Branding: Create Zealots for Your Brand, Your Company and Your Future.* New York: Free Press, 2006.

Hart, T., J. Greenfield, and S. Haji. *People to People Fundraising: Social Networking and Web 2.0 for Charities.* Hoboken, NJ: John Wiley & Sons, 2007.

Harvard Business Review on Marketing. Boston: Harvard Business School Publishing, 2001.

Heath, C., and D. Heath. *Made to Stick: Why Some Ideas Survive and Others Die.* New York: Random House, 2007.

Holland, D. *Branding for Nonprofits: Developing Identity with Integrity.* New York: Allworth, 2006.

Janes, R. *Museums in a Troubled World: Renewal, Irrelevance or Collapse?* London: Routledge, 2009.

Jolly, R., and J. Grant. *UNICEF Visionary.* Florence, Italy: Tipografia Giuntina.

Kim, W., and R. Mauborgne. *Blue Ocean of Strategy: How to Create Uncontested Market Space and Make the Competition Irrelevant.* Boston: Harvard Business School Press, 2005.

La Piana, D. *The Nonprofit Strategy Revolution: Real-time Strategic Planning in a Rapid-Response World.* Saint Paul, Minn.: Fieldstone Alliance, 2008.

Li, C., and J. Bernoff. *Groundswells: Winning in a World Transformed by Social Technologies*. Boston: Harvard Business School Publishing, 2008.

Neal, W., and R. Strauss. *Value Creation: The Power of Brand Equity.* Mason, OH: Texere, 2008.

O'Reilly, T., and S. Milstein. *The Twitter Book.* Sebastopol, CA: O'Reilly Media, 2009.

Pelosi, P. *Corporate Karma: How Business Can Move Forward by Giving Back.* Toronto, Canada: Orenda, 2007.

Piasecki, B. *World Inc.: When It Comes to Solutions—Both Local and Global—Businesses Are Now More Powerful Than Government.* Naperville, IL: Sourcebooks, 2007.

Quelch, J., and N. Laidler-Kylander. *The New Global Brands: Managing Non-Government Organizations in the 21st Century.* Mason, OH: South-Western, 2006.

Ragas, M., and B. Bueno. *The Power of Cult Branding.* New York: Crown Business, 2002.

Roberts, K. *Lovemarks: The Future beyond Brands.* New York: PowerHouse Books, 2005.

Runte, A. *Yosemite: The Embattled Wilderness.* Lincoln: University of Nebraska Press, 1990.

Senge, P., B. Smith, N. Kruschwitz, J. Laur, and S. Schley. *The Necessary Revolution: How Individuals and Organizations Are Working Together to Create a Sustainable World.* New York: Doubleday, 2008.

Silverman, L. *Wake Me Up When the Data Is Over: How Organizations Use Stories to Drive Results.* San Francisco: Jossey-Bass, 2006.

Spence, R., with H. Rushing. *It's Not What You Sell, It's What You Stand For.* London: Portfolio, 2009.

Tybout, A., and T. Calkins. *Kellogg on Branding: The Marketing Faculty of The Kellogg School of Management.* Hoboken, NJ: John Wiley & Sons, 2005.

UNICEF United States Fund. *Life Stories.* New York: UNICEF United States Fund.

Van Auken, B. *Brand Aid: An Easy Reference Guide to Solving Your Toughest Branding Problems and Strengthening Your Market Position.* New York: AMACOM, 2003.

Wheeler, A. *Designing Brand Identity: A Complete Guide to Creating, Building, and Maintaining Strong Brands,* 2nd ed . Hoboken, NJ: John Wiley & Sons, 2006.

Wheeler, C. *You've Gotta Have Heart.* New York: AMACOM, 2009.

ARTICLES

Agres, B. "Community Building in Hawaii." *Nonprofit Quarterly,* Summer 2005, 36–37.

Bemporard, R., and M. Baranowski. "Branding for Social Good: Strategies for Harnessing the Power of Your Brand." A BBMG report available at http://www.bbmg.com, September 2008.

Bemporard, R., and M. Baranowski. "Branding for Sustainability: Five Principles for Leveraging Brands to Create Shared Value." A BBMG report available at http://www.bbmg.com, September 2008.

Cone, in collaboration with Intangible Business. "The Cone Nonprofit Power Brand 100." Report, June 2009.

Editors. "Nonprofits and Philanthropy: Scenario II—An Interview with Ralph Smith." *Nonprofit Quarterly*, Winter 2008, 38–42.

Editors. "Seizing the Day: Opportunity in the Wake of Crisis—An Interview with Lester Salamon." *Nonprofit Quarterly*, Winter 2008, 34–37.

Enright, K., and C. Bourns. "The Case for Stakeholder Engagement." *Stanford Social Innovation Review*, Spring 2010, 40–45.

Fisman, R., R. Khurana, and E. Martenson. "Mission—Driver Governance." *Stanford Social Innovation Review*, Summer 2009, 36–43.

Foster, W., and G. Fine. "How Nonprofits Get Really Big." *Stanford Social Innovation Review*, Spring 2007, 46–55.

Fournier, S., and L. Lee. "Getting Brand Communities Right." *Harvard Business Review*, April 2009.

Goggins Gregory, A., and D. Howard. "The Nonprofit Starvation Cycle." *Stanford Social Innovation Review*, Fall 2009, 48–53.

Kriegel, M. "From Legacy to Leadership: Is Philanthropy Ready for the New Consumer?" A BBMG report available at http://www.bbmg.com, 2009.

Light, P. "Social Entrepreneurship Revisited." *Stanford Social Innovation Review*, Summer 2009, 21–24.

Martin, R., and S. Osberg. "Social Entrepreneurship: The Case for Definition." *Stanford Social Innovation Review*, Spring 2007, 28–39.

McKee, S. "How to Build Brand Friendship." *BusinessWeek*, May 9, 2008.

Nambisan, S. "Platforms for Collaboration." *Stanford Social Innovation Review*, Summer 2009, 44–49.

Pratt, J. "NPQ's Illustrated Nonprofit Economy." *Nonprofit Quarterly*, 2008, Insert.

Rangan, V., and B. Kasturi. "Go Red for Women: Raising Heart Health Awareness." *Harvard Business School Case Study*, September 21, 2006.

Renz, D. "The U.S. Nonprofit Infrastructure Mapped." *Nonprofit Quarterly*, Winter 2008, 17–20.

Sargeant, A., and J. Ford. "The Power of Brands." *Stanford Social Innovation Review*, Winter 2007, 40–47.

Schwartz, N. "Nonprofit Taglines: The Art of Effective Brevity." *Nonprofit Quarterly*, Fall 2008, 72–75.

Wei-Skillern, J., and S. Marciano. "The Networked Nonprofit." *Stanford Social Innovation Review*, Spring 2009, 38–43.

■ **WEB SITES**

Wikibranding—www.wikibranding.net

All about Branding—www.allaboutbranding.com

Mud Valley Brand Marketing Community—www.mudvalley.co.uk

About the Authors

■ JOCELYNE DAW

Jocelyne has over 25 years, experience in nonprofit leadership positions. She has successfully helped create a brand for a national grassroots movement, revitalize a cherished institution's brand, and reposition two organizations' brand after major mergers.

Jocelyne is a recognized pioneer in the evolution of business-community partnerships and the integration of non-profit marketing and fundraising. She is author of *Cause Marketing for Nonprofits: Partner for Purpose, Passion, and Profits* (Wiley, 2006). Jocelyne works with business and nonprofits to build community strategies that strengthen brand identity, connections, and trust.

■ CAROL CONE

For more than 25 years, Carol Cone has created substantive partnerships between companies and social issues. As Founder of Cone, Inc., she led the development of cause initiatives for Avon, Reebok, ConAgra Foods, PNC, and the American Heart Association, helping raise awareness and more than $1.2 billion for various social issues.

In 2007, *PR Week* called her "arguably the most powerful and visible figure in the world of Cause Branding." In 2010 she joined Edelman Public

Relations to continue her journey guiding groundbreaking brand and corporate citizenship efforts.

■ KRISTIAN DARIGAN MERENDA

Kristian is an acclaimed cause expert whose work is featured in President Bill Clinton's *Giving*, Philip Kotler's *Marketing: Improving the Quality of Life*, and case studies published by Harvard Business School and the United Nations, among others. She is senior vice president, Edelman Good Purpose Labs.

■ ANNE ERHARD

Anne Erhard, vice president at Cone, consults clients toward industry-leading results including her work on the American Heart Association's award-winning *Go Red For Women* movement. Specialties include integrated marketing communications, corporate philanthropy and social responsibility, nonprofit cause branding, and public/private partnerships.

For more information, please see each author's profile page at LinkedIn .com

AFP Code of Ethical Principles and Standards

ETHICAL PRINCIPLES • Adopted 1964; amended Sept. 2007

The Association of Fundraising Professionals (AFP) exists to foster the development and growth of fundraising professionals and the profession, to promote high ethical behavior in the fundraising profession and to preserve and enhance philanthropy and volunteerism. Members of AFP are motivated by an inner drive to improve the quality of life through the causes they serve. They serve the ideal of philanthropy, are committed to the preservation and enhancement of volunteerism; and hold stewardship of these concepts as the overriding direction of their professional life. They recognize their responsibility to ensure that needed resources are vigorously and ethically sought and that the intent of the donor is honestly fulfilled. To these ends, AFP members, both individual and business, embrace certain values that they strive to uphold in performing their responsibilities for generating philanthropic support. AFP business members strive to promote and protect the work and mission of their client organizations.

AFP members both individual and business aspire to:

- practice their profession with integrity, honesty, truthfulness and adherence to the absolute obligation to safeguard the public trust
- act according to the highest goals and visions of their organizations, professions, clients and consciences
- put philanthropic mission above personal gain;
- inspire others through their own sense of dedication and high purpose
- improve their professional knowledge and skills, so that their performance will better serve others
- demonstrate concern for the interests and well-being of individuals affected by their actions
- value the privacy, freedom of choice and interests of all those affected by their actions
- foster cultural diversity and pluralistic values and treat all people with dignity and respect
- affirm, through personal giving, a commitment to philanthropy and its role in society
- adhere to the spirit as well as the letter of all applicable laws and regulations
- advocate within their organizations adherence to all applicable laws and regulations
- avoid even the appearance of any criminal offense or professional misconduct
- bring credit to the fundraising profession by their public demeanor
- encourage colleagues to embrace and practice these ethical principles and standards
- be aware of the codes of ethics promulgated by other professional organizations that serve philanthropy

ETHICAL STANDARDS

Furthermore, while striving to act according to the above values, AFP members, both individual and business, agree to abide (and to ensure, to the best of their ability, that all members of their staff abide) by the AFP standards. Violation of the standards may subject the member to disciplinary sanctions, including expulsion, as provided in the AFP Ethics Enforcement Procedures.

MEMBER OBLIGATIONS

1. Members shall not engage in activities that harm the members' organizations, clients or profession.
2. Members shall not engage in activities that conflict with their fiduciary, ethical and legal obligations to their organizations, clients or profession.
3. Members shall effectively disclose all potential and actual conflicts of interest; such disclosure does not preclude or imply ethical impropriety.
4. Members shall not exploit any relationship with a donor, prospect, volunteer, client or employee for the benefit of the members or the members' organizations.
5. Members shall comply with all applicable local, state, provincial and federal civil and criminal laws.
6. Members recognize their individual boundaries of competence and are forthcoming and truthful about their professional experience and qualifications and will represent their achievements accurately and without exaggeration.
7. Members shall present and supply products and/or services honestly and without misrepresentation and will clearly identify the details of those products, such as availability of the products and/or services and other factors that may affect the suitability of the products and/or services for donors, clients or nonprofit organizations.
8. Members shall establish the nature and purpose of any contractual relationship at the outset and will be responsive and available to organizations and their employing organizations before, during and after any sale of materials and/or services. Members will comply with all fair and reasonable obligations created by the contract.

9. Members shall refrain from knowingly infringing the intellectual property rights of other parties at all times. Members shall address and rectify any inadvertent infringement that may occur.
10. Members shall protect the confidentiality of all privileged information relating to the provider/client relationships.
11. Members shall refrain from any activity designed to disparage competitors untruthfully.

SOLICITATION AND USE OF PHILANTHROPIC FUNDS

12. Members shall take care to ensure that all solicitation and communication materials are accurate and correctly reflect their organizations' mission and use of solicited funds.
13. Members shall take care to ensure that donors receive informed, accurate and ethical advice about the value and tax implications of contributions.
14. Members shall take care to ensure that contributions are used in accordance with donors' intentions.
15. Members shall take care to ensure proper stewardship of all revenue sources, including timely reports on the use and management of such funds.
16. Members shall obtain explicit consent by donors before altering the conditions of financial transactions.

PRESENTATION OF INFORMATION

17. Members shall not disclose privileged or confidential information to unauthorized parties.
18. Members shall adhere to the principle that all donor and prospect information created by, or on behalf of, an organization or a client is the property of that organization or client and shall not be transferred or utilized except on behalf of that organization or client.
19. Members shall give donors and clients the opportunity to have their names removed from lists that are sold to, rented to or exchanged with other organizations.
20. Members shall, when stating fundraising results, use accurate and consistent accounting methods that conform to the appropriate guidelines adopted by the American Institute of Certified Public Accountants (AICPA)* for the type of organization involved. (* In countries outside of the United States, comparable authority should be utilized.)

COMPENSATION AND CONTRACTS

21. Members shall not accept compensation or enter into a contract that is based on a percentage of contributions; nor shall members accept finder's fees or contingent fees. Business members must refrain from receiving compensation from third parties derived from products or services for a client without disclosing that third-party compensation to the client (for example, volume rebates from vendors to business members).
22. Members may accept performance-based compensation, such as bonuses, provided such bonuses are in accord with prevailing practices within the members' own organizations and are not based on a percentage of contributions.
23. Members shall neither offer nor accept payments or special considerations for the purpose of influencing the selection of products or services.
24. Members shall not pay finder's fees, commissions or percentage compensation based on contributions, and shall take care to discourage their organizations from making such payments.
25. Any member receiving funds on behalf of a donor or client must meet the legal requirements for the disbursement of those funds. Any interest or income earned on the funds should be fully disclosed.

A Donor Bill of Rights

PHILANTHROPY is based on voluntary action for the common good. It is a tradition of giving and sharing that is primary to the quality of life. To assure that philanthropy merits the respect and trust of the general public, and that donors and prospective donors can have full confidence in the not-for-profit organizations and causes they are asked to support, we declare that all donors have these rights:

I.

To be informed of the organization's mission, of the way the organization intends to use donated resources, and of its capacity to use donations effectively for their intended purposes.

II.

To be informed of the identity of those serving on the organization's governing board, and to expect the board to exercise prudent judgement in its stewardship responsibilities.

III.

To have access to the organization's most recent financial statements.

IV.

To be assured their gifts will be used for the purposes for which they were given.

V.

To receive appropriate acknowledgement and recognition.

VI.

To be assured that information about their donations is handled with respect and with confidentiality to the extent provided by law.

VII.

To expect that all relationships with individuals representing organizations of interest to the donor will be professional in nature.

VIII.

To be informed whether those seeking donations are volunteers, employees of the organization or hired solicitors.

IX.

To have the opportunity for their names to be deleted from mailing lists that an organization may intend to share.

X.

To feel free to ask questions when making a donation and to receive prompt, truthful and forthright answers.

DEVELOPED BY
Association for Healthcare Philanthropy (AHP)
Association of Fundraising Professionals (AFP)
Council for Advancement and Support of Education (CASE)
Giving Institute: Leading Consultants to Non-Profits

ENDORSED BY
(in formation)
Independent Sector
National Catholic Development Conference (NCDC)
National Committee on Planned Giving (NCPG)
Council for Resource Development (CRD)
United Way of America

Index